PRAISE FOR

The Deep Well of Time

Michael Dorer's *The Deep Well of Time* will be welcomed by parents and educators; it's a well written defense of the use of story, and includes both a rationale for this important way of learning and practical information on how to become a storyteller. The majority of the book consists of stories, many of them taken from or created in relation to Montessori curriculum, especially Montessori for children from 6 to 12 years. This book joins those of Keiran Egan at Simon Frasier University and Godly Play creator Jerome Berryman in championing the importance of this way to give children what Dorer calls the gift of the memorable.

—John Chattin-McNichols, Ph.D., Associate Professor of Education and Director, E.M. Standing Center for Montessori Studies, Seattle University, AMS 2014 Living Legacy, Author: *The Montessori Controversy*

What a priceless gem Michael Dorer has given to adults and children alike. Through his personal memories of the stories his grandfather told him, his insightful depth and appreciation of the wealth of oral stories, his relevant research, his clear organization, and his storytelling experiences with his students, he inspires us to recall those magical oral stories of our youth and provides a path for us to wander that will take our children away from the "screen" to the *Deep Well of Time* where their imagination and creativity thrive.

—Judi Bauerlein, AMS 2010 Living Legacy

Michael Dorer's book makes a valuable contribution to the Montessori community in highlighting the importance of storytelling in our pedagogy and providing a wonderful selection of model stories. We applaud his clear message that the "Great Lessons"—or any of the other traditional Montessori stories—have no set script and that every story needs to reflect the personal delivery of each teacher and the current findings of science.

—MICHAEL AND D'NEIL DUFFY, authors of *Children of the Universe: Cosmic Education in the Montessori Elementary Classroom*

~

What a gift this book is, on so many levels! *The Deep Well of Time* is a gift to teachers, an opportunity to learn the craft of storytelling from an experienced guide. It is a gift to students, the lucky listeners who will be touched profoundly by new connections to the world around them. However, even more importantly from my perspective as a parent in the trenches of raising three children, it is a gift to me: not only does it provide a sneak peek into the goings-on of their Montessori classrooms, but it both inspires me to tell my own stories and provides me with the nuts and bolts of how to start spinning those yarns.

—TREVOR EISSLER, author: *Montessori Madness! A Parent to Parent Argument for Montessori Education*

~

Children love to learn through stories. The stirring of children's imaginations through the telling of a well-crafted story brings power to their learning. In *The Deep Well Of Time* Michael Dorer brings us more than stories. Michael helps us understand how to tell stories that speak to the minds and hearts of children. This is a book that every Montessori elementary teacher should have as an essential resource. Once Michael gets you telling stories, you may never want to stop. Lucky children! Lucky you!

—MAREN SCHMIDT, author of *Kids Talk Newsletter, Understanding Montessori: A Guide for Parents, Building Cathedrals Not Walls, 7 Parenting Problems You Can Avoid*

~

In Montessori, we weave a tapestry of stories that ignite children's curiosity and sense of wonder and lead to thoughtful conversation and life-long learning. Michael Dorer is a gifted storyteller. In *The Deep Well of Time* he helps us to find our own path to becoming a weaver of stories that capture children's imagination.

—TIM SELDIN, President, The Montessori Foundation; Chair, The International Montessori Council; Head of School, The NewGate School

~

Children love stories. Stories help them to travel across time and distance. Listening to a good story allows them to feel free from obstacles and constraints. It stimulates their imagination and creativity. It helps them to become themselves at a critical moment of their intellectual development. For many years, Michael Dorer has observed how children react to stories. His book is a gift for teachers and a joy for children.

—ANDRE ROBERFROID, Past President Association Montessori Internationale

~

An *outstanding* book about storytelling and its capacity to mesmerize us with ALL subjects. Imagine how different education would be if teachers taught everything through story, this most ancient and truly effective way of learning that fascinates and connects us to everything ... truly amazing ... such a comprehensive approach ... one comes away with the idea that storytelling can, and should, be used for every subject.

—JENNIFER MORGAN, president, Deep Time Journey Network; and author, Universe Story Trilogy (*Born With a Bang, From Lava to Life, Mammals Who Morph*)

~

As in everything he does, Michael Dorer has created excellence; this time in the form of a powerful book about storytelling. To the Montessorian this collection of stories in one volume is inspiring and invaluable. Thank you, Michael for this gift of stories and for the instruction on how to tell them.

—JOYCE S. PICKERING, President Board of Directors, American Montessori Society; Executive Director Emerita Shelton School and Evaluation Center, Dallas, TX

~

Michael Dorer has demonstrated that his own "transformative" compilation of story-upon-story is part of a deeply lived and deepening spiral of a world view that is not only Montessori but a projection of his whole identity in the context of his personal life.

—DAVID KAHN, Executive Director of the North American Montessori Teachers' Association

~

Michael Dorer is a gifted storyteller who shares the secrets that can help his readers make the magic of storytelling happen in their classrooms. The stories he shares are themselves a generous gift that will help all of us become more effective in using the art of storytelling to delight, enthrall and inspire children for years to come.

—FELAND L. MEADOWS, PH.D., President, Pan American Montessori Society; Goizueta Endowed Chair of Early Childhood Education at Kennesaw State University, Kennesaw, Georgia.

THE DEEP WELL OF TIME

The Transformative Power of Storytelling in the Classroom

MICHAEL J. DORER

Foreword by Paul Epstein, Ph.D.

A division of Montessori Services
www.montessoriservices.com

Book design by Robert and Erik Jacobson
LongfeatherBookDesign.com

Author photo by Rebecca Zenefski
ByRebeccaStudios.com

Paperback ISBN: 978-0-939195-48-0
Ebook ISBN: 978-0-939195-49-7

Library of Congress Control Number: 2016909158

This is for Rose.

"There have been great societies that did not use the wheel, but there have been no societies that did not tell stories."

—Ursula K. Le Guin, American author

Contents

Illustration List

Foreword

I am a student of children. For more than forty years and throughout the world, I have observed them, presented to them, and made presentations about them. I have, however, undoubtedly learned more *from* them.

One of the lessons children have taught me is that we are indeed designed to constantly learn throughout life. As our nervous systems run automatically, sometimes we learn without awareness, but in times of deeply transformative learning, we are brought to new awareness that takes us to the awakening "I didn't know that I didn't know." I have watched children encounter these kinds of moments: their expressions include a combination of disbelief, wonder, and even rapture. Their incredulity gives way to understanding. And with understanding comes capability. In the voice of a child, we hear a resounding, "I *can* do it!" We hear the child proclaim, "I know it!"

Constant learning is necessary if we are to become truly able. Although I have met countless educators, many have missed this enduring mandate of childhood. Michael Dorer is not in that group. He understands children. He is a children's guide. He knows how to assist children as they pursue their quest of becoming, determined to persist and resolve challenges. One of Michael's most profound gifts is his masterful use of storytelling to support and aid children in their transformative learning. Michael understands the power of stories and their ability to take us to real and (perhaps) mythical destinations, break speed and time barriers, and connect and immerse us in that which "cannot be directly touched, sensed with our normal senses, or retrieved with mundane tools" (Dorer xxxvii). Michael is right: we often do come back from a story having traveled throughout the Deep Well of Time.

As Michael tells it, "stories have powers to illuminate, elucidate, motivate, spark creative imagination, and touch the spirit of the children ..." Take note of these qualities. These are among our best human qualities. Stories take us into realms of human experience that differ from that of mainstream education so narrowly and damagingly focused on fear-based achievement and testing by demand and mandate. That is just one reason why this book is so important.

This is a book of stories, and this is a book about how to tell stories. Just as stories are meant to be heard again and again, so, too, is storytelling meant to be learned and improved upon with practice: it is an essential tool for any educator or parent—anyone who has any connection to children—at any stage of their career or relationship with children. In essence, a book for everyone.

Educators of every background will relish this rich collection. These stories are written by Michael; guest authored; adapted from Dr. Maria Montessori's ideas, lessons, and stories; and enhanced by Michael's annotative comments about background content and the structure and purposes of the Montessori elementary curriculum.

The stories in this book form a web that connects all areas of the Montessori elementary "story-centered" curriculum: mathematics, science, history, language, geography, and autobiography. There are myths, legends, and folktales. There are stories about origins, secrets, and the sacred, too. Some of the stories teach us about linguistic and mathematical conventions and inventions. Organized and classified as Great Lessons, curriculum stories, origin stories, biographical histories, personal stories, character development stories, and creative dramatics, Michael's story collection is paired with illuminating pedagogical explanations and, often, illustrating figures that further bring the stories to life.

Michael's tremendous experience with children is present throughout these pages, which recognize education's purpose to touch, as Dr. Montessori once wrote, the vast human potential possessed by each child. Apparent is his understanding of what matters to children, what captures their interest, and what entices their wonderment and imagination, the first pedagogical step in a journey of understanding. As a form of transformative learning, a listened-to story takes us far beyond capturing our attention, entertaining, and instructing. Stories help us learn to listen, develop imagination, receive cultural values and wisdom, and build character.

Our cultural and historical heritages come to life when we participate in stories. So too do mystery and a reverence for life. In this book, you will come to understand Michael's regard for storytelling as a spiritual act, a premise with which I completely agree. Inviting a deep relationship between the storyteller and the audience, a story actively engages and transports. During and after a story, the storyteller and the listeners are not quite the same.

Michael is a true Montessori educator, adhering to and promoting the principles and best practices of our Montessori legacy. His teaching roles have involved him with children and adults in early childhood, elementary, secondary, and university classrooms, and he speaks to audiences throughout the world. When he works with learners of any age, Michael is engaged and exacting. His knowledge and experience run deep, and he has originated curriculum including, as you are about to read, numerous and wonderful stories. I also have the good fortune that Michael is my friend. I learn from him when I ask for and follow his advice.

I have enjoyed hearing Michael tell stories to children. He can be serious, then suddenly humorous. As a storyteller, he playfully teases, then is mysterious and enticing. We get immersed and caught up in his characters, their purposes and challenges, their adventures, their mistakes, and their triumphs. We come out of the story satisfied with new understandings about events and ourselves. We're often hungry with more questions, too.

As you may know, a Montessori curriculum guides children to develop their unique capabilities. Dr. Montessori called this work a child's noble task. Children seek to understand themselves and their purposes and contributions, asking, as Dr. Montessori noted, "What am I? What is the task of man in this wonderful universe? Do we merely live here for ourselves, or is there something more for us to do? Why do we struggle and fight? What is good and evil? Where will it all end?"* We cannot directly answer these and other related questions. As Michael so well teaches, storytelling will assist children with their own explorations of life's fundamental questions. When a child listens to a story about

---

*Montessori, M. (2003, first published 1948). *To Educate the Human Potential.* Oxford, England: Clio Press. p. 6.

a hero, for example, she may imagine herself in the role, holding the power to affect the entire world. Michael reminds us that when we tell stories, we intentionally offer children the "Gift of the Memorable." It is a precious gift.

There is so much to learn in the following pages. I am confident that you will enjoy and be enriched, as I have been, by this transformative exploration of stories and storytelling throughout the Deep Well of Time!

Paul Epstein, Ph.D.
Speaker, Consultant, Writer
Author, *An Observer's Notebook: Learning from Children with the Observation C.O.R.E.*
Winona, Minnesota
April 2016

Preface

Once upon a time, long ago, far back in the mists of time, an ancient Pleistocene shaman sat by a flickering campfire surrounded by attentive members of his tribe. He looked at the people around him, catching their eyes. With a mysterious look and a commanding voice, he began to tell a story of the great hunt.

Or perhaps he spoke of where and how to find certain non-poisonous foods. He may have spoken of dangers like fearsome animals. Possibly, he described the successes and failures of finding a mate. Maybe he told of one who offended the traditions or violated the taboos of the tribe—and the frightening consequences this traitor faced.

These were stories, and they are still familiar to us as stories. Humans have been sharing narrative presentations for thousands of years, and just like our ancestors thousands of years ago, we still tell stories and find them strangely compelling. It is as if there is something within us that only stories can reach.

In this book, I examine stories and storytelling in classroom and school settings, as well as in homes and home-school settings. The intent of this book is to reach teachers of all sorts—Montessori teachers as well as their more traditional colleagues. It is also suitable for school leaders, administrators, board members of every sort, parents, and higher educators, including professors of education in colleges or schools of education across the world. In fact, it is meant to reach anyone who is interested in children, learning, and stories: anyone who wants to bring stories and narratives to children or learners of all ages.

At heart, this is a book about the exceptionally valuable uses of narrative in human learning. Our stories recall that ancient Pleistocene shaman who was preparing to tell a prehistoric story. Today still, storytellers of all kinds enthrall and co-create memorable stories with their audiences. Every one of us can participate in this uniquely human venture. That is the subject of this book.

INTRODUCTION

"Our minds make stories, and stories make our minds."

—Terry Pratchett, British author, and Ian Stewart and Jack Cohen, British scientists and authors

THIS IS A BOOK ABOUT STORYTELLING. More than that, it is a book for teachers telling stories and about special stories for special purposes. This book is about using storytelling with children in schools, homeschools, and classrooms to inspire, explain, and motivate. It is about the power of stories to address difficult curricular elements and realize otherwise unachievable student comprehension and understanding.

The word *story* comes to us originally from the Latin word *historia*, meaning "history," "account," "tale," or "story." Storyteller Paul Clement Czaja writes, "The word *story* comes from the ancient Greek word *histor* and means literally 'a narration from a learned man'" (2003, p. 69). The Oxford English Dictionary (1989) dates the word as entering the written English language from the early thirteenth century. The term *storyteller* dates only from 1709 (Oxford English Dictionary, 1989).

Most of this book is made up of actual stories to be told orally in schools. In this way, with the aim of meeting special purposes, they are distinctive. These are not the usual, ordinary stories frequently associated with childhood.

Those more familiar, traditional stories are certainly needed. There is an important place in schools and homes for the telling of well-known, time-tested stories, like myths, legends, fables, folktales, parables, and fairy tales. These *Gifts of the Past*, stories from many cultures and historical eras, continue to shape us as they have long shaped human cultures. They expose children to tales of heroism, courage, integrity, kindness, fair play, and love. These story types comprise a vital element of our collective written and oral literature and should be regularly shared with children.

Yet, the stories in this book are different. Almost every narrative presented herein links to a particular element of school curriculum: mathematics, history, language arts, or some other topic. Which particular curricular link is not the concern. Most important is that each story has a connection with the curriculum.

I have also included a small selection of autobiographical stories, which I have done because children love to hear of the world as it was when the adults in their life were young. They enjoy tales of our experiences and what we may have learned from them. These stories serve as examples of personal history: the stories of one life lived. In this way, they connect to the history curriculum. In Montessori schools, children regularly create personal histories, develop individual timelines, and research family history and family stories. Children may use these models to create their own life stories.

Stories are entertaining. They are enjoyable for the listeners and storyteller alike. The plain fact of stories' great fun is what makes them so usable in the classroom. Children simply like to hear them. Most children will happily gather around a storyteller to listen to tales being told and retold. As they do this, children express the joy of listening to a story, which is not only an individual pleasure, but also a group enjoyment. It is a feeling shared by each listener and, not insignificantly, the storyteller him or herself.

Listening to a story is not a passive act. On the contrary, it is participatory, a mutual exchange that engages imagination and abstraction. It can be visceral, cerebral, and often emotional. The storyteller's art creates a community of the teller and the listeners. Together, they share a meaningful and powerful experience.

Stories allow us to share in one of the most primal and uniquely human experiences—oral communication. The human gift of oral communication transcends history. Unlike literacy, a relatively recent invention, speech leaves no fossils, records, nor scrolls. Our oral tradition is not subject to archeological discovery. Instead, we are, ourselves, the archeological resource. The capacity for sharing oral literature lies as much within us as it did for Aesop. We only have to begin telling.

My Grandfather's Gift

I found my own storytelling beginnings as an impassioned story listener. I was very lucky to have an extraordinary grandfather, and some of my earliest memories are of him telling me fantastic stories. In addition to my grandfather's role of paterfamilias, warmly looking over all of his flock, he was a published author of poetry and prose, an early environmentalist, and an avid patriot. He expressed broad life experience, speaking of nature, conflict, and human struggle. The stories that he crafted were rich in poetic cadence, sonorous rhythms, and enthralling vocabulary, and they offered, even to a young child such as myself, glimpses of what I could hope to be as an individual.

Every evening at bedtime, my grandfather would lie down on the bed next to me and begin a story of the little people. There was no book. There were no pictures or video. There was only his voice in the warm, dark bedroom, and his tales came to vivid life in my mind. As I got older, the magical characters in his tales grew, and their exploits broadened, in mirror of my own development.

My grandfather's stories gave rhythm to my nights. They filled my dreams and enriched my imagination with allegory and metaphor. Each day I looked forward to the nighttime arrival of the *droons,* as my grandfather called the magical little people in his stories. It was certainly no coincidence that their leader was always named Michael (or some variant thereof).

Inevitably, I would quietly fall asleep at some point during the tale, and this is the point where my grandfather would take it up the next night. There was never any need to persuade or force me to go to bed; I was always eager to find out what would happen next.

Now, many years later, I realize what an astonishing gift I was given. Strange as it may seem now, we had no television, no computer, and no video games. Although we were a family of great readers, in my estimation, my grandfather's stories—his patience, his voice—surpassed any literature. I owe so much to his rich imagination; it captured and directed my own.

~

My background, as a teacher and as a storyteller, is within the Montessori tradition. I will admit that when I first discovered Montessori education, I was initially reticent—perhaps almost put off—by its emphasis on stories, fables, and myth for the elementary school years. Somewhere along the way, I must have lost contact with the rich imagination of youth; I had forgotten the effects that my grandfather's stories had on the young me.

The Montessori elementary teacher education process placed great emphasis on stories and the power of the creative imagination, and we teachers-to-be heard and explored a wide range of stories for children. Some of the stories were powerful and compelling, yet others seemed comparatively light, almost inconsequential. Not only was I not persuaded that my future students would be able to accept many of these stories, but I really could not understand how I could actually tell them.

However, as I began, tentatively, to tell stories to my students, I discovered the joy of not only listening, but also telling a variety of tales. I began to work on embellishment, vocal dynamics, facial expressions, and gestures. Stories started to actually become enjoyable, for the children and for me. Once again, I was falling in love with story.

Most importantly (and to my amazement), the stories worked. They brought children to lessons in an anticipatory mood, excited to be a part of the storytelling experience. They not only loved the stories that I perceived to be powerful and compelling, but they also loved those that I had believed to be trivial or corny. They simply loved stories—all of them. Stories were fun!

If stories are fun, can they be educational, too? Can children really learn from stories? If they do, what will they learn?

Indeed, stories seem to do much more than any other single curricular element. They motivate and inspire, and well-told stories contain touch points for children to identify throughout the more traditional pedagogy of the school.

I can no longer imagine a school without a rich shared collection of stories. Such a place would be insufferably sterile and dull.

~

Montessori schools use stories at all levels, but there is a special emphasis on them during the elementary years. In fact, because of the extent of its basis upon certain key stories, the entire curriculum for the elementary years could be called the *Story-Centered Curriculum.* This book presents stories that fit within the Montessori curriculum and thematic plan. Some of these are traditional Montessori stories that go back many years and which I have represented here with nods to tradition and to modern consciousness both. Also in this book are stories that I have developed and written to bring the power and richness of oral literature to new areas of the Montessori curriculum.

Regardless of this book's Montessori focus, almost all of the stories herein could find a useful place within conventional classrooms—though organizing and centering a curriculum around the creative device of story would soon guarantee that those classrooms were no longer conventional!

Paradoxically, using stories can make classrooms (and schools) more progressive and more traditional at the same time. The progressive element lies in utilizing the child's imagination as the driving impetus to education. With imagination captured, inner curiosity and questioning are activated, and education truly becomes a lifelong process.

At the same time, classrooms that use stories become more deeply traditional. Storytelling extends our long, great human tradition of oral communication. Even before the Bronze Age, the storyteller was the educator, the keeper of tradition, and sometimes even the priest or shaman in human communities. Modern teacher-storytellers join and carry forward that ancient and venerated tradition.

In our pre-modern eras, before the widespread growth of literacy, the storyteller provided history, tradition, entertainment, education, values, and morals—the preservation of culture—to the audience. Paul Clement Czaja (2003, p. 69) writes, "Since the beginnings of human time, noble men and women who had survived life long enough to be old would share stories of wisdom to all who would gather around the fire and listen."

In traditional cultures, storytelling held a central role. On this, Sri Lanka studies specialist Patrick Harrigan of the Living Heritage Trust, reporting to the Sri Lankan paper *The Island* (1994, p. 2), comments, "The ancient art of storytelling is highly regarded in traditional cultures where it is often the principal vehicle for the transmission of in-depth understanding as opposed to the mere accumulation of bits of information."

Thinking of storytellers of the past, and especially those of Sri Lanka, Harrigan says "... traditional storytellers wove fact and fiction together as the warp and woof of a single, all-inclusive fabric of reality" (1994, p. 2). Elements of early storytelling included repetition, rhythm, gesture, chant, alliteration, key phrases, movement, memory, sounds, pantomime, and even dance. Some or all of these components can still enrich the experience of storytelling in the classroom.

~

This book was not begun with the intent of being spiritual or including a spiritual element. Yet, I can see that even without trying, it has happened. This is because storytelling is more than a mere art: it is a spiritual act. Storytelling enriches the spirit of the teller, and stories touch the spirits of the children who are listening.

It is in this context that Montessori educator Phyllis Pottish-Lewis (1994, para. 1) writes, "Storytelling brings to the listeners heightened awareness, a sense of wonder, a sense of mystery, a reverence for life. It is through the stories themselves, and through the interaction between teller and listener, that storytelling goes beyond the surface child to speak to the inner child."

Stories, like all art, open our minds to the strange and wonderful world (and universe!) that surrounds us. Speaking of myth, Georgia College folklorist and professor Mary Magoulick (2006, para. 8) writes, "One of the functions of all art is to reconcile us to paradox. Another is to suggest fundamental patterns of life and the universe." For children and adults, becoming aware of and addressing fundamental paradoxes is a spiritual journey. This journey is unequivocally aided by story.

~

Many people tell me that they are visual learners. From the numbers who approach me with this observation, I am led to believe that visual learners are at least a plurality among our population. To help and instruct the visual among us, as well as to clarify complicated tellings, this book contains a number of graphics and illustrations in the section called *The Stories* (p. 59). I hope that you enjoy them and that they enhance your enjoyment of the stories.

Finally, please tell stories to children. Tell them at bedtime, tell them after dinner, tell them in the car, and certainly do tell them in the classroom. Stories bring us together in ways that no other medium can. Enjoy.

The Reason for the Title

This book's title, *The Deep Well of Time*, is meant to invoke the deep tradition of storytelling that connects us to our historic and even prehistoric past. It refers to the connection between stories and the deep understanding and inspiration that can be drawn from them, like water from a well.

The inspiration for the title came from the traditional nursery rhyme "Jack and Jill":

Jack and Jill went up the hill
To fetch a pail of water.
Jack fell down and broke his crown,
And Jill came tumbling after.

Have you ever wondered what it was that led Jack and Jill up the fabled hill to fetch water? Wells are not normally found on the top of hills. Since water flows downward, wells and springs are usually located toward the bottom of a slope. Presumably, they could have found some source of water without their ill-fated climb up that hill. What lured the children up?

A vital insight is that this legendary source was not an ordinary well, nor did it contain ordinary water. The mystical well on top of the hill must have been the sacred well bearing the water of life (or knowledge)—a well not bound by normal physical constraints. It is safe to presume that Jack and Jill were seeking wisdom, insight, knowledge, power, or more from the fabled water of the wondrous hilltop well.

The origins of this nursery rhyme are disputed, but at least one of the possibilities is ancient (Cassidy, 1951).

In very early Norse mythology, we meet Hjúki and Bil, brother and sister, who climbed a hill to try to steal from the sacred well of Byrgir. In this version of the tale, the well's liquid is not simply water but a sort of sacred and wonderful golden mead described by the mythological term *soma*, the creative sap of nature and inspiration, which rose from a subterranean source of unknown depth to hydrate the middle root of the world-tree.

Hjúki and Bil never returned from their expedition to the hallowed well; the moon-god took the children and the sacred golden liquid of Byrgir for himself. Thus it was that the Norse gods of Asgard were able to partake of this numinous drink of wisdom and knowledge.

The deep well that had been sought by these Jack and Jill precursors was no ordinary water source. As a sacred well of inspiration, wisdom, and knowledge, it represents a fount that humans throughout time have sought—and still continue to seek. I call this deep spring of human experience the Deep Well of Time.

Stories are our way today to plumb the depths of this deep well and share them with one another and with children. In the oral tradition of stories, legends, and myth, we seek our beginnings as well as inspiration, knowledge, and wisdom. Some of our origin stories plumb deeply into the well of time, while other tales only skim the pellucid surface.

I enjoy the metaphor of the Deep Well of Time because it helps me in understanding the remarkable power of story. Unlike Hjúki and Bil's elusive golden mead, a real, drinkable creative fluid is obtainable to us through the extraordinary vessel of story. Story has the power to reach deeply into the imagination within each and every one of us. In my metaphor, story is a bridge between our everyday existence and the well of universal human experience.

The stories captured in this book are offered as a beginning of the learning process—a first bucket eagerly dipped into the waters of the deep and cavernous well. It is my hope that they will engender many more stories for young people, and invigorate and recreate education.

~

This book begins, appropriately I think, with a story, or fable. Like the other stories in this book, it is meant to be told aloud and listened to. As you read ahead, experiment with speaking the words; allow yourself to experience the cadence and musicality of oral language. I hope that you enjoy it.

The Fable of the Well

Once upon a time, in what may seem to be a distant land, there was a wondrously curious and unusual place. When I describe this place, people are surprised to find that they know it, yet often this spot cannot be found. Come and join me as we voyage together to find and explore this strange location. Our journey is a short one, but it brings us to an extraordinary and wondrous setting, much closer than we may realize. It is an odd and marvelous place, but at the same time, it is somehow familiar.

Here, sheltered in twilight, and guarded by the muse, Mneme[*], is a magical structure: the Deep Well of Time. The Well lies under a mossy stone arch, decorated with fragrant flowers and boughs of trees. It is bordered with wild green hydrangeas and red daisies.

Mystically, the water in the Deep Well is somehow more than simple water. Those who drink of it find refreshment and a conscious feeling of hope, faith, and purpose. The golden waters of this Deep Well are mixed from two sources in fantastic nearby springs.

The first cool spring lies deep in shady greenery. It is the Spring of Hope, its water colored a pale green. It is the source of expectation, trust, wishes, dreams, and aspirations. Its waters offer anticipation and faith.

The second spring, called the Spring of Love, is warm, its water very slightly tinted red. This soothing water nurtures the spirits of passion, adoration, and worship. It is the source of courage, compassion, kindness, charity, fondness, and romance. Running through all these feelings and binding them together is the warm power of Love.

As they run their course toward the mystical Well, the waters of these two springs pass through challenges and obstacles including the thorns of anger, the mire of hatred, the fog of prejudice, the sting of fear, the scorn of contempt, the malice of cruelty, and the gloom of pessimism.

Eventually, the cool green stream and the warm red flow find each other. Joyfully, they mingle. In unification, their waters magically acquire a golden color yet also retain a crystal transparency. This brilliant, glowing new stream emerges into the Deep Well, where it collects and offers inspiration for all humanity.

---

1 Pronounced M nEEM ee

The Well itself is mysterious, reaching far beyond ordinary and natural depths into unmapped subterranean territories. Penetrating the Well is the strong central taproot of the magnificent Tree of Creativity, which drinks deeply and constantly of the Well's amazing waters. Also fed by Imagination and Abstraction, this wondrous Tree bears marvelous branches in the arts, sciences, literature, religion, games, images, languages, and more.

The Deep Well lies at the center of this remarkable landscape. Let's choose a mystical bucket to plunge into its profound, hidden depths. The marvelous golden liquid promises unequaled refreshment from its powerful source, deep beneath us.

A magical property of the Deep Well is its ability to quench both our collective and our individual thirsts for memory. In its waters are origins, beginnings, sources, changes, recollections, experiences, knowledge, beliefs, and understanding. Many have even experienced powers of forgiveness and healing from a taste of its golden waters.

At its most profound reach, the Deep Well of Time leads to a gateway where the wells of all humanity, personal and collective, present and past, join to a single source of collective meaning. Here exists a foundation of shared remembrance and mutual recollection. It is here that we find the sources of wonderful myths and sacred stories concerning the origins of the world, the creation of life, the beginnings of humanity, and how the world and all of its creatures have come to be as they are today.

At the Deep Well of Time's foundation are the secret stories of our greatest inventions, like the mysterious and fascinating story of human language, including the first human word, the origins of sign and symbol, and the discoveries that led to alphabets. Here, too, we find the fascinating tale of mathematics: the human quest to number, to count, and to record.

In this Well are the roots of faith and belief, the origin stories of tribes, ancient cults, and those who welcomed the first wolves into human partnership. Here are stories of the original farmers, the beginnings of villages and cities—the inception of culture.

Along with the wonderful, the Deep Well of Time also contains the terrible. Here the seeker may locate night terrors, horrifying creatures, and human suffering, anguish, fear, panic, and dread.

The Deep Well of Time plunges into ancient and archaic eras, long before recorded history began. Its tributaries extend far beyond the limitations of each individual's own personal history.

No ordinary bucket or pail can draw the mystical golden waters from the Well, and no single draught will be, by itself, complete. Obtaining the priceless fluid of the Deep Well requires the ancient container called Story, a wondrous chalice embedded with the sparkling filaments of Imagination.

With the vessel of Story, each person may retrieve the holy waters of the Well. Thus, the artist may bathe his eyes so that he sees anew. Drinking deeply, the adventurer finds renewal and purpose in his quest. The inventor finds that hands dipped in these waters restore the nimble powers of distant ancestors. To scholars, bathing in the waters offers new and unique insight. The holy seer discovers in the sacred fluid inner truth, coupled with devotion and fidelity. These mystical waters offer teachers assured fluency tempered by thoughtful kindness. Immersed completely in the welcoming waters, children may travel unheard of distances to see the past and sight the yet unknown future.

Known also as myth, legend, fable, folklore, and tale, Story gives to humans the means to probe the Well's depths and draw from it that which we seek. Story gives us also the mysterious power to revel in the waters even while we are using them. Amazingly, our use of the Well never depletes the availability of the waters, but instead, strangely, renews their power and bounty.

Stories that access this Well of memory and time allow humans to encounter that which cannot be directly touched, sensed with our normal senses, or retrieved with mundane tools. However, no single story is complete or perfect. It is the collective impact of all story, myth, folklore, and legend that reveals the riches of the mystical Well.

When you are ready, your senses sated, you may return with me from the Deep Well of Time, from the two springs, crimson and emerald, and from the watchful eye of Mneme. Remember the verdant Tree of Creativity and its broadly spreading branches. You may keep Story, the wonderful and beauteous bucket. With it, you are now free to seek its magnificent riches at any time.

PART I

STORYTELLING

> "People are hungry for stories. It's part of our very being. Storytelling is a form of history, of immortality too. It goes from one generation to another."
>
> —Studs Terkel, American author and broadcast personality

Do we have time for stories? Can teachers, school leaders, and busy parents afford the time needed to be storytellers?

It might be that the business of schools and education is so critical that there is no time to tell a story. It certainly seems that way at times.

This might be true if stories were only a simple form of entertainment and nothing more. However, in truth, stories are much more than that. They may represent the most effective and powerful approach to learning available to us, even today in a quickly moving electronic and information age.

The great power of storytelling makes it especially suited to any situation involving learning, whether for toddlers, teens, or everyone else. This section of the book explores the background of educational storytelling—why, how, and when stories should be used, particularly their use in schools, including Montessori schools and more.

What is Storytelling?

Storytelling is an ancient and universal art.

"Storytelling is a uniquely human behavior, and anthropological evidence indicates that it is not a recent development—humans likely began telling stories tens of thousands of years ago" (Scalise Sugiyama, 2009, para. 1). As an oral medium, it uses voice, expression, movement, and gesture. Stories offer narratives concerning events that are fictional, factual, or mythological—or any combination thereof. As stories are told, the teller may involve embellishment and improvisation, or they may adhere closely to a set text. In any case, storytelling is universal. It has existed around the world in every culture.

Stories are tremendously important to us as human beings. They are also unique to human beings. In other words, telling stories is a mark of our humanity. This suggests that as a human characteristic, stories and storytelling are universal. They are part of every culture and, in fact, accessible to all individuals within that culture. On this topic, Michelle Scalise Sugiyama, a research associate at the University of Oregon, writes:

> Literate or not, all societies practice some form of storytelling. Moreover, the capacity for narrative is found universally across individuals within cultures. Although narrative skill varies from person to person, the ability to generate and process narrative is not limited to the exceptionally intelligent, nor is any formal instruction necessary for the acquisition of this faculty. (2001, p. 1)

Recognizing this universality, authors Terry Pratchett, Ian Stewart, and Jack Cohen suggest, in their 2002 science fiction novel, *The Science*

Of Discworld II: The Globe, that the human species be renamed from *Homo sapiens* (wise man) to *Pan narrans,* the storytelling or narrative ape. "We are not Homo sapiens, Wise Man. We are the third chimpanzee. What distinguishes us from the ordinary chimpanzee Pan troglodytes and the bonobo chimpanzee Pan paniscus, is something far more subtle than our enormous brain, three times as large as theirs in proportion to body weight. It is what that brain makes possible. And the most significant contribution that our large brain made to our approach to the universe was to endow us with the power of story. We are Pan narrans, the storytelling ape" (p. 325).

In his review of *The Science Of Discworld II: The Globe*, critic Steven Silver (2002, para. 4) writes that the authors "… show how humans use stories to explain the world around them and learn from these stories."

Although storytelling has a literary and linguistic component, it must be considered separate from reading, aloud or otherwise. Reading is an indispensable personal, family, and classroom activity, and it is one of the great outgrowths of literacy. Reading is essential in modern culture, but it is not storytelling. As storyteller Sally Crandall (2007, para. 6) writes, "Storytelling is not reading. It feeds on the natural brain paths already laid down from the beginning of human communication." In fact, storytelling is a non-literate art; it involves essentially different mental activity than reading; this is what makes it so vital and exciting.

Confusing the telling of stories with reading can lead us to ignoring orally-told stories, as unfortunately happens in many homes and classrooms. The stories in this book, and in other collections for telling, should not be read aloud, nor should they be recorded and played back electronically to children. Simply, they are to be told. This is the unique place of oral literature.

This is not to suggest that the practice of reading aloud be discarded. Reading aloud has its own essential merits: it allows the children and the reader to experience great literature with the cadences of oral language informing the story. Through reading aloud, we uniquely connect with authors and illustrators that speak to us from eras past and present. Reading aloud with children should be a daily activity. However, it is still a distinct exercise. It is not storytelling.

Storytelling is also not a recitation of memorized poetry or prose. Again, the memorization and recitation of selected literature is admirable and should be encouraged. Recitation can deepen our appreciation of literature. However, it is also not storytelling, and we should be careful not to confuse the two.

Storytelling is also related to the art form known as spoken word. Also with its own unique oral tradition, the modern form of spoken word evolved from troubadours, *trobairitz*, and *jongleurs* of the Middle Ages. Troubadours were artists who composed and recited poetry, often with music. Jongleurs were performers who did not compose their own poetry but performed by "covering" the compositions of others.

Both models (composer-performers and cover-performers) survive in today's spoken-word movement. Some artists invent or create narratives on the spot, in front of an audience. Others recite previously created compositions or perform works from others. Spoken-word performances are often poetic, although the genre is not limited to poetry.

Storytelling, as described in this book for an educational setting, is a spoken-word art, usually involving the delivery of material previously composed and practiced. It may include original stories or those composed by others. In other words, storytellers may be modern troubadours, trobairitz, and jongleurs.

Storytelling, as oral literature, involves listener and storyteller in ways that can only be compared to other interactive arts such as dance and drama. Like the dynamism of good conversation, a superior story is not one-sided. The response of the audience is essential to the art. A gasp, a sigh, a cry, a giggle, or a laugh: these all inspire the teller and inform the continued story. An audience may respond with words, gestures, movements, or facial expressions, and they are also certainly responding in ways that we cannot see. In fact, it is this inner response, the vital hidden happenings of the mind, that story can stimulate so well.

Like other lively arts, the art of storytelling is temporal. Linked to an actual, specific time, it is not an art form that can be hung in a gallery or mounted in a scrapbook. When the story has been told, it has moved from the mind of the teller into the minds of the audience members. Like music, it resides there to come to consciousness periodically. In our imaginings, the story can be revisited again and again, and through this revisiting it can have a transformative effect, causing us to revise and review thoughts in the light of the elements of the story.

Of course, no art simply exists in a vacuum. The intensity and power of the arts lies in the communication that they create. This is often a personal conversation between the artist and the recipient, but, particularly in an art like storytelling, it can also be a mutual, shared communication between all participants, or recipients, of an artistic product.

With storytelling, the audience is left with a shared experience—the story. The story, therefore, is a catalyst in community building. This is one of the great powers of storytelling. The collective strength of narrative and oral literature brings children, classes, and schools together in a kind of society with a shared identity.

All classrooms and schools need to build community, and they always benefit from a clear, defined identity. What better and more direct medium exists than oral storytelling to achieve these dual goals?

Finally, storytelling has a spiritual power. It is no accident that some of the most ancient storytelling may have included prehistoric drawings and early cave art as a visual element. Modern children too have spiritual needs and drives that are encouraged and developed through the narrative power of orally told stories.

When a powerful story is told, a special bond is formed between the teller and the audience. When that audience is a classroom of impressionable children, then that bond is special indeed. In Montessori schools, children in the Children's House (preschool)[2] and Elementary levels stay with the same teacher and continue together as a group over a three-year period. This is an essential element of the Montessori approach that allows community and spiritual bonds to be deeply nurtured over an appropriate amount of time. In any classroom or school setting, whether Montessori or not, this bond is intensified and strengthened through the shared tradition of stories.

The special relationship between the audience of children and the

---

[2]Maria Montessori used the Italian term *Casa dei Bambini* to name her program for young children. This is usually translated into the English term "Children's House" or "House of Children." Many Montessorians prefer this name, or the even simpler *Casa,* for the three- to six-year-old environment. A large number of Montessori professionals avoid the word *preschool,* since they argue that the experience is, in fact, "school." While the word *primary* is also used for this level in many areas, this is problematic in that "primary" refers to the lower grades in many states and to the elementary years in many countries. Finally, some groups, such as the American Montessori Society, call this level *early childhood.* Even this term is sticky, in that it most generally means the period from birth to age eight, not just the three to six age span. In this book, I use the terms *Children's House* and *preschool* synonymously.

storytelling teacher is one of mutual trust. On one hand, the child trusts in the meaning and depth of the story. On the other hand, the adult performs an act of faith and trust in offering the story. As in all art, there is an element of risk, as storytelling requires a certain amount of baring one's soul. The reciprocal trust and communion over shared experience are enhanced and strengthened every time a story is repeated.

Storytelling is a gift that the storyteller gives to the audience. In the case of the classroom, the gift is given to the children and to the future. It is a gift of self, of spirit, of excitement, and of love, yet ironically, it is not completely altruistic or selfless. The gift of story enriches the storyteller as much as the audience. In this, it is one of our greatest artistic techniques. All who participate gain from the experience.

Stories for the Montessori Classroom

Stories are vital to the Montessori experience. More than that, they are an indispensable element of every childhood, as they always have been. With the youngest infants, toddlers, and preschoolers, as well as with older, sophisticated adolescents, stories have a place, and it should be a prominent one. Stories enhance and deepen the educational experience, and they enrich the culture of any classroom and any school. Most importantly, they nurture the spirit of the child, offering insight, perception, relaxation, entertainment, and plain enjoyment.

The Children's House

In the preschool or Children's House level of Montessori, great emphasis is placed upon reality. This means that the presentations of educational material in the classroom are precise, meticulous, and exact. All classroom work at this level has its roots in concrete objects—real things.

Correlated with this emphasis on reality, a central focus of the Montessori Children's House is to offer young children the opportunity to identify, clarify, and name fundamental impressions that they receive through their senses. Montessori at this level also aims to educate or refine the senses so that the child becomes capable of making finer and more precise discriminations, as well as gaining and using rich accompanying vocabulary.

Montessorians describe their approach for the young child as *sensorial* in nature; it is based upon what can be seen, heard, tasted, felt, or smelled. A second and equally important focus of Montessori is to assist children in developing independence and self-reliance.

Maria Montessori brought the sensorial approach to the fore as a central tenet of her method, but she did not originate the concept. In 1862, lifelong educator Adonijah Strong Welch wrote a perceptive, influential manual for elementary school teachers while he was principal of Michigan State Normal School (later Eastern Michigan University). The book, *Object Lessons,* contains much that seems to augur Montessori's ideas to come. Welch, who subsequently became the first president of Iowa State University, wrote,

> The first instruction given to the child in school should be based on the fact that his intellectual activity consists in seeing and hearing rather than in reasoning and reflecting... Since the senses of sight and hearing are first in exercise and development, the first step in school training should be to give them a systematic culture. (1862, p. iii)

An emphasis upon the senses necessarily suggests, as Welch later argued in *Object Lessons,* that things—objects—form the basis of early education (1862). Because of this direction and in acknowledgement of the natural instincts of children, the stories told in the Montessori Children's House tend to emphasize reality and sensorial experience; they reference images that can be identified by children and verified by their senses. This does not mean that all images are familiar, but unfamiliar ones are enriched by sensorial language that emphasizes color, shape, size, texture, scent, sound, temperature, weight, or taste. This is meant to engage the emerging power of the children's senses in facilitating their understanding of the story.

Excellent stories for the Children's House level may be relatively short—perhaps the oral equivalent of just one or two paragraphs. These may include accounts of simple everyday events, autobiographical or biographical anecdotes, animal stories based on real animals or animal development, or stories from science. They may be fictional, but they should always have a sensorial foundation.

The Elementary Level

Montessori elementary classrooms are designed for children with an approximate age range of six to twelve years old. The stories offered at this level (and older) should emphasize the imagination. This is the time to introduce legend, myth, fable, folklore, and fancy. Elementary classrooms also provide the right moment for the uniquely specialized, imagination-based *curriculum story.* These are specially developed stories directly related to elements of the school curriculum.

In the elementary years, children shift from purely sensorial experience to an emphasis upon higher-order thinking, which educators call *cognition.* Using the sensory understandings that they developed in the Children's House, or preschool, children leapfrog to new thinking ability, contemplating questions of meaning, our beginnings, and our possible futures. The elementary years begin as an age of imagination and later transform into an age of abstraction. Sensorial elements at this level are always applied to higher-level conceptualization.

These developmental shifts have led to a Montessori approach for elementary children that is by nature *holistic*—a notion that actually has two meanings. The first is that, whenever possible in a first or very early presentation of a material, some means must be exploited to offer the children the largest possible overall conceptual impression. The second implication of the *holistic* descriptor is that the child is offered activities that lead to the children so immersing themselves in that which is being studied that, figuratively speaking, they become the thing that is being studied, rather than simply studying about it.

Never as precise or exacting as Children's House presentations, elementary presentations of Montessori learning material can almost always be enhanced with stories, origins, art, etymologies, imaginative posters, music, movement, or commentary from the adult or other children. More, the two aforementioned holistic objectives are often best addressed through story.

A story offers a virtual experience of things that cannot concretely be brought into the classroom. Impressions, feelings, historical events, mythological creatures, possible futures, and the substance of the cosmos can all be offered in this creative, intentionally metaphorical way. Stories can even be used to create familiarity with concrete items, like geological artifacts, that are rare or unobtainable. Through correlated creative drama, children can act out or perform the stories they have heard, in effect "becoming the thing" and fulfilling the second holistic objective.

In her book *To Educate the Human Potential* (1996), Montessori (recalling a nearly 100-page chapter in her 1916 work *The Advanced Montessori Method, Volume 1*) discusses the topic of imagination. In this lengthy discussion, Montessori addresses the importance of imagination not only to the child but also to all of humanity. In fact, she makes the case that all of human progress is due to imagination. Here she asserts that the correct time for imaginative stories and other activities that develop imagination is during the elementary school years, a period Montessorians refer to as the *Second Plane of Development*.

Much of the remainder of *To Educate the Human Potential* is then taken up with Dr. Montessori's transcriptions of a set of stories including the beginning of the universe, the creation of the Earth, the eras of prehistoric humans and early civilizations, as well as accounts of many important human advances. The elements of these stories were later incorporated into a more formal group of specific stories that elementary Montessorians call the *Great Lessons* (Duffy & Duffy, 2002).

The importance of *To Educate the Human Potential* to the development of Montessori's elementary program cannot be overestimated. Through its emphasis on narrative story and storytelling to nurture the imagination and communicate essential curricular elements, the book serves as the philosophical and theoretical basis of the entire Montessori elementary approach.

There are innumerable outstanding stories for the elementary level, ranging in length from a few brief minutes to narratives of up to half an hour. These stories may include metaphor, myth, invention, imagery, parable, personification, anthropomorphism, and zoomorphism. Elementary stories sometimes include props, art works, or simple costumes.

When preparing learning activities, one should always be sure to consider all the possible stories that might fit. You may use a story that you already know, or this may be the opportunity to create a new or special story tailored to the learning experience.

In any case, be sure to somehow record the stories that you use in your classroom. Children will eagerly request the same stories time and again. They will want to hear about their favorite characters, funny incidents, and stories that you have told or performed in particularly memorable or pleasing ways. Sometimes a child will surprise you with a request for a story that you thought did not work. Despite your impression of failure, that "flop" somehow struck a chord.

Stories are never a one-time thing; they grow, and often change, through repetition.

Technical and Psychological Lessons

In every school, be it Montessori or more conventional, lessons are regularly offered to children. In addition to all of the presentations in diverse subject areas, there is instruction aimed at the development of independence, character, and other developmental qualities.

A classification scheme is very helpful when thinking about the countless lessons that schools offer. Most presentations can be broken into two large groups: the technical lessons and the psychological lessons.

Technical lessons involve a sort of education that many of us would recognize immediately. These familiar lessons aim to teach things like the multiplication facts, different kinds of nouns, great poets in British literature, musical notation's treble clef, or the climate of Australia. In other words, these technical lessons focus on knowledge, procedures, reasoning, or specific learning materials. In Montessori classes particularly, many presentations involve the uses and applications of the numerous, specially designed Montessori learning objects. These presentations are clearly technical in nature; literally, they emphasize "technique."

Technical lessons are the "meat and potatoes" of the classroom. They make up the majority of lessons in almost any school group, Montessori or otherwise. Technical lessons represent most of what we conventionally think of as "curriculum," and they focus on instruction, process, explanation, facts, nomenclature, understanding, and manipulation of objects.

In great contrast to the technical, psychological lessons function to strike the imagination, inspire, invigorate, animate, surprise, and awaken or develop a sense of wonder. This is the category where *curriculum stories* belong. Like any lesson, a curriculum story is a gift, but it is a special one that balances the curriculum and activates both sides of the child's brain.

Psychological lessons do not attempt to present techniques or procedures. Instead, their aim is to approach the child's spirit with a buoyant and uplifting element that utilizes the power of the imagination. When spirit and imagination are actively engaged, children's learning is deeply enhanced and empowered. While these psychological lessons do not represent the "meat and potatoes" of the child's intellectual meal, they are like the herbs and spices. Only a sprinkling is needed, but its effect can be powerful, and it can elevate the mundane to the sublime.

In addition to stories, other psychological lessons may use imaginative posters, timelines, musical instruments, movement, visual art media, and other specialized materials. Yet, while stories are not the only psychological lessons, they are probably the most accessible.

It is important to understand the imperative that not all lessons fall into the psychological group, nor should they. Although this could be exciting for children, it would lack the thoroughness and substance provided by technical lessons, which constitute the vast majority of instructional presentations.

On the other hand, an intellectual diet made up solely of the technical would be bland—unappetizing in the extreme. The result of an all-technical curriculum would be boredom and disassociation from learning. Sadly, this force-fed diet of the technical is not uncommon in many conventional schools, and even some Montessori schools fall victim to this problem.

The key to a well-ordered classroom is to strike a balance. When the technical lessons inform the bulk of the intellectual curriculum, the goals of instruction, process, explanation, nomenclature, understanding, and proper manipulation of objects are achieved. At the same time, a vigorous component of psychological lessons inserts the energy of imagination and visualization in developing dynamic motivation and excitement, as well as an affirmative attitude toward school and learning.

Why We Use Stories: *The Gift of the Memorable*

Det er nåtidens plikt å ta vare på fortiden for fremtiden.

"It is the duty of the present to convey the voices of the past to the ears of the future."

—Norwegian saying, translated by Kari Lie Dorer

Memory is a tricky thing. As we recall the past, certain events stand out, usually for a powerful reason.

We all have particular memories that we carry with us from our early schooling. Some of these memories are bright, wonderful, and delightful. Other memories are darker; they may be of failure, sadness, or pain. Most of us retain very few memories of commonplace or routine childhood events. It is a trick of our memory that it emphasizes recollection of the more extraordinary and powerful events.

I would like to suggest that, as dedicated parents, teachers, and school heads, we are called to intentionally offer children unforgettable moments, small capsules of brilliance, and remarkable experiences that will resonate within them for years. These vital moments cannot occur every minute, every day, but offering them is one of our greatest obligations. I call this the *Gift of the Memorable.* The outcome of this gift cannot be measured on tests or report cards, but it is possibly the greatest impetus we can offer to lifelong learning. Without these brilliant flashes, the young person's education will be desolate, bleak, and unmemorable.

The Gift of the Memorable certainly can and should be given through other arts, exercises, or lessons; however, a primary value of storytelling is that it is an art most accessible to adults and that children are most ready to unquestioningly receive. It usually takes little more than the words *Once upon a time…* to signal to the children the wonder that is to come. There is no necessity for them to study story appreciation to gain joy from a narrative tale. They are already primed for it.

The Gift of the Memorable offers a tremendously important value implicit to storytelling. However, it is by no means the only value one can find in narrative. Indeed, this value is just the first of nine values that I will discuss.

~

Stories can offer a way to appreciate, grasp, or absorb an entirety or whole so large that it is otherwise practically beyond comprehension. This second value of story is called *holism*. Holism essentially means presenting the whole before the parts. Instead of beginning with details, the minutiae are presented later, in relation to the whole. Deriving from *hólos*, a Greek word meaning "whole," "all," or "entire," holism is the idea that all the properties of a system cannot be determined or explained by the sum of its component parts alone. Therefore, the system can best be understood as an entirety.

In his 1926 book, *Holism and Evolution*, the South African statesman Jan Smuts coined the word *holism*, which he defined as "the tendency in nature to form wholes that are greater than the sum of the parts through creative evolution" (Smuts, 1926, p. 88). Millennia earlier, Aristotle had summarized what would become the central idea of holism in the *Metaphysics*: "The whole is more than the sum of its parts."

As holism suggests starting with the biggest possible picture or approach before later narrowing the focus, the Montessori elementary curriculum is plainly holistic in nature. In the Montessori elementary method, almost all topics are approached holistically, with the widest view possible. The idea is always to begin a lesson with a presentation of an entire concept, or at least a vision of the whole. To do this, it is considered best, when possible, to bring the real thing into the classroom and use it as a starting point. A real canary can help a child to understand the meaning of *wing*, or a model can assist in identifying the parts of a glacier.

But what do we do for lessons on occurrences that are conceptual, not physical? Teachers need to present a multitude of things that simply cannot be brought into the classroom, things for which there is no model or picture available. If we are offering a lesson on the concept of time, or the beginnings of agriculture, or something as major as the creation of the universe, models simply will not do.

These are the moments in which a story can provide the big holistic picture that cannot be otherwise easily grasped. This has always been the task of myth, to offer seekers a big-picture explanation of the origins of things. Our modern stories can be as holistic as ancient myths.

Award-winning author Stephen Denning writes in *The Secret Language of Leadership* (2007, p. 205),

> When we hear a powerful story, we have the feeling that it is somehow unique, somehow without precedent. We perceive a sense of the "newbornness" of the entire world, as if there has been nothing like this, ever, anywhere. It is the same feeling that we get when we perceive a beautiful object that "fills the mind and ...gives the 'never before in the history of the world' feeling."

This may well be one of the essentials of holism and the holistic approach—the idea that we are collaborators in creativity, that we are part of an ongoing work of creation.

~

A third value of storytelling is the development of the skill of careful listening. Really an art in itself, listening requires, and thrives upon, repeated practice. Stories give children the opportunity to develop their listening ability in a non-threatening context in which there is no test, assessment, or worrisome judgment.

Additionally, stories introduce non-literate children to the entire structural range of literature. Children unfettered by their ability to read or sound out alphabetic characters can experience all the setting, organization, rising action, and the denouement. Every one of these elements, keys to analyzing and understanding later literature, can be absorbed by children while simply enjoying a story. As stories are offered as uninterrupted wholes, not chopped up like the chapters of a book, the storyteller contributes to the sense of holism experienced by the children.

Thus, a powerful fourth value of story: the development of literacy. Listening to and participating in stories develop comprehension skills that will ultimately be transferred to reading. Bruce Marbin, administrator of the Corvallis Montessori School in Corvallis, Oregon, affirms, "The thing with the tradition of storytelling is that they, the children, have to make the pictures in their head. It kindles the spirit of literacy" (2006).

Well-crafted stories powerfully assist in growing the child's vocabulary, another part of successful total reading. Phyllis Pottish-Lewis writes, "Children should have continuous practice in hearing stories told so that their vocabularies will grow as well as their abilities to comprehend the meaning of the spoken word. Moreover, a word that has been heard and understood is more easily recognized when a child encounters it in print" (Pottish-Lewis, 1994).

~

A fifth value of storytelling is the compelling engagement of the imagination. Like many educators, Montessorians believe that the elementary years are a particularly rich and fertile period for imaginative growth. Speaking of elementary children, Montessori wrote, "Not only can imagination travel through infinite space, but also through infinite time; we can go backwards through the epochs and have a vision of the earth as it was, with the creatures that inhabited it" (Montessori, 1996, p. 10). Herein lies the imperative to offer overtly creative components of the curriculum such as narrative stories.

In the collection that follows, some of the stories such as *The Family Gallery* (p. 219) may not properly be called stories, but instead are more accurately described as *narrative*. These narratives offer an effective way to increase a lesson's imaginative appeal by transforming it into a narrative form.

However, stories do not only stimulate the imagination of elementary children. They serve the same purpose when offered to preschoolers, middle school students, and even adults. We are none of us immune to the power of story. The plain fact is that, as noted by Maria Montessori in *To Educate the Human Potential*, stories help in the development of the imagination, regardless of age.

Nationally acclaimed storyteller and author Heather Forest put the case for imagination well when she wrote,

> Both telling a story and listening to a well-told tale encourages students to use their imaginations. Developing the imagination can empower students to consider new and

> inventive ideas. Developing the imagination can contribute to self-confidence and personal motivation as students envision themselves competent and able to accomplish their hopes and dreams. (Forest, 2000, para. 3)

Stories develop the imagination because the young people listening literally create their own images from the words that they hear. Even when the storyteller uses pictures or models, educational materials, or other props, the children are still busy with the mental work of creation. Likewise, the storyteller is engaged in a similar creative, imaginative activity. This act, the creation of images, is at the heart of imagination. Supporting this idea, Phyllis Pottish-Lewis writes, "The ability to visualize that which is not tangible is the basis of creative imagination" (Pottish-Lewis, 1994).

Montessorian Paul Clement Czaja corroborates this notion in writing of the act of storytelling: "A story well told has the power to set imaginations aflame, to engage the listener's feelings, to become a matter of life revealing life" (2003, p. 69).

There is a somewhat widely held misconception that Montessori schools and Montessorians avoid a focus on the imagination. In fact, it is a Montessori tenet that stories and activities engaging the direct input of the senses create the basis for future, critically important flights of the imagination.

Plainly put, very young children are busy identifying elements of their surroundings. They sense them, classify them, and build a vocabulary around them. Thus, the stories that are told to preschool children build their imagination when referencing these same sensorial points from the surrounding environment. These stories develop imaginative powers precisely because of their basis in reality.

Older children, in a less sensorial plane of development, need—and love—stories that stretch their deepening imagination. Although sometimes referencing sensorial cues, these stories can now deal with the fantastic, extraordinary, or out-of-this-world.

Stories help to develop creativity. The storyteller is a creative artist, but so is every listener-participant. They create the images and context of the story as it is narrated. Stephen Denning wrote on this subject,

> Story stimulates creativity. It causes us to gape and suspend analytic thought, to set aside the inclination to slice and dice experience into abstract categories. Instead, the mind is prompted to search backward to earlier examples and parallels. And simultaneously we are prompted to new acts of creation, to imagine other analogous examples in the future. (Denning, 2007, p. 205)

~

Storytelling's effectiveness in addressing state, county, or district standards represents a sixth value of storytelling. Throughout the United States, most standards address the development of speaking and performance abilities. Involving students in storytelling experiences may be a way to satisfy these requirements.

~

Stories are a tremendously effective method of passing on culture. This is a seventh benefit of storytelling. Embedded in stories are ideas, attitudes, knowledge, and wisdom of multitudes of people who have lived before us. Many of the standard Montessori stories are traditional and carry these values. New stories can do this as well by being careful to include cultural values and knowledge.

Part and parcel of cultural values is the development of character building. This represents storytelling's eighth role. Curriculum stories that offer knowledge and wisdom that encourage specific, prosocial behavior can have lasting effects beyond the targeted lesson or even beyond the school years. Character-building stories of the sort told by master storyteller Jonathan Wolff offer a peaceful way to help children in developing positive personal and societal values. They do this by presenting situations in which good choices made by some characters can be contrasted with poorer choices made by others. Children use their imaginations to connect these to their own situations.

~

Finally, stories should be used simply because children love them. They are a tremendous source of entertainment. "A good story, after all, is both entertaining and instructive at the same time," writes author Patrick Harrigan. He continues, "Moreover, it may be told and retold in any number of ways. And stories may serve as bridges of understanding between people, for a good story may be enjoyed and appreciated by young and old or rich and poor alike, each according to his or her own level of appreciation" (Harrigan, 1994, p. 2).

There is no doubt that stories are one of the most popular classroom activities. I have found that if I begin a story in some classroom corner with a small group of children, others will soon gather around, even if they have heard the story before—possibly *because* they have heard the story before! These children may not be in the group to whom this story is directed, but they want to be part of it, to join the community that is emerging around the story. They may say, "Oh, I love this one," or "This one is so silly."

Even those who do not come over are often involved, from a distance, across the classroom. I see them following along, even mouthing favorite parts. From their own work places in other parts of the room, they are transported by the power of story.

Children love stories. Stories are incredibly effective. Stories help to develop the imagination. Stories lead to literacy. Stories can offer wisdom and build character. Stories help perfect listening. Stories speak to the spirit. With all of these benefits and more, it is clear that stories and storytelling deserve a central role in our schools. The mystery is that story is used so little. We need to use story widely and well.

When Should Stories Be Offered?

There are multiple places for stories throughout every school day, not to mention throughout every school year. Many of these opportunities spring up organically and spontaneously. Still, many teachers want to know specifically when, and to whom, various stories should be told. This can be essential for planning lessons, preparing materials, and for engaging in the necessary practice that should precede any storytelling session.

One excellent use of curriculum stories is as an introduction to a topic or lesson set. Because stories offer holistic views, they can be delivered at the beginnings of units or chapters, often preceding the presentation of materials. In other cases, they may be coupled with material presentations or demonstrations. In Montessori schools, as in other schools, there are many sub-units or strands within major subjects. For example, in geometry, elementary school Montessorians address topics like fundamental geometric ideas, kinds of triangles, measurement of area, and many others. The beginning of each of these segments is an ideal spot for a narrative tale.

Curriculum stories can also be used in summary or conclusion. Toward the end of a unit or chapter, there is a natural need to sum up, to relate what has been accomplished to other curricular elements. This is also a good time to tell a story—again because of the holistic powers that stories possess. One excellent practice is to retell the same story that was used at the beginning of a unit. This can lead to interesting, dynamic group discussions, especially among older elementary children.

This should not indicate, at all, that there are any bad times for stories. I cannot imagine a poor moment to insert a story into a curriculum. Because stories have powers to illuminate, elucidate, excite, motivate, spark creative imagination, and touch the spirit of children, they may well be used throughout the entire curriculum.

It must also be recognized that, realistically, teachers will be doing many other things every day besides telling stories. This is why I have tried to identify absolute "don't-miss" spots for creative storytelling. When using stories in these curricular places, a teacher will develop experience, comfort, and confidence in storytelling; this may well lead to the teacher's ability to use stories much more extensively and spontaneously.

In addition to the times of day that are appropriate for stories, teachers may also question the best use of stories within the wider academic calendar. Are stories better placed at the beginning of the year because of their holistic value? Would they better conclude the year because of their summative power? Perhaps they belong mid-year, or possibly somewhere else.

The answer is that certain curricular stories do fit better at certain times of the school year. One example is the group of five fundamental story-centered presentations used in Montessori elementary programs—the Great Lessons. Profoundly holistic in nature, these powerful stories are invariably to be told at the beginning of the school year as they foreshadow and anticipate the entire curriculum to come.

Other stories may deal with specific holidays, festivals, or anniversaries. These, too, have natural, "right" times to be told. A story about the vernal equinox naturally falls on that specific day, just as we may tell a story about snow as the season's first flakes gently drift down outside the window.

Most curricular stories, however, should follow the flow of the curriculum. If an introduction to the geometrical concept of area is planned, then this is a logical time to offer the story *Measuring the Farm* (p. 248). Later, as the topic is concluded, it may be appropriate to offer that same story a second time.

A great characteristic of most stories is that they offer flexibility and need not be rigidly tied to a prepared monthly or annual schedule. The place for most curriculum stories will become evident as the curriculum proceeds throughout the year.

Allied with the question of when to tell a story is the related question of who should comprise the audience. Should it include the preschoolers? What about middle school? Should it be limited to any particular age group?

Oral stories and narratives offer benefits to all children, but the age(s) and developmental level(s) in any particular class or group should often determine considerations about content and length. The stories that are offered need to be appropriate to the developmental level of the children.

In the Montessori context, stories for preschool children should have a clear basis in reality. This is not to indicate that they may not be fanciful, fun, creative, or funny—they may be any or all of those things. What this means, however, is that they should appeal to the children's senses—and to experiences to which they can relate through their senses. To many Montessorians, this rules out fantasy and anthropomorphism in stories for this age group. Instead, appropriate preschool stories emphasize nature, pets and farm animals, and children. Preschool stories might be biographical or autobiographical, or they might originate from within that very classroom.

Stories for elementary children may include all of these topics but also involve ancient peoples and the origins of anything and everything. At this level, it is effective to use myth, fable, legend, and much more in the purely imaginative realm. This correlates to the Montessori understanding of the middle years as a period of explosive growth in children's creative imagination.

Whereas the preschool child was a sensorial explorer, the elementary child is moving beyond perception of the world only through the senses to bring new mental powers to use. Montessorians characterize the mind of the infant and preschooler as an *absorbent mind.* This is meant to suggest that the primary means by which young children acquire information is by simply "soaking it up"—absorbing it. This absorbent mind of the young child changes with maturity throughout the elementary years, becoming a *reasoning mind*, similar to that of an adult. This new reasoning mind is characterized by the twin powers of imagination and abstraction, which represent new means to gain and manipulate information.

What this means for the elementary school child is that reality is only a launching pad. With imagination and abstraction as fuel, the reasoning mind can travel unfettered throughout the vastness of the universe.

Furthermore, the older child is clear on the differences between reality and fantasy. As soon as words like "once upon a time" are uttered, these children enter into what poet Samuel Taylor Coleridge called the "willing suspension of disbelief" (Coleridge, 1817, p. 174). This stimulates the motivation of a story listener to accept and enter into the world of a fictional or fantastical tale as if it were literally true even while he or she fundamentally understands that it is not. Children in the elementary years relish this distinction just as we adults do when we enjoy novels, theatre, and film.

Maria Montessori herself devoted attention to the importance of imagination in six- to twelve-year-old children when she wrote, "The secret of good teaching is to regard the child's intelligence as a fertile field in which the seeds may be sown to grow under the heat of flaming imagination" (Montessori, 1996, p. 11). This parallels the power of the imagination to the sun itself, offering radiance, inexhaustible energy, light, and brilliance to the fertile fields of the child's developing mind.

Montessori metaphorically suggests that without imaginative energy, the intelligence of the child, no matter how fertile, will not produce. Like the sun, this flaming imagination provides the heat and energy to promote growth.

This understanding indicates that elementary teachers must do everything they can to encourage the development of rich and powerful imaginations, as well as offer frequent opportunities for students to exercise their burgeoning imaginative powers. In Montessori schools, one approach that is utilized for this purpose is called *Cosmic Education.* Briefly, Cosmic Education is Montessori's term for her entire approach to education at the elementary level. It involves the integration of subject matter in a thematic approach, emphasizing relationships among all things throughout history. Montessori's book *To Educate the Human Potential* is devoted entirely to Cosmic Education.

Cosmic Education encapsulates the holistic idea of giving to children what Montessori called a "vision of the whole universe" (1996, p. 5). Because of the immense totality of the universe, there is only one way in which a holistic understanding of it can be introduced to anyone, child or adult. This is to make use of the imagination. To do so, teachers must employ devices such as narrative, symbolism, metaphor, myth, imagery, visualization, supposition, zoomorphism, and anthropomorphism. What are these but the elements, the tools, of storytelling? Narrative stories provide the opportunity for children as well as adults to drop the constraints of reality, willingly suspend disbelief to travel to otherwise unattainable worlds, meet impossible people, visualize fantastic and wondrous animals, travel through time to the distant past or the remote future, and address problems and find solutions to the greatest challenges facing humanity.

The Storyteller

> "The purpose of a storyteller is not to tell you how to think, but to give you questions to think upon."
>
> —Brandon Sanderson, American novelist

In most elementary and preschool classrooms, the teacher (or *guide*) is a generalist. He or she offers all of the core subject areas—mathematics, language arts, science, and social studies. The adult models for the children the love of many subjects and offers diverse ways for the children to interact with each subject. By being the storyteller, the guide includes one additional facet of personality to offer young scholars.

The art of storytelling requires that you come to see beyond the literal meanings of things. It requires that the storyteller learn to view subject matter, curriculum topics, and the material itself metaphorically, symbolically, and/or allegorically. On becoming a storyteller, Paul Clement Czaja writes, "The primary problem to overcome by anyone moving to take the first steps toward becoming a storyteller is how to move away from the strong habit of conceptualization (surface-thinking) which our past schooling has laid on us all" (2003, p. 69).

This is exactly the direction in which we must move in order to increase and develop our inventory of character, representation, metaphor, and impression. We must let go of the literal, didactic form of learning with which most of us grew up and strive for deeper forms of thought in which symbols matter, feelings are significant, and imagery is emblematic of hidden meanings.

~

The role of the storyteller is essential. It is critical. What is wonderful is that as teachers, parents, and other adults who work with children, we are all storytellers. This is one of most appealing attributes of the art of telling stories: storytelling is universally accessible.

There can be great rewards in bringing in professional storytellers, talented specialists, or gifted parent volunteers as guests. You will probably be thrilled by their performance, as will the children. There is no doubt that this should be done occasionally. However, curriculum stories must be integrated into the everyday events of the classroom, and the real benefits of Cosmic Education require your full, deeply engaged, and engaging participation.

A fundamental ingredient for the successful and natural ongoing storytelling culture is that the adults who are close to the children are the ones that tell the stories. Storytelling is a relationship-based art; it is enhanced by the deep and deepening bond that develops between the storyteller and the listening child. Time, love, and experience support this vibrant art as an endeavor with mutual benefits. This means that telling stories is, and must be, a primary task of the regular classroom teacher. The best storyteller in your classroom is you!

Offer stories regularly and with the liberal injection of your own personality. With a schedule of storytelling at least weekly, possibly even more frequently, you will gain the experience to quell any stage fright you may have. Your personality brings a distinctive life to the story. It adds verve, spice and a unique quality that only you can add. This can only be done with orally told stories, not those read aloud or recorded.

As a storyteller, you must not only have a large number of stories at the ready, but you need to be prepared to bring them up at nearly any moment. You might use some of the stories found in this book, but you will also develop other stories of your own over time. Start with one story that you particularly like and with which you feel comfortable. Offer that story to the children. Then, incrementally, add new tales to your repertoire. Eventually, you will begin to find new stories coming to you regularly and spontaneously.

We know that in conversation, in gesture and expression, and in sharing both everyday and life-changing moments or events, we all practice storytelling all the time. For most of us, however, the challenge arises when we begin to think about formally creating or telling a story. It does take a certain amount of daring and nerve to begin.

It is possible that you are fearful, or feel particularly challenged in offering a story. The excellent news is that the children will be deeply accepting of all of your efforts. They are in this with you. They want the experience to be good.

I recall Coleridge's remark on "the willing suspension of disbelief." It suggests to me that storytelling requires not only the suspension of our disbelief in a work of fiction, but also the suspension of disbelief in ourselves. We all can become successful storytellers when we suspend the disbelief that interferes with our courage and self-confidence. Suspend that disbelief and let the inner storyteller within you emerge.

Myth and Truth

In everyday modern usage, the word *myth* tends to mean an unwitting falsehood or even an outright deception. This definition underlies idiomatic concepts such as *myths in advertising*, *food myths*, and even such oddities as *shopping myths*. Perhaps you are familiar with the popular television program, *Mythbusters,* that aired on the Discovery Channel. It focuses upon debunking modern urban legends and other questionable tales. All of these examples demonstrate a common modern conception of *myth* as an untruth, subject to being "busted."

In fact, the word *myth* is of ancient origin, stemming from the Greek word *mythos*, meaning "story" or "word." In the primary and academic sense of the word, a myth is a symbolic story, often from the distant past. Myths explain origins, beginnings, and why the world is as it is. I like to explain that myths are actually sacred stories, which may have been, or may now be, holy to some tribe, group, nation, culture, or religion. Far from being false, they represent humanity's best creative efforts to bring sense and meaning to a chaotic world.

As sacred narratives, myths are sometimes associated with the beginnings of any number of specific religions. To the practitioners or followers of a religion, its particular myths may have the power of truth, or the myth may involve faith and belief. Others who hear these myths might not hold the same faith-based beliefs, but in all cases, it is crucial that we approach myth with the profound respect any sacred story deserves.

In addition to their correlation to religious belief, myths, in some ways, are also similar to science. Both myth and science offer accounts of the beginnings of the universe, the origins of life, and the creation of humanity, as well as of the meaning of life itself. In both myth and science, we can find truth as well as speculation.

The established, technical facts of science are external truths. They are testable, verifiable, and quantifiable. These truths reside properly in the brain—when I discuss these with children and parents, I point to my head.

Conversely, the certainties contained in myth, as in religion, are internal truths, and they reside not only in mythology but also in parable, allegory, fable, folktale, and legend. The honesty of story is not testable but is metaphorical and impressionistic. These are truths of the heart, so I point to my chest when discussing this equally valid knowledge.

The aim of this line of reasoning is to focus on the metaphorical and impressionistic power of story. The stories contain truth, but it is frequently of the internal sort, which bypasses the conscious reasoning intellect and instead addresses the inner person, the heart, or the soul. It may not be subject to verification in the laboratory, but this, too, is truth.

In Patrick Harrigan's words, "The world's greatest stories have their roots in truth, and the greatest storytellers have always insisted that they speak only words of truth" (1994, p. 2). There is little purpose in worrying about whether an oral narrative is absolutely true in the scientific sense. Like our distant ancestors who created much mythology we still share, children have no trouble with metaphorical thinking. They hear it and know it for what it is. It speaks to them through their hearts.

Kinds of Stories

Students of storytelling have created various classification systems to categorize different types of story throughout history. Some writers, like the wonderful Minnesota storyteller Kevin Strauss, list many kinds of stories, including fables or anecdotes; fairy tales; folktales; *pourquoi*, which are *why* stories, origin stories, or *explanation* stories; myths and legends; tall tales; personal stories; and histories (2006, pp. 21–22). The *pourquoi* stories are especially interesting because they are essentially the same as Montessori origin stories, discussed below. They offer an explanation of why something is as it is in a way that may be legendary, fanciful, or grounded in history. The common element to both kinds of stories is the explanation, answering the question *why*.

I use a unique story classification system. It is tremendously useful in my Montessori school setting, and I believe it is wholly applicable in other school settings as well. My classification scheme is very broad—more inclusive than exclusive. It includes seven major story types that are used in the Montessori class, and there is distinct overlap: a single story may fit in several categories. Over time, I have developed the following seven groupings for story categorization:

- Great Lessons
- Curriculum Stories
- Origin Stories
- Biographical Histories
- Personal Stories
- Character Development Stories
- Creative Dramatics

The Great Lessons

Montessori elementary programs offer a thematic approach to learning. Each year, five main themes are introduced narratively through the *Great Lessons* (pp. 65-139), sometimes called the *Great Stories*. These are five impressionistic dramatic stories or story sets that provide a unifying structural framework for all other lessons. All of the Great Lessons are, in fact, origin stories, but their importance in creating a framework for study sets them apart from other stories of beginnings.

The central themes addressed by the Great Lessons are: the development of the universe and the Earth; the beginnings, development, and diversity of life; humanity and human evolution; human languages and all uses of language; and the history and development of mathematics, including number systems as well as geometry. These themes are organized into the following five Great Lessons:

1. *The Story of the Universe.* This story (p. 65) takes children back more than thirteen billion years to the creation and early development of the universe and, eventually, our planet Earth. The lesson includes work with specific impressionistic experiments and charts.
2. *The Coming of Life.* This story (p. 75) offers a look at the beginning of life, the first living beings, and evolution up to humanity. This lesson is accompanied by an illustrated Mural of Life.
3. *The Coming of Humans.* This story (p. 101), accompanied by a timeline, focuses upon human origins, evolution, and development. It spans the development of the earliest human beings to the earliest civilizations, with an additional focus on the development of the essential needs of people.
4. *The Story of Language.* This story (p. 111) represents stories of origin of the first parts of what Montessorian Paula Polk Lillard calls the "tools of human communication, that is, language and mathematics" (Lillard, 1996, p. 58). This lesson includes an overview of the first speech, the development of the alphabet and beginning writing, and an introduction to reading.

5. *The Story of Mathematics.* This final great lesson (p. 125) focuses on the history of counting and our system of numerals. Many teachers include a story of geometry as well. This story of mathematics concludes the accounts of the origins of the tools of human communication.

All of these great lessons are told aloud; they cannot be read. The storyteller uses a dramatic, even exaggerated manner. During the story or sometimes in preparation for it, the teacher may utilize visual aids such as posters, pictures, or charts with impressionistic images. In some cases, special experiments or demonstrations are also included. However, the emphasis is always on telling the story in a way that engages the children's imagination.

For example, the First Great Lesson, *The Story of the Universe* (or for some, *The Creation of the Universe*), begins with the teacher speaking the following words (with variation, according to their own personality and preference):

> *Look all around you. Aren't we lucky to have all of the plants and animals? We also have buildings, streets, our own homes, and our families.*
>
> *Once there was a time when there were no buildings at all. Can you imagine this time? It was long, long ago, even before your mother was born, before your grandmother was born. Before that time, there was a time when there were no people, no people at all. Even before that time, there were no animals, no plants. In fact, there was a time when there was no Earth at all.*
>
> *In the beginning, it was very, very cold. Colder than the coldest cold that you have ever known. It also was dark. Darker than any night could ever be. It may have seemed that there was nothing there at all in this very dark, very cold space that was everywhere. Nevertheless, eventually there was something ...*

The story continues to present the formation of the chemical elements, the stars, and the planets. It places particular emphasis on the coalescence of planet Earth and its cooling, involving volcanoes, mountain formation, and the development of the atmosphere and hydrosphere. The story ends with the Earth being proclaimed ready for life.

The Great Lessons are integrative by nature. Presented as they are in a narrative storytelling format, they involve language, grammar, science, mathematics, and history. The Great Lessons lead to the introduction of specific work for the children. They are offered regularly, to all of the elementary children, on an annual basis.

Curriculum Stories

A curriculum story is like a gift to the children in a classroom. Specifically linked to constituent elements of the curriculum, these stories can be about mathematical operations, parts of speech, historical events, or other curriculum content. Most stories in elementary Montessori classes are of the curricular type. These stories are often coupled with specific learning objects or artifacts. This special category of curriculum story is called an *object story*.

Curriculum stories are somewhat unique to Montessori in that each story is individually tied to some specific concept, lesson, chapter, or unit in the Montessori curriculum, but they may also be linked to particular learning materials or presentations. Still, this same concept of creating specific stories linked to the curriculum can be used in any school, not only Montessori schools.

The purpose of curriculum stories is manifold. They inspire, animate, strike the imagination, invigorate, motivate, balance the curriculum, and involve both sides of the brain. They are used to introduce new concepts as well as to summarize, and no matter what, they always aim to deeply involve the children.

Origin Stories

Origin stories speak eloquently to deep-seated human curiosities: why are we the way that we are? What caused us to be this way? Have we always been like this? Through origin stories, we can learn how things came to be.

To scholars of mythology, origin stories are also known as *etiological tales*. From the Greek word *aitia*, etiology has come to mean the study of causes, beginnings or origination. In everyday usage, I find that the term *origin story* communicates more easily, so it is the term I generally use when explaining story types.

Rudyard Kipling's wonderful *Just So Stories* (1907) are literary examples of one sort of origin story. Among these famous tales are *How the Camel Got His Hump* and *How the Leopard Got His Spots*. These are a sort of origin story that rely upon a fanciful, entertaining narrative.

Like Kipling's stories, some of the origin stories used in classrooms may be fanciful in part, but they should contain a central nugget of truth in their impressionistic, allegorical, or metaphorical idea of how something came into existence or began to be used.

Other origin tales attempt to provide a more scientific or historical explanation. They may be based upon actual science or they may be drawn from legend. On the other hand, they can simply be informal discussions of different possible explanations for how something started. This approach may feel less like an actual story and more like an improvised conversation; however, because of its narrative nature, it may still be classified within the idea of origin stories.

Children want to know why we do what we do, why we speak with the words that we use, why we act in particular ways, and even why our bodies are shaped as they are. Origin stories offer a narrative peek into the beginnings and explanations of many elements of humanity and human culture. In addition to these stories, elements of origin are widely exposed to the Montessori child through literature, etymologies, myths, legends, folktales, and scientific theory.

Biographical Histories

Biographical histories are stories about great or famous real people. The subject of a biographical history story might hail from the distant past, such as Pythagoras, Eratosthenes, or Euclid. Subjects might also be people from a more recent time, such as Susan B. Anthony, Maria Montessori, Marie Curie, Albert Schweitzer, or Martin Luther King, Jr. This category also may include people living today, such as religious, political, or scientific leaders—or even celebrities.

Often, these stories will inspire or amuse. Children find the story of Archimedes running naked through the streets shouting "Eureka!" terribly funny, but through it, they also discover essential nuggets of instruction. Other stories, like those of Schweitzer or King, Jr., inspire young people and may lead to a profound desire to emulate the examples of helping and serving others.

Personal Stories

Personal stories involve the storyteller sharing some incident or tale from his or her own life. Autobiographical in nature, they offer small glances at the character of the storyteller as well as anecdotes that children can relate to their own current experiences. They often deepen the bond between student and teacher.

Children love to know more about their teachers, and learning about how it was "back in the day." In this book, I have included a few personal stories from my own life. My personal stories are not meant for you to tell in your own classroom, but they are intended to show how the incidents of our lives can be developed into story form. I invite you to create similar small stories from your own experience to share with the young people in your class.

Character Development Stories

Honesty, kindness, gratitude, strength, bravery, fairness—these are just some of the elements of good character. Tales that speak to moral development help children to focus on virtues within the safe and familiar context of story, removing the "preachy" qualities with which such instruction is often associated.

Neither lectures nor sermons, character development stories speak directly to a child.

They are often presented as parables or fables, and they may use animals or plants as lead characters. Even though cloaked in image, or perhaps because of that, these stories are particularly effective. Master storyteller Jonathan Wolff has written many stories in this genre. One of them, *The Little Red Spoke* (p. 303), graciously contributed by Jonathan, is included in this collection.

Creative Dramatics

The art of Creative Dramatics is not in and of itself a category of story classification, but it fits with storytelling in that it is an effective technique to bring stories vibrantly to life. Children use creative drama to bring themselves into the stories that they love. Instead of simply hearing a story, with creative dramatics, the child really *becomes* the story. At the same time, the story becomes the child. This unity transcends any form of book-based or lecture-based learning.

After hearing a curriculum story, many children enjoy assuming a character and acting it out. Performing a skit or a small quasi-spontaneous play is an essential element of a successful Montessori elementary classroom. The creativity displayed by young people in bringing these tales to life can be astounding.

A second form of creative dramatics is even more extemporaneous. Children may be presented with a situation, an element of a story, or a character within it, and asked to bring it to life.

> *What do you think it might have been like to be an early fish trying to creep up on the shore? Let's figure out how they felt as they became amphibians!*

Using this sort of directive, the children can develop a storyline and play it out in action.

Preparing to Tell a Story

In my experience, fully preparing to tell a story is more than essential, it is indispensable. A good story does not simply "happen," but depends, like any successful aspect of the school day, upon conscious mindful practice. Storyteller Aaron Shepard (1990, Part 2) puts it well: "... you must absorb the story until it becomes second nature. Find the best way for you."

For me, it is best to organize the story and practice telling it silently until I really feel that I have understood it. This means grasping the inner meaning, the nuance, and the imagery. Through this initial work, I begin to feel that I really have the words right, the sequence down, and the characters or sounds well planned.

Next, I practice the story aloud—usually in front of a mirror. Some storytellers use a video camera or a voice recorder, but, for me, a simple mirror has proven to be best. I tell the story in this way, paying particular attention to the flow and any difficult transitions, until I feel confident that I have it down vocally. I also use this time to experiment with any gestures, sounds, special voices, or tones that I may want to use.

Next, I perform the story for my family and possibly for friends. They can be excellent critics because they have heard all of my stories—including those that did not work and ended up being abandoned or completely reworked. Over the years, members of my family have also appeared as characters in some of my stories, such as the story *Measuring the Farm* (p. 248).

Once I pass the family test, I know that the time has come to try the story in the classroom. The first time is especially stressful for me, as it probably is for nearly all storytellers, but I have found the children to be a particularly forgiving audience. In fact, the appreciation of the children has helped the first time to almost always go well.

After the children, my stories usually find yet another audience in adult learners. This final offering can be the most difficult, as adults may not be as appreciative as previous listeners. Still, telling the story to adult groups invariably helps my delivery and technique immeasurably.

The object of all this practice and work is for the story to really become yours. It should become a part of you that you can access easily, at any time—the story must be embedded within you. It is at this point that the story becomes part of your repertoire and you are ready to begin the process anew with a fresh story.

Telling the Story

"You shouldn't tell a story unless you really believe in it. Your own credibility is always crucial, and the moment people sense that you are having them, they lose interest."

—Garrison Keillor, American radio personality, storyteller, author, and humorist

Once preparation is complete, the time has finally come to offer the story to the most important audience, children. The question is, how do you do it successfully?

It is important to let children know whether and how they are expected to interact with your story. I like to have a very quiet atmosphere before beginning, so that the children are concentrating and focused on the story and on me—the storyteller.

For small children, such as those in preschool, I sometimes encourage them to a quiet attentiveness by using imaginative props—for example, a very small bell can be effective. Tell the children that before you begin, you would like everyone to be able to hear the story, so you are going to try a *quiet spell.* Get the children's attention and cooperation by saying that everyone needs to concentrate for the magic to work, and once you have relative silence, ring the bell and begin the story (National Literacy Trust, 2015).

The first and most important rule is to *tell* the story. Do not read it aloud or refer to notes. A story is meant to be told. Reading is simply not the same thing and will not have the same results. If you are in doubt, you have probably not prepared enough. Spend some more time practicing, but then plunge in. You don't have to worry if the story does not seem perfect or if you forget or misstate some little part. Minor imperfections are of little consequence; what matters is that you tell your story.

As you tell it, try to make direct eye contact with as many members of the audience as possible. Remember that storytelling is an interactive, relationship-based art. Consciously creating an intimate bond with children is deeply meaningful to them and makes the magic of storytelling happen.

It is important to be sincere in your delivery. Whether the story is humorous or serious, it requires a heartfelt approach. Any story worth telling possesses an inherent strength; a wholehearted telling will allow that strength to emerge. Paul Clement Czaja notes, "The art of storytelling involves the storyteller filling the story with vitality. When the storyteller tells a story rather than merely reciting the cold facts, he or she recreates a human experience that has vibrant existence" (2003, p. 69). Note Czaja's emphasis on *telling* the story rather than simply *reciting* it. Allowing the story to emerge from the heart, the teller transcends the limits of recitation and emerges with the potential to offer a true Gift of the Memorable.

At the same time, telling a story is a joyful art. Embrace the story. Fall in love with the flow, plot, characters, situations, and conclusion. Very few classroom stories are sad or tragic. Certainly, these stories do exist; however, for young children, stories of this sort can be frightening. Our classroom focus on upbeat, positive tales allows for happiness and joy to permeate the telling. While stories are serious business, they are also sources of great pleasure.

Most stories benefit from an animated and enthusiastic approach. Try to intensify the story with dramatic language. There are certainly some stories, like *The Love Story of the Lines* (p. 214), in which a subdued demeanor is part of the humor. Most stories, however, gain from your complete and passionate involvement. Apathy has no place in classroom storytelling.

Voice is one of the most significant elements in storytelling. Your voice must offer characterization, demonstrate emotion, create atmosphere, and move the story forward. This requires vocal dynamics. The idea of vocal dynamics involves volume, resonance, pitch, quality, pace, and intonation.

Intonation

Intonation emphasizes the way in which we say things, rather than what is being said. Without intonation, it is impossible to interpret the expressions and ideas that lie under the words. The basic elements of intonation are timbre, tone, variation of pitch, and volume.

The rising and falling sounds of the voice when speaking, as well as its general quality, are the essential elements of intonation. Without intonation, it is impossible to interpret the expressions and ideas that lie under the words.

Intonation can be purposeful, the intentional management of your voice's volume, pitch and tone. There are few things more dramatic than a loud, room-filling voice followed by a tiny, quiet or whispering voice. Vocal contrast creates interest and helps the tale unfold. Equally striking is the small, quiet voice succeeded by a big, loud voice, as is used to relate the story of the Big Bang in the First Great Lesson, *The Story of the Universe* (p. 65). The essence of intonation is variety; no story can succeed in a monotone. Such tellings are, in point of fact, monotonous! A change in intonation will create interest. A dynamic voice brings the story to life.

Timing

The pacing of your delivery can add tremendously to the story. Timing refers to the rate at which you speak, as well using tempo and rhythm to augment the story.

Be careful to avoid speaking too quickly. If you are new to the story, unsure, or nervous, you may unconsciously increase your rate of speech; in fact, this pitfall is common even for seasoned storytellers. It is often effective to intentionally speak slowly. It may well not seem slow to your listeners.

The pacing of your storytelling will powerfully affect the way in which the story will reach the listeners. Making use of well-timed dramatic pauses can be very effective. Combining a deliberate pause with a quizzical expression or other look suited to the story's content will make that moment particularly memorable.

Characterization

Modulating your voice is essential to bring individuality to different characters in a story. This is called voice characterization, and is closely related to acting. Giving a distinctly unique voice to each character can be extremely helpful to listeners as they work to sort out who is speaking. However, if you do not feel capable of pronounced accents or voice distinctions, even small variations in vocal quality or intonation can help the listener in visualization.

Some stories also make use of unusual sound effects. You may need to sniff, click, pop, hiss, yelp, growl, or make other interesting sounds! These may be the factors that bring vitality, life, or humor to a particular tale. For example, the story *The Point, Line, Surface, and Solid* (p. 206) uses a vocabulary of four different sounds to portray the ideas of a point, a line, a surface, and a solid. These four concepts are hard to characterize without some device to assist in labeling them. Unusual vocal sounds accomplish that task. In a sense, they give voice to characters who are otherwise simply geometric ideas.

You must be immune to embarrassment when experimenting with this sort of vocal characterization. Keep in mind that children will enjoy seeing you completely immersed in the story, and remember this quotation from Canadian comedian Red Green, who often ended his television show by saying, "Remember, I'm pulling for you. We're all in this together" (Green & Smith, 1997–April, 2006). The children are like that. They are pulling for you too—they know that you are all in the classroom together.

Physicality and Movement

Beyond your voice, remember that your entire body can (and should) be actively engaged in the art of storytelling. Facial expressions are tremendously important in offering a tale: smiles, frowns, displays of happiness, bewilderment, or even disgust can all enhance your story. Animation will add marvelously to your audience's enjoyment of your story—and it may enhance their understanding and recall as well.

Your movements, gestures, and posture will also help children visualize the story. Bodily movements are particularly effective if matched with certain characters or inserted at dramatic moments in the tale.

An additional consideration is to make use of what is called the *Storytelling V*—a technique in which the teller pivots the direction of his or her body about 45 degrees as characters change back and forth. With this technique, the teller is still facing the audience, but the alteration of stance helps children define exactly which character is speaking.

Props

Some people question if (or what) props are appropriate in telling a story. While props may add interest, it is important to remember that the essence of storytelling is oral narrative. Be careful that any props you choose do not become overwhelming and inhibit the advancement of the storyline.

Some stories, however, actually require certain artifacts or props. *Measuring the Farm* (p. 248), *The Chicken or the Egg* (p. 184), and *The Very Thirsty Man* (p. 238) are just three examples of this kind of story, which is often referred to as an *object story* because it relies on one or more objects as an essential component of the story itself.

I generally argue against props when they are used simply as visual aids. Even when a prop is essential to the story or a material found in the associated curriculum, the focus of the story should be, as much as possible, its oral aspect. This is fundamental to the children's ability to perform the creative visualization that is their task as audience members.

If additional props like puppets or flannel boards are used, they often create the image for the child, rather than allowing the child to create it mentally. Later, creative dramatics or opportunities with art media can allow children to firm up their creative images and express them to others. Thus, I urge any storyteller to carefully and thoughtfully evaluate whether a prop is necessary.

Scheduling

Stories as psychological lessons should be almost always be told before technical lessons. As prefatory elements, they set the mood, motivate, and create anticipation. Consider telling a story even a day or two prior to its corresponding technical lesson. It is also possible to offer the story immediately before the technical component. You should experiment with story placement. See what works in your setting; it will not be the same for all stories.

Stories can also be very useful after a lesson or unit is complete. Here, it is usually appropriate to offer a reiteration of the story rather than a first telling. In this way, the story acts as a sort of parentheses, framing the technical elements. It also highlights the relationship between certain elements of the narrative and related components in the technical lesson. Be careful that the second telling still has enthusiasm and verve. Do not allow the story to become dry simply because it has been told before.

Duration

A good story has no set length. The stories in this book vary tremendously in the time that it takes to tell them. Although the average time is about ten minutes, the shortest takes only two or three while the longest runs for almost twenty-five. No attempt should be made to standardize story length. One part of the charm of stories is their innate variety.

That said, stories nearing a half hour in length, like some of the Great Lessons, should be told infrequently.

One good generalization about story length is: the younger the children, the shorter the story. I have watched Montessori toddler teachers give wonderful, captivating stories in two minutes or less. I have also seen upper elementary students fascinated by *The March of the Three Kings* (p. 258) as it goes on for twenty minutes or more.

You will know if you start to lose your audience. Fidgeting, inattention, even rolling on the floor should tell you that there is an issue. It may be the length of the story. If so, trim the delivery to be more concise.

The guidelines for length are logical: the age of the audience and the content of the story. Let the story flow, but know your audience. If you lose them because of the length of the story, it is difficult to regain their attention. Your experience will help you find the right length for stories. When stories (and their teller) are clever, engaging, and animated, a longer length may work very well.

The Teller's Experience

Above all, make sure you enjoy telling your story. Children are deeply perceptive. They will know when you really like a story and they will mimic your enjoyment. They will also know if you are "faking it." We are transparent to children. Although they may not do it consciously, they see beyond our exteriors to the real people inside. When we are honest in our delight in a story, they will enjoy it with us. If you find that your storytelling is not working, look at yourself first and work to become personally engaged. Your level of interest is communicated to the children and is inherently correlated to their involvement in the story.

Remember that storytelling is an art. It takes time and practice to polish your talents and skills as a storyteller. It also requires commitment. You must also take the time to reflect upon your successes and setbacks as a teller. Experience and reflection will sharpen your skills and confidence; it will bring a naturalness and ease to your presentations.

After Telling the Story

Generally speaking, there should be no assignment or other follow-up work after a story presentation. There are exceptions to this rule, but it is essential to remember that the most creative follow-up happens within the mind of every child who listens to the story.

The Great Lessons, particularly, are examples of stories that do not and should not have direct follow-up work. Instead, expect children to surrender to the rhythm and magic of the narrative. The real follow-up is the entire remaining school and learning experience in which the child will engage. No single assignment can capture the magnificent scope of the Great Lessons.

If the expectation is created that assignments follow stories, children will stop really listening to the story and become unable to lose themselves in the power of oral narrative. Instead, they will listen for the assignment, keying into what they will have to do later rather than what is happening right now in the story. They are no longer in the present, but planning for what will come. Focusing on assignments can entirely demolish the power and wonder of the story.

It is possible that, at times, some post-story work may be appropriate. However, one must be cautious that this is infrequent.

If you want a follow-up, the best possible work is usually in the arts. For example, one might offer a particular art medium, such as paint, clay, or pastels, to the children. Should they choose, allow them to express their responses to the story artistically or in drama. Note my emphasis on not requiring this—art that is mandated is not actual, authentic expression.

Of course, certain curriculum stories do lead to lessons—they exist and are structured this way in order to introduce specific lesson components. In this case, an assignment or follow-up work may ensue after the lesson, but it should not come directly after the story.

It is important to remember that telling a story is an art form. It is meant to bypass the conscious mind and speak directly to the oral level within us; that is, it should speak to the heart. This is a vital, yet delicate, operation. Treating a story as though it is nothing more than direct instruction can easily spoil it.

Let the story settle within the mind of the listeners. There, it will grow, ferment, effervesce, and develop. Have faith that this is, in fact, the true follow-up activity.

Creating Your Own Stories

Many of us need to create new stories for our curricula. Revising a lesson that needs more excitement, or simply experiencing a moment of artistic insight, can lead to a new story's creation. When we do find the right opportunity for a new story, however, the question is often where and how to begin.

As an example from my own teaching, I can recall my frustration that the geometry lesson that focused upon the four fundamental ideas of geometry—the point, line, surface, and solid—was very hard to do well. The children did not seem to understand these very abstract concepts. That was the spark that led me to write *The Point, Line, Surface, and Solid* (p. 206). It worked, and children were suddenly thrilled to get this lesson.

Consider the following points for starting and developing your own new stories.

Base It on a Folktale

One of the best ways to begin is to base your creation upon an established story such as a familiar folktale or fairy story that you know or can find in literature. This is one reason why reading many folktales is so valuable: a wide vocabulary of children's literature will lend invaluable help as you plan your new narrative.

As an example, the traditional Russian folktale *The Fool of the World* served as an inspiration for the story *Measuring the Farm* (p. 248). Of course, I did not steal the story, but it offered me a basic theme and structure for my own tale. *The Fool of the World* tells of a couple that had three sons, the youngest of whom was a fool. All three sons go to seek their fortune, but it is the youngest, the fool, who succeeds—despite all odds.

This very simple theme offers many levels of interpretation. I chose it for *Measuring the Farm* because it suddenly seemed to fit perfectly and my story began to flow. Had I not been familiar with *Fool,* I could not have written *Measuring the Farm* as I did.

Details

In writing the story, do not be afraid to make up or create details. I may say:

> *There once was a small tribe of people who lived on the side of a great and tall mountain called Mount Sapone. A fresh and gushing stream coursed down the slope in front of their tiny village.*

These details, like the name of the mountain, the fact that it is "great and tall," the "fresh and gushing" stream, and the "tiny" village add to the listeners' ability to visualize the narrative. The trick here is to choose details that add richness and texture and enhance the storyline without distracting from the main direction of the tale. Often, it is a memory of some specific detail that leads a child to remember the story or its critical themes.

Names

Character names are essential to stories and should be chosen deliberately. Some names are important because they have a secret meaning that can be discovered by the child at some future time. This is why *The Piece of Paper that Sees and Speaks* (p. 118) uses the name *Phyllis,* which comes from Greek and refers to *a lover of plants or foliage*; or why the insightful hero of *The Ox and the House* (p. 114) is called *Alim*, an Arabic and Swahili word meaning "wise one," "learned," or "scholar."

Choosing names that carry etymological meaning allows children to make discoveries that they bring back to the story as an epiphany. Their realizations may occur many years after the story has been told, but they will still cause the individual to experience an aha moment.

Other names hold power because of their very direct and stated meaning. For example, the English name *Margaret* originally comes from the Greek word *margarités*, which means "pearl."

In telling a story about *Margaret*, I might say, "*On the day that the small child was born, her father found a tiny, white, luminous stone in a shellfish that he caught. This omen of beauty led him to name her Pearl to honor the moment*." Later, I could remind the children that, over time, the Greek word for pearl evolved into our modern name *Margaret*.

Most traditional as well as popular names have meanings behind them. These meanings were clear to the ancients who chose names according to traits that they observed in the child or qualities that they hoped the child would demonstrate as he or she grew.

In stories for children, it can also be effective to name a character with qualities rather than with a regular name. This convention can seem to bring the story back to an older time, and it creates a unique feeling around the name. Thus, a character may be called *Curious One*, *She Who Hunts*, or *Strong Arms*. These names are different and memorable.

Use creative names that offer a special connotation. Unless the name has an etymology of particular interest, it is generally wise to avoid currently popular names. If a child in your audience shares that name, or knows someone with that name, he or she might lose focus on the story as their thoughts drift to their other associations with the name.

The Hero

Character is an essential component of story. In my school and classroom stories, I frequently cast a child as the lead character to speak more effectively to my youthful audience. Characters may also be geometric figures, plants or animals, or even parts of speech. In that case, we frequently use a device called *anthropomorphism*—giving human qualities to non-human characters.

In some circumstances, such as personal stories, you will have little choice about the main character of your story. However, in other cases, you do have the freedom to be creative with your hero or lead.

Making a child the hero or heroine of a story allows the children in the class to imagine themselves in that role. A child might imagine that she or he could achieve something in the same way that the hero of the tale accomplished something wonderful. This gives power to youth, to childhood, and to innocence.

I have also created a great number of tales in which the lead character is someone who, at first, seems of small consequence and less important than others. Hearing about a character's journey from insignificance to importance or success helps in the development of hope. Almost all children in your audience will have felt unimportant or ignored at some point or in some situation. To learn that characters, like Cinderella for example, have felt that way and then succeeded sends a powerful, fundamental message.

Starting with the Personal

There is a multitude of possible topics for your stories. For your first time creating a new story, it can be best to begin with something easy, such as a personal story from your own history that that you already know well and can share with your young audience.

When a story is familiar and real, writing it and embellishing it with detail should come naturally. Because of your enjoyment, your students will love hearing it and may well ask for it repeatedly. I have been asked many times to retell the story of the watermelon, a simple chronicle of a dropped and broken fruit. I believe that my pleasure in telling and essentially reliving the story leads to the pleasure that the children take in it.

Object Stories

The Montessori teacher often constructs stories surrounding a particular Montessori material or a particular lesson. To the Montessorian, these materials are not considered props, but valuable and central learning materials. When the materials are a central component of the story, used as a visual or tactile element, the story functions as a type of *object lesson*.

Object lessons are not unique to Montessori schools. For example, most geometry teachers will use three-dimensional objects while teaching the names of the solids, and science teachers may use models of the eye or other body parts in anatomy classes. These are, to some extent, object lessons because an object or objects are used to flesh out the presentation. To fully classify them as object lessons, the students need to touch or handle the objects at some time.

Adonijah Strong Welch discussed these special lessons in his book *Object Lessons* in 1862, eight years before Maria Montessori was born. However, the object lesson has a special place in the Montessori setting, for two reasons. First, the objects utilized are usually Montessori materials, unique artifacts linked to specific presentations in Montessori schools. A second distinction is that these are stories, not simply lessons. That means that they must be told orally, and that the materials or objects play a supporting role to the story. Because of this special distinction, I prefer not to call them object lessons. Instead, I use the modified term *object stories*.

In this book, there are several object stories. *The Rebellious Pronoun* (p. 163), *The Story of Tan* (p. 227), and *The March of the Three Kings* (p. 258) are all examples of this genre.

When you write an object story, begin with the piece of material or object that will be used. Nearly every piece of Montessori material has a tale to tell. Other materials in non-Montessori classrooms should have their own backstory as well. Think, why is it made this way? Why does it have its particular shape? Why was this color scheme chosen? What is it supposed to teach or demonstrate?

Remember to think in metaphor, or in visual images. Could this represent something else? Might it stand symbolically for something? Could it relate to a story or folktale that I know? For example, the red sphere of the verb represents energy and motion. The bright red color and its round shape do then have symbolic meaning. Find these meanings and capitalize on them.

A good story will not be a mere recitation of historical facts. Give it vitality by bringing the material to life. This may involve anthropomorphizing the material, as is done in *The March of the Three Kings* (p. 258). It might involve a plot with characters as in *The Rebellious Pronoun* (p. 163) or *The Story of Tan* (p. 227). The key is to avoid presenting the material in a direct and dry manner. Bring it to life.

Old-Fashioned Language

Creating a sense of timelessness or tradition within your story can be difficult. The story will not seem to have come from "long ago and far away" if it is replete with modern idioms and colloquialisms. If you are trying to present something ancient such as an origin story, carefully review your tale, trying to identify and remove modernisms.

Think of ways in which antiquated, archaic, or more formal-sounding language could be inserted. For example, a character might state, "I'm going to town to get a job." Instead, consider, "I shall travel to the great city to seek my fortune." This makes it sound old or antiquated, because few people today use the word "shall," nor do they state that they plan to "seek their fortune" in the "great city."

Dramatic Irony

Dramatic irony is a literary and storytelling device in which the audience knows more about the situation than the characters do. A good example of dramatic irony is in *The Piece of Paper that Sees and Speaks* (p. 118). In that story, the child messenger cannot understand the concept of markings upon paper; he cannot see how they might communicate. The children in the audience do know that it is writing—sometimes they even shout it out, so eager are they for him to know.

Dramatic irony can be very powerful. It helps involve the audience by seeming to give them special, almost secret knowledge. It helps to focus the attention of the listener upon the story.

As you write, consider places in which dramatic irony could be a powerful addition to your story. What might your audience know or recognize that the story's characters themselves may not know? Is there something that is obvious to the audience but simply not stated in the story?

When I wrote the story of *The Four Strange Brothers* (p. 196) I decided to use this device. I wanted to use colors and terms that would let the listeners know what each brother signified before it was actually stated. For this reason, I cloaked the brothers in colors associated in Montessori schools with the four arithmetic operations: red for addition, gold for multiplication, green for subtraction, and blue for division. I then had each brother wear a "strange emblem" or badge that the children immediately recognize as a plus sign, a times sign, a minus sign, or a division sign. The brothers seem happily oblivious to the deeper meaning of their decorative ornaments.

When I tell this story, I always notice that some of the listeners immediately catch on and show this understanding by exchanging looks and smiles. They are verifying with one another that they share a knowledge or insight superior to the characters; they are "in on the secret." This brings them into the story in a compelling way.

Repetition

Repetition can have powerful effects on both the flow of a story and on its meaning. In fact, it is a dominant stylistic element in many traditional folktales and sagas. Consider *The Kalevala*, the epic poetic saga of Finland.

The ancient Finns used rhythm and repetition to create a sonorous beauty in their great epic. In the following excerpt from John Martin Crawford's translation (1888, p. 14), listen for the repetition of sow, seed, and the alliterative "s" sound in general.

> Who should sow the vacant island,
> Who the forest seeds should scatter.
> Pellerwoinen, thus consenting,
> Sows with diligence the island,
> Seeds upon the lands he scatters,
> Seeds in every swamp and lowland,
> Forest seeds upon the loose earth,
> On the firm soil sows the acorns,
> Fir-trees sows he on the mountains,
> Pine-trees also on the hill-tops,
> Many shrubs in every valley,
> Birches sows he in the marshes

The repetitive and resonant elements of this piece lend it power and a chant-like character. I tried to use this element in *The Point, Line, Surface, and Solid* (p. 206). In this, each time a new concept is introduced, the same phrases are repeated. "Maybe they liked each other and were friendly. Maybe they were in love." The repetition becomes a part of the story that the children may even chant along with the teller.

Suitability

Think carefully about the audience for your story. If aimed at a preschool audience, it must be created differently than if it were to be offered to elementary children or older students. The appropriateness of the story may be determined by its theme and intellectual content, the word choice, and/or its use of fantasy or imaginary components.

In discussing suitability, Heather Hansen explained that the storyteller must know the audience—in this case, the children. Hansen wrote:

> When telling stories it is really important to know who you are telling them to and have an idea of how they might react to them. Age group … and culture are extremely important factors; make sure your story is appropriate for your audience. Even when you are telling a "tried and true" story, what might be appropriate and funny for one group, could be distasteful and unacceptable for another. Take care when choosing the topic of your story and the language you use to deliver it. (2010, para. 1)

Starting a Story

It is important to begin the story in a way that lets the listeners know that this is indeed a story and not some other lesson. I often begin physically by briefly turning my back and taking a breath or two to compose myself and adjusting my expression or otherwise getting into character. After this momentary preparation, I turn to the children and begin. I only do this when storytelling, so it is a reliable cue—they know what is to come.

There are also certain phrases that can assist in setting the mood. It may seem that "Once upon a time …" is too hackneyed to work, but this is actually not so. On the contrary, this well-worn phrase serves the purpose of letting the children know that a tale is about to unfold.

Ending a Story

Just like beginnings, appropriate endings are important. There must be some signal that the story has concluded. On this subject, master storyteller Tim Jennings (2009, para. 1) comments, "Traditionally told tales often end with a conventional tagline, to let listeners know the story is over, bring them back to earth, and ease the transition to normal conversation—or whatever conversation is involved in getting the next one started."

We have all heard this ending to fairy and folktales: "they lived happily ever after." While this still works for some stories, in many cases, it does not fit the model of a curriculum story. You may also simply want something different.

Many curriculum stories traditionally end with an introduction to the related material or to the curriculum component to follow. These endings may be as simple as: *And now, that is exactly what we are going to work on!* This sort of ending is designed to use the motivating effect of narrative story in bringing the children to a work or study project. This is not the same as an assignment. Children will not be questioned about the story or asked to write a summary. The ending simply assists in directing their motivation to a related project.

PART II

THE STORIES

"The shortest distance between a human being and the truth is a story."

—Anthony de Mello, Indian Jesuit priest and psychotherapist

"Nothing you do for children is ever wasted."

—Garrison Keillor, American radio personality, storyteller, author, and humorist

The rest of this book consists of actual stories to be learned and told to children in classroom settings. These are all stories that have actually been told, exactly as they are written, in real classrooms. They are purposely written in an oral style, taken from transcripts of orally told stories. You are, of course, free to modify them to adapt to your class and to your own voice.

Each story has an introduction with some background and helpful information. Many are illustrated. Enjoy!

The Stories

Welcome to the world of stories. Enjoy your plunge into the Deep Well of Time.

The stories that follow are of three very general types:

- Those entirely original to me, which I wrote.
- Those that are traditional Montessori ideas, lessons, or stories, which I have rewritten or substantially adapted.
- Those written by guest authors, used here by permission.

Introduction

Every story in this collection has an introduction and a source reference that gives the origin of that particular story.

When you see text like this in the margins, it is meant to be a direction or other information to you, the teller. These margin notes are not to be read aloud or told, but are there only to supply information to the teller.

Story

Following that introduction is the story itself in an oral style, as it is to be told. The beginning of the actual story is marked by this symbol of a well. So, when you see that symbol, get ready to start telling.

I have tried to refrain from too prescriptively designating age levels for the stories. In general, the stories involving myth or imaginative images are aimed at the elementary school years or above. They certainly may be adapted for the preschool, if one wishes. The autobiographical stories originated for younger children, but I have found that elementary-aged children enjoy them as well. I suggest that you be the judge of the appropriate age level. The only exception to this is the collection of Montessori Great Lessons, which are specifically aimed at elementary students and above.

Some of what I have collected in this book would obviously and conventionally be called stories—that is, they have a plot and characters. In other places, these elements are absent, and I have chosen to call these pieces of text narratives. Because the narratives are meant to be presented just like the stories, and are received as such by children, I have included them in this collection. They help to demonstrate that almost any concept can be shaped to a narrative structure.

I am responsible for having reinterpreted and rewritten the traditional Montessori stories or presentations. That means that the stories are my interpretations, and may differ considerably from versions told by Montessori practitioners around the globe. Teachers, parents, Montessorians, and storytellers are certainly free to find their own constructions and tell those. There are many ways to tell stories, and for these classroom stories, I welcome alternatives and variation. As an example, note that *Cinderella* has 345 documented variations (Cox, 1893), and probably more undocumented variations exist. No single variant of any story should be considered the definitive and final adaptation.

You may be interested to note that many story characters have specific assigned genders. These include the main characters in *The Piece of Paper that Sees and Speaks* (p. 118), *Dawn Child* (p. 125), *Measuring the Farm* (p. 248), and several others.

Additionally, some anthropomorphized characters also have gender specific names or titles. These include the noun and the verb in *The Noun and the Verb* (p. 157), the king and the prince in *The Rebellious Pronoun* (p. 163), the three kings in *The March of the Three Kings* (p. 258), and some others.

These genders are entirely arbitrary, and you should feel free to either keep the stories as they are written or alter the characters, including gender, as you prefer. Like most elements of the stories, these may be modified or personalized. When you tell stories, they belong to you.

Make these stories your own. Use them and their various versions with children. The rewards, both for the teller and for the children, are enormous.

The Great Lessons
(Elementary Levels)

> "If you're going to have a story, have a big story, or none at all."
>
> —Joseph Campbell, mythologist

What teachings are the most important or most significant in Montessori schools for elementary ages? How should they be taught, and when?

The answer lies in the Montessori *Great Lessons*. There are five of these Great Lessons in the traditional Montessori curriculum. These are the biggest and arguably the most important presentations in the entire Montessori elementary legacy. All five are presented in the form of stories—great stories. These stories encapsulate the entire curriculum, and some would argue all human knowledge.

The Great Lessons are presented in order, from first to fifth, to the entire elementary class every fall. These lessons represent a vital and central element of holism in offering a vision of the whole or entire picture before dwelling on the parts. They are also an umbrella for the curriculum. In a sense, they also represent a sort of ritual, in which the same gift of story is offered annually and received as a key element of the school culture and tradition.

The five Great Lessons are:

- The First Great Lesson: *The Story of the Universe* (p. 65)
- The Second Great Lesson: *The Coming of Life* (p. 75)
- The Third Great Lesson: *The Coming of Humans* (p. 101)

- The Fourth Great Lesson: *The Story of Language* (p. 111)
- The Fifth Great Lesson: *The Story of Mathematics* (p. 125)

It is important to recognize that the stories are offered to all three age groups in the elementary class, all together. This is a shared large whole class group that Montessorians call a *collective.*

However, only certain age groups or levels pursue the specific curriculum elements that represent a direct follow-up to the stories. In particular, this means the Second Great Lesson, *The Coming of Life*, and the Third Great Lesson, *The Coming of Humans,* are linked to particular components of the history curriculum.

Although *The Coming of Life* is offered annually, it is linked to the lessons and exercises of a history material called the Timeline of Life. This timeline is an object or artifact used with numerous history lessons for the second-year students, referred to as second grade in graded schools. It is revisited in the fourth year (fourth grade) with a more in-depth approach.

In the same way, *The Coming of Humans* is offered annually, but also has a link to the Timeline of Humans, which is studied throughout the third year of elementary (third grade). It also is revisited in the fourth year (fourth grade) in greater depth.

The other two annual stories, *The Story of Language* and *The Story of Mathematics,* also lead to major parts of the curriculum, but these are taught across all of the years or grades of this elementary schooling.

When these stories are presented, the storyteller must remember that they are meant to awe and inspire the children, not merely to transmit information. They should enthuse and excite the children and their imaginations, motivating them to further study and investigation.

The teller must remember that the very bigness of these tales is a huge part of what makes them so inspiring. Never try to simplify, shorten, or condense the Great Lessons. Instead, plan to put your heart and soul into it and go all out.

The First Great Lesson: *The Story of the Universe*

(Elementary Levels)

Introduction

The Story of the Universe, alternatively called *The Story of Creation*, is the first Montessori Great Lesson. Before presenting the Story of the Universe, there are twenty special science demonstrations, called history experiments, which are offered in Montessori classes.

The history experiments are demonstrations that give an impressionistic background and setting for the First Great Lesson. They are meant to introduce matter from which the children can abstract the makings of our Earth, solar system and galaxies in general (Nolan, not dated).

These history experiments are key, concrete, sensorial experiences for this tale. They also go hand in hand with the first six Impressionistic Geography Charts, which are referenced below.

Some teachers present some of the experiments during the story, but I have adhered to a more original version of the story in which the history experiments have been presented before the story is told. When the experiments have been presented in advance, the storyteller can refer explicitly to the experiments as he or she tells *The Story of the Universe.*

There are several key points associated with the telling of this story:

1. The time is established as "very long ago."

2. Particles were attracted to one another.
3. The Big Bang occurs.
4. The gases expand and coalesce.
5. The Sun and planets are created.
6. The Earth cools.
7. The rain falls.
8. The stage is set for life.
9. All events follow an absolute obedience to the laws of nature.

This story, like all of the Great Lessons, is to be told at the beginning of the school year in an elementary classroom. In advance, approximately two related experiments can be given per day. At that rate, it will take about ten days to complete the required preliminary work. Like an annual ceremony, then, this lesson will generally be presented during the third or, at the latest, fourth-week of school.

Six special charts or posters called the *Impressionistic Geography Charts* accompany this Great Lesson.

Each impressionistic chart has two titles. The first one, which is used with the children, is called the *Sensorial Title.*

Chart Number	Sensorial Title	Technical Title
1.	How Small the Earth Is!	A comparison of the size of the Earth to the Sun
2.	The Sun's Family	The solar system
3.	The Cosmic Dance	The beginning of the cooling process
4.	The Time of the Volcanoes	Volcanism and the cooling process
5.	The Sun's Beautiful Daughter	Cooling and filling the oceans
6.	What's Inside the Earth?	Geochemical constitution of the Earth

It is meant to appeal to their imagination and interest. The second name, called the *Technical Title,* gives a better idea for adults and older children of the actual content contained within the charts. At left (p. 66) is a listing of the six charts with their titles.

These charts are all illustrated in the written text of the story at the appropriate moments. You can make these posters for use in your classroom. In order to make the deepest impression on the students, they should be large, at least 20 x 24 inches.

Avoid any follow-up work or assignments based on this story, except, perhaps, certain artistic, musical, or dramatic activities. You could make art media and tools available to the children, then suggest that if they wish, they may choose to use them to react creatively to the lesson.

There is also quite a bit of interesting and complementary literature that many children will enjoy. Of particular interest are the many creation myths of people from cultures around the world. While these do not demonstrate a scientific approach, they do indicate to the children that the question of *how it all happened* or *what was the beginning* has been asked by all peoples. This can be aided by making available creation stories from many cultures around the world, past and present.

Source: *The Story of the Universe* is a traditional Montessori Great Lesson that I have significantly updated and reworked.

STORY

Look all around you. Look at all of the plants that you see. They have beautiful colors and provide us with food. We also live among many animals, from tiny insects to huge mammals. Aren't we lucky to have all of the plants and animals?

We are surrounded by wonderful things that people have made and built—the building that we are in, our streets, and our own homes. We have our families as well, our parents, and grandparents.

I want to take you far back in time. This will be a long trip, into a time long ago, before your mother was born, before your grandmother was born, even before your grandmother's grandmother was born.

There was once a time, long, long ago, when this building that we're in had not been built. In fact, there were no buildings at all. No buildings at all! Anywhere in the whole world! Can you imagine that time?

Now, we will go even further back, before that time, to a time when there were no people, no people at all, anywhere. Before that time, there were no animals and no plants, and there was even a time before there was any life at all. There were no living things anywhere.

There was no water, no stone, no sand, and even no air. In fact, a long, long time ago, there was a time when there was no Earth at all.

In this ancient beginning time, it was very, very cold. Colder than the coldest cold that you have ever known. It was so cold that the coldest thing that you have ever known would seem hot compared to this cold.

It also was dark—such a black dark that not a single spark of light existed in the whole universe. It was darker than any night could ever be.

And it was quiet. So still, that there was absolutely no sound. Just silence.

It may have seemed that there was nothing there at all in this very dark, very cold, silent space that was everywhere. But actually, eventually, there was something …

At first there were little particles—teeny, tiny particles that were attracted to one another and pulled together. They were attracted to each other because they had to follow the laws of particles, which say that when particles are attracted to one another, they pull together. As more and more pulled together, they created a stronger force. This force became stronger and stronger until all the particles of the entire universe came crashing together. All the particles finally crushed themselves into a mass smaller than a grapefruit. Imagine—all of the particles of the universe, everything in every star, every galaxy, and every planet—all compressed into a body smaller than a grapefruit!

The gravity must have been a powerful, crushing force. Tremendous! It tied the particles together until they lost all identity. Tied them together until it couldn't hold anymore. And with a great explosive force—BANG!—it blew apart, and the particles spun out in this *big bang*. As they expanded in huge expansive spirals, they held the explosive fiery heat of this big bang and it caused them to turn into a gaseous form. And gases expand; again, because of the obedience to the law, they have to expand. So these gases expanded—over hundreds, thousands, millions, even billions of years. As they expanded in that way, they cooled and coalesced, and this caused the formation of suns, stars, and even planets and moons. Asteroids, comets, and even cosmic dust were formed! These were all created from this expanding, gaseous material that had totally come out of this big, big explosive bang.

Now, in one corner of the universe, something very interesting occurred. One star—our Sun—formed, and all around it formed masses of particles that were large—large enough eventually to be called planets. One of those planets, the third planet out, was destined to be special. This special planet is our Earth.

Although the planet Earth seems large, even huge to us, it is tiny compared to the Sun—it seems like a little particle next to the gigantic Sun.

Display Chart 1: How Small the Earth Is!

Figure 1. Impressionistic Chart 1: How Small the Earth Is!

And our little Earth is not alone out there with the Sun. The other planets are also whirling and revolving around the Sun. It is as if the Earth is a member of a great solar family: *The Sun's Family!*

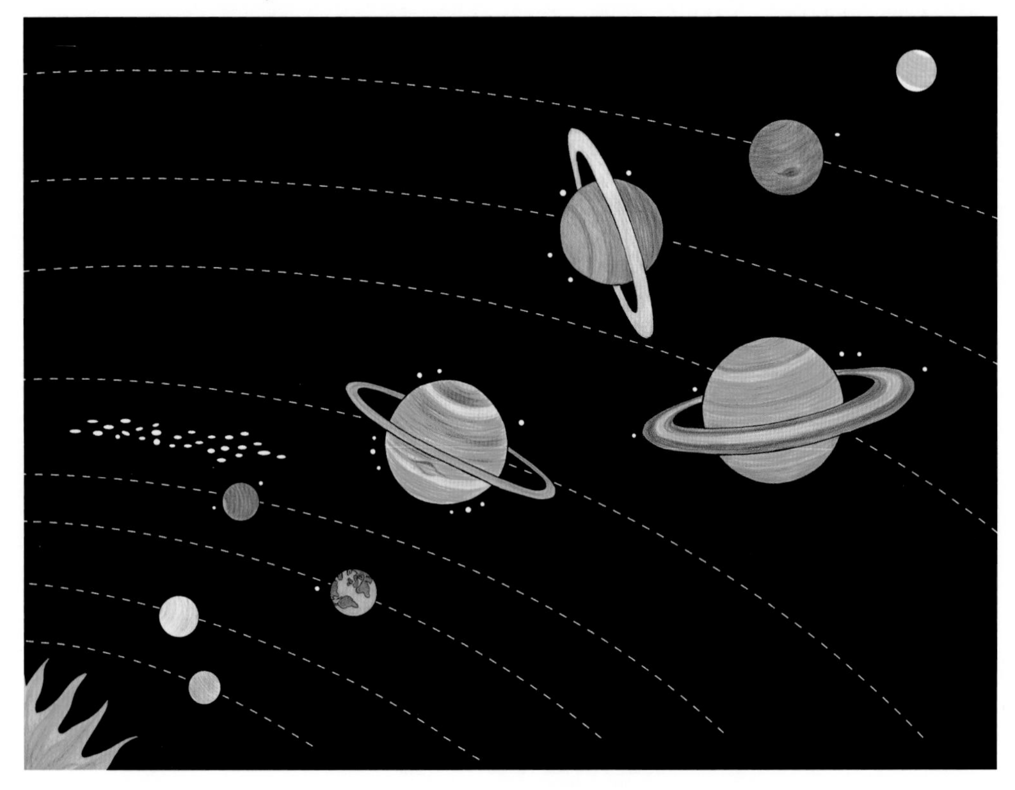

Display Chart 2: The Sun's Family.

Figure 2. Impressionistic Chart 2: The Sun's Family.

All of these planets, even every asteroid, every chunk of rock, and even bits of dust in the Sun's family make up our *solar system*.

Although the Earth itself was formed at this time, it was nothing like the Earth as we know it today. Instead, the Earth was hot from its formation out of these terribly warm gases. It was hot from coalescing. The surface of the Earth must have been nothing but molten, boiling lava. Think of it; covered in hot lava, the whole surface was fiery molten rock. There was no soil, no life, and there was not a single drop of water on the Earth. And the atmosphere—well, there was no atmosphere around the Earth at this time. There was no air. You couldn't breathe. No one could have lived there at this time; you would have died if you had been there.

We know that heavy things have to descend or fall down and light things have to float or rise. This is the law. So as the Earth slowly cooled, the heavier things descended to the core, or center, of the Earth and the lighter things floated and came up to the top. This created an Earth with a heavy, hot molten core and a surface of lighter rock and metals, also still hot and molten.

We also know that heat rises, according to the law, so heat began to rise from the hot surface of the Earth.

Display Chart 3: The Cosmic Dance.

Figure 3. Impressionistic Chart 3: The Cosmic Dance.

At the same time, the gases that were in the atmosphere rose and began to cool. As they cooled, they descended again, creating a kind of convection current that rose and carried the heat away from the Earth. It was like a dance of the atmosphere, a cosmic dance! Slowly, very slowly, this caused the Earth to cool.

But, before it cooled, there were volcanoes. Remember that there was a super hotness at the center of the Earth. With the thin, mostly molten crust at the surface, that hot interior would bubble up and burst through the surface every once in a while. All over the Earth, these volcanoes erupted, blasting out rocks

Display Chart 4: The Time of the Volcanoes.

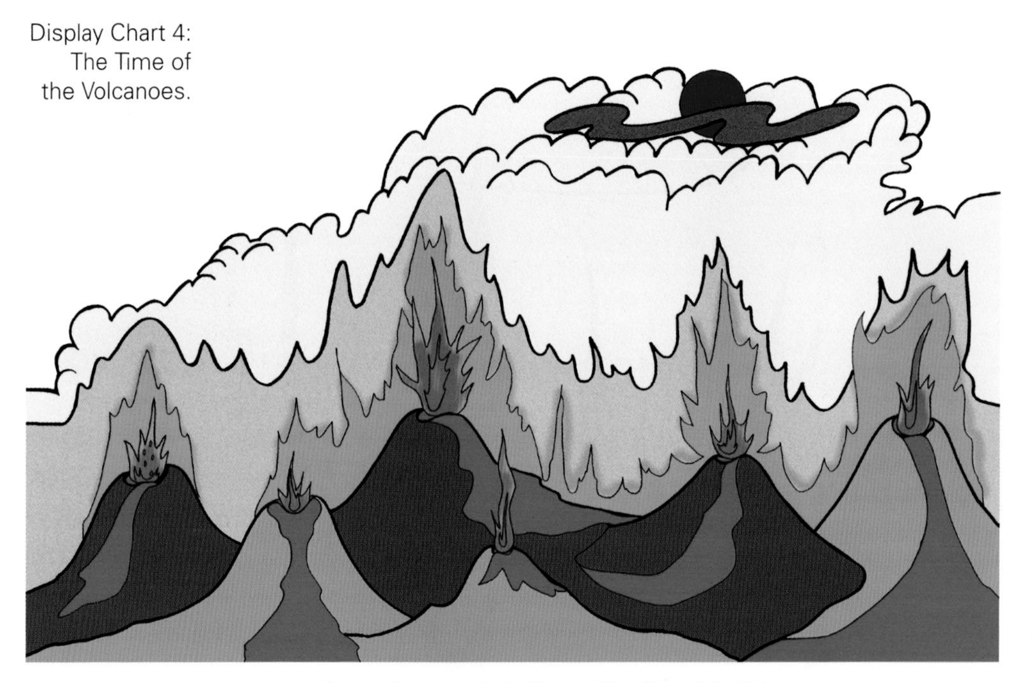

Figure 4. Impressionistic Chart 4: The Time of the Volcanoes.

and stone, lava, gases, and ash. This created clouds of ash, which shadowed much of the Earth and captured moisture, high in the sky. The shadows of these clouds helped to cool the Earth even more. Imagine that, the entire sky darkened with ash that blotted out the Sun.

Finally, from those clouds that hovered above the surface of the Earth, something happened. Eventually, a raindrop fell. But the Earth was too hot, and as the rain fell, it evaporated before ever reaching the surface. But the rain did, over millions of years, cool the atmosphere. Finally, there had to be a very first raindrop to make it to the surface. Imagine, the world's very first raindrop ever. It came out of the sky, *pshhhooo*, and touched the surface of the Earth. Instantly, immediately, it evaporated. The first raindrop to touch our Earth. Instant evaporation!

I don't know how many raindrops fell through the atmosphere and evaporated before they could reach the surface of the

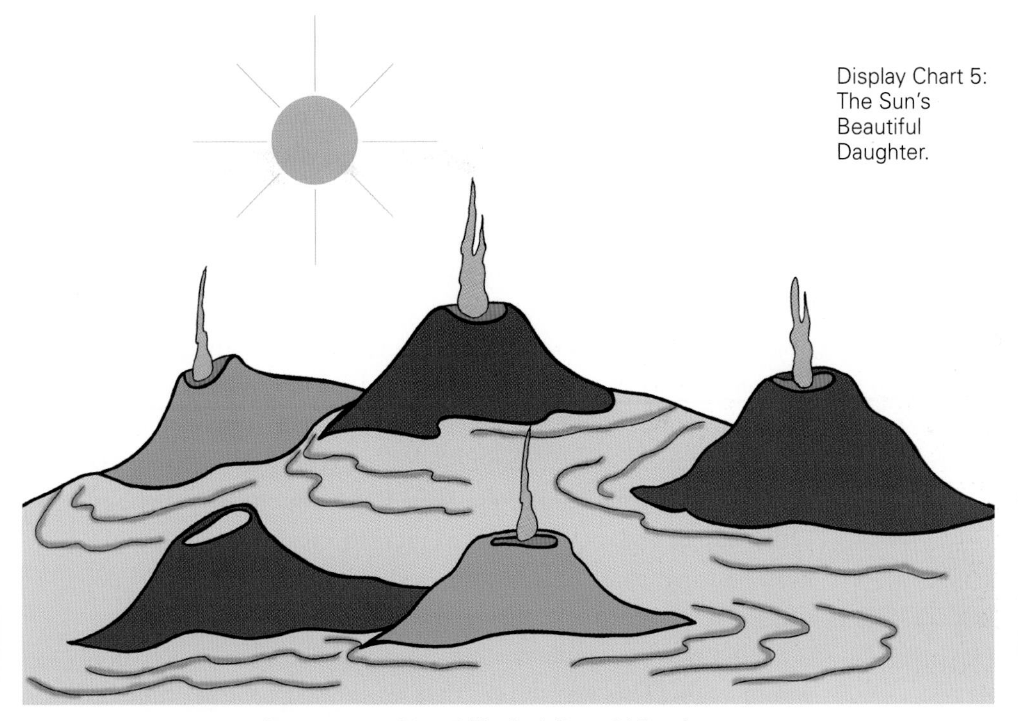

Figure 5. Impressionistic Chart 5: The Sun's Beautiful Daughter.

Earth. Billions and billions of them, I'm sure, fell and fell and fell for millions of years before, finally, one could reach the surface of the Earth, *pshhhooo*, instantly evaporating. Then a second raindrop fell, *pshhhooo*, and another. As the rain fell, the surface of the Earth began to cool even more. The water that fell evaporated, becoming a gas and creating more clouds above the Earth.

These clouds hid the sun and allowed Earth to cool even more. Until, finally, one drop of water did not evaporate, but stayed on the surface of the Earth.

One drop, and one more, and then one more, and the drops of water began to accumulate. It rained and rained and rained; furious storms seethed over the Earth. The water began to flow into all the low places, making hot, muddy puddles, sludgy and dirty with ash.

The puddles flowed together, creating warm, thick lakes. The lakes grew into a large sea filling up all the low places—a muddy, sludgy sea of very warm water mixed with ash from the volcanoes.

This great world sea was shallow and warm—warm from the surface of the Earth—and sludgy from all of the ash from the volcanoes. It must have looked like a great dirty pond, a great shallow sea, filthy with ash, but richly filled with minerals. Even so, it was beautiful, like a cradle—a cradle for life.

The sky above, with its thin atmosphere, still did not have oxygen. It had a dilute atmosphere of some sort, but it was not dense enough to block out rays, cosmic dust, meteors, and other objects from space. So, this warm world sea was barraged with showers of particles from space, exposed to energy rays from the Sun, and bombarded with meteorites that came from afar.

This was our world, about 3.8 billion years ago. Coming up from the water, here and there, were the remnants of volcanoes. Other stones and rocks may have emerged, creating stony islands, even housing lakes. There was no soil, no plants, no animals, no life—just volcanic rock and sludgy, warm water.

This was the cradle for life. This was the place where life would begin. This was the era that set the stage for the time of living things. The Earth was ready to receive life.

The Second Great Lesson: *The Coming of Life*

(Elementary Levels)

Introduction

This story, *The Coming of Life*, is the second Great Lesson. It is accompanied by the Mural of Life, a long impressionistic chart, printed in vibrant color, illustrating many of the events discussed in the story.

Figure 6: Mural of Life on pages 78-81.

After this story is told, the mural becomes a centerpiece in the Montessori classroom for a while, allowing other lessons to focus upon it. Eventually, it can be replaced by a more detailed chart, the *Timeline of Life*, which contains text as well as images.

Figure 7: The Timeline of Life on on pages 98-99.

This story, like all of the Great Lessons, is usually told in the fall, quite early in the school year. It is a sort of annual ritual in which the children may participate. Two related stories, *The Creatures on a Quest* (p. 88) and *The Great Invasion* (p. 94), are part of the second Great Lesson and also appear in this section.

Generally, there should be no follow-up work to this lesson. The exception could be work in the arts. Some teachers like to set out a set of pastels or other drawing media with paper and suggest to the children that they may wish to respond artistically to the story. Others may find interesting literature or music that complements the story.

Source: *The Coming of Life* is a traditional Montessori Great Lesson that I have significantly updated and reworked in a narrative form.

STORY

Remember when I talked to you last about going far, far back in time? We went back to a time when the whole universe was created with a bang, and then we talked about how the Earth was created, and then we talked about the time of the volcanoes, and then finally we talked about how the rains came and how the warm, murky, shallow sea was formed.

Now let's go back to that story and see where we can go from there. Remember that I told you that the warm, shallow sea covered most of the surface of the Earth, and the water was rich in minerals from the volcanic ash. The sea also had some places where rocks stuck out, making islands from small to very large.

There were no plants, there was no life on the Earth, and there was no life in the water. There was no soil or dirt on the Earth, just rocks. And in that silent sea, in that quiet ocean, nothing lived. Nothing lived on the rocks or stones, or in the lakes, or in the atmosphere. There was no movement, there was no sound. The atmosphere was thin so that things from outer space would come in: dust, rays, and meteorites.

The waters were warm, rich in minerals, and set just perfectly for life, but there was no life. Now, we don't know exactly why this happened, and we don't know exactly how this happened, but inside that warm, nurturing, mineral-rich water, bathed in rays and materials coming in from space, yet contained within the safety of our planet, something happened. Something began to move.

I don't know how many times this movement might have happened. Maybe whatever it was that moved had lived for a short time and then died. And maybe a million years later, that happened again. And maybe it happened many, many times—we don't know. We do know that eventually something moved and kept moving. That something was life. Life.

People don't actually know how it happened. Some say it just happened. Some say God made it happen. Some say it was destined to happen. Some say that there were waves and materials coming in from outer space, and something in those materials and forces seeded the ocean. We really don't know for sure.

But we do know that it did happen. That is what we do know for sure—that somehow, some way, something began to move there in the water. This earliest form of life was only a little tiny, tiny, tiny, tiny cell—so small you couldn't have even seen it without a microscope.

We really don't know what the first living things were like. Life may have begun at deep underwater hot springs that spewed hydrogen-rich molecules.

Another idea is that life started because of comets that brought energy and caused chemical reactions, producing chemicals essential to life.

Or maybe life started with small molecules that interacted with each other. These may have been enclosed in simple cases like the outsides of cells.

Still other people believe that some early life may even have been remotely plant-like, or that there were simply forces that we can't understand at work.

Eventually, as life evolved, it began to gain its energy by basking in the light of the Sun. The Sun shone on it and it gained energy. There were minerals available, and with the Sun's energy, life could form food. At some point, the living thing felt within itself a pull—a pulling apart—a pull that caused it to almost tear in two. In fact, it did split in two—and both of its halves were still alive. And that happened again and again, and that's how it reproduced. And that's how life grew, by splitting in two, again and again. And again and again. It was as if life had felt a command to reproduce. Divide. Make young. And that is exactly what happened

New living forms continued to come from the first living forms, and over time, life seemed to hear another command that said, "Adapt and change." Some of the forms changed in one way, and some changed in another way, so that life became different. Even so, all of the living things still lived in the water and gained their energy from the Sun.

Then some living forms heard commands that said, "Work

together, cooperate, and collaborate." So some of the cells joined together so that they could share their strengths and abilities—one set of cells could do one thing and other cells could do another. In this way, they could become specialists, and they worked together.

Then life felt another great command: "Take for yourself and give back." Life must do this, and so these living things heard this command and took food, nutrition, minerals, and chemicals for themselves. At the same time, they gave back those same things, by excretion and by death, because even these living things learned that out of death comes more life. In this way, a circle was created.

Now, millions and millions of years later, a time came when some of the living things had a new and different idea. I don't know why, but I do know that they had a different notion. Instead of just lying there in the water, basking in the Sun and letting its

Figure 6.
The Mural of Life.
Continued on pages 80-81.

rays cover and warm and heat them and give them food, some of the living things had the idea to let others lie there in the Sun and gain energy. When the others had done it, these living things would eat them. They would wait until others had gained the energy of the Sun, and then they would eat those others.

Hmm. It's a little bit scary, but you do it, too. You might lie in the Sun yourself, but all that happens to you is that you get a tan, or maybe a burn. You can't gain your food that way—but a plant can. You get the energy of the Sun when you eat the plant.

Those first living things that did that—eat others to get energy, instead of just getting it directly from the Sun themselves—we call animals. An animal gets its energy by eating something else that gained its energy from the Sun.

Another command came to all living things that they had to heed. And that command was *love*: "Create a more efficient love." As they heard this command to create a more efficient love,

some of them started to care for their young. We do this to this day, because we care for our young in a way that is very different from the first things that lived.

At this time, all life lived in the water because life began in the water. Some of them, the animals, thought of not only eating the plant-like things, but also of eating other animals. They thought they might as well eat anything that they could eat. And many of the animals began to do things to protect themselves as well.

Display the Mural of Life. The next several paragraphs will require interaction with the mural, pointing out specific animals as you continue to tell the story.

Let's look at this beautiful mural. Way over here at the left end, we see early animals and plants growing in the water. Some have many, many cells, and are very big. Some of the animals, like this trilobite, were covered with a hard shell. That helped to protect it from others that wanted to eat it. It grew the hard shell so that it could live. It might be able to live without the shell, but not when someone else wanted to eat it. This shell protected it.

Some animals that look something like plants are standing here. These are crinoids and sea lilies. Even though they may be called lilies, they are not plants; they are actually animals. They stand hooked to the sea floor with their mouths open and their little fronds on the side forcing food and water toward them. That's their whole life—standing and waving their fronds toward their open mouth—but, since they don't move from place to place but are rooted to one spot, to them it's an interesting life.

Others, like these jellyfish, float about, waving fronds underneath in the hopes that they'll bump into something and be able to catch it and eat it. Because eating is one of the first things that all life has to do—a living thing won't live very long unless it can eat somehow.

You'll see that everything is in the water—all life is in the water. Some creatures, like these bivalves, are like mussels or

oysters, protecting themselves completely with hard shells. They lie down on the ocean floor where maybe nobody will see them, but some other animals became specialists at finding them—like this one, the terror of the sea, the great giant nautiloid. The nautiloid is a huge cephalopod that comes sailing out on the hunt. Look, his tentacles come out from his head. That's why he is called a cephalopod—it means "head-foot." It's as if his legs sprout from his head.

The cephalopod is over fifteen feet long, with a great biting beak and arms that catch and grab. You wouldn't want to swim in that ocean. You wouldn't want to be there and have that great cephalopod think, "What a tasty morsel you look like," and grab you and have you for dinner, perhaps. But of course, in this sea, at this time, there were no people.

These animals and plants that lived at this time lived entirely in the ocean. They started from that single little plant-like thing, and over hundreds of millions of years, developed into animals that eventually started to look something like fish. These early fish were a great advance, and I'll tell you a wonderful secret about them. This is a fishy secret, but it's an important one: they have bones! They came up with a great idea: bones. They were the first animals to have a skeleton inside themselves!

These other animals have a skeleton on the outside of their bodies. Can you imagine wearing a suit of armor and being glued to the inside of the suit? You wouldn't have any skeleton inside you, but you would be glued to the inside of the armor and hang from it. That's the way their life was—their skeleton, their support, is outside, and hard like armor.

Well, the fish came up with a different idea. They didn't want to leave the armor off, so they kept hard, heavy armor on the outside of them as well. These are called armored fish, because they go around with big heavy plates of strong material on the outside. They have names like *pteraspids* and *cephalaspids*. Not only did they have a skeleton on the inside, but they also had a heavy suit of armor on the outside. This heaviness made them slow. It was hard for them to get away. Other animals were able to get them and break through the armor. Before long, some fish began to lose the armor. This made them much faster—now they were able to get to food more quickly. The armored fish all died out. They didn't succeed very well because they were too slow. It turned out that, for fish, it's better to be fast than to be armored. It works so much better.

There came a certain time, which we'll talk about a lot more later, when there was a drying up—a great drying up of many centuries. This was a time when there were glaciers—great amounts of frozen water locked up in certain parts of the world. When huge quantities of water were tied up as glaciers, the seas became shallower and shallower. In some places, the glaciers took so much water away from the seas that the oceans began to dry up in many areas.

Life was threatened, as living things lived only in the water. Now, some living things needed to find another place to live, another place to go. The first things that did this were probably bacteria and algae. Then came plants that lived very close to the edge of the ocean, where their bottoms could be in the water and their tops could be up in the air. They were very small at first, only a few centimeters high. They had no roots, leaves, or flowers like modern plants, but plant life had arrived on land.

We still see plants something like that growing on the shore. Sometimes if it dries out a little bit, they can still live, but other times, when it's wet, they can survive in that, too. These plants eventually moved a little way out of the water, or possibly the water moved away from them. One way or another, they moved up into the cracks and holes on the land.

One of the first pioneers that lived completely out of the water, on stones or sand, was a kind of plant-like organism called *lichens*. Lichens are actually a cooperative life form usually made up of a fungus and algae. These lichens lived on rock or stone and they break it down—they actually eat the minerals in the stone and break the stone down. Eventually, the lichens die and their bodies, including the minerals they've broken up, decay and become soil. Lichen have no roots, but once the lichens die, plants with roots can begin to grow in the same area, and over time organic matter builds up. This allows other plants to begin to move up onto the ground, and before long, animals that eat plants will appear.

Probably the first animals that wanted to eat parts of the new land plants were small arthropods, like mites and some primitive insects that came up onto the land. Then, of course, when the insects arrived, other insects wanted to come to eat them. Like that giant dragonfly, can you imagine—its wingspread was more than thirty inches! That would be a huge insect to see buzzing around. Its wings were like this. Bzzzzzz! Can you imagine seeing a dragonfly moving with wings this big? It must have had to eat many other insects, but dragonflies do eat other insects, so that's what it did.

Spread out your arms, and move about while making a buzzing sound.

Fish like to eat insects, too. In fact, fish eat many, many insects. But once many of the insects were on land, the fish couldn't get to them up there. This, plus the fact that the some of the water was drying up, caused some of the fish to begin to move to try to get out of the water some of the time. Many scientists think that there was a kind of fish called a lungfish that could come out of the water for short periods of time. Then it could go back into the water, out again, and back.

Who knows how many fish died trying to climb onto land? Who knows how many of them didn't make it? Nobody knows. Nobody knows how many fish tried and tried—how many flopped up onto the land, ate an insect, but couldn't get back to the water. Did that happen a thousand times? A million? Who knows? Probably many times. But eventually, there were fish that managed to stay out of the water for longer and longer periods, and they had some kind of lung as well as gills. This was the first lung in the whole animal kingdom.

When we see salamanders today, they are very like that. Some of the simplest ones have gills that we can see, as well as lungs inside their bodies. They can swim in the water and breathe with their gills, or they can come out of the water and breathe with their lungs. They have two lives, wet and dry. That's what *amphibian* means, and that's what these fish became. They evolved into some kind of amphibian, an animal with two lives: a wet life and a dry life—water and land. And amphibians love to eat insects! They were drawn to the land by the insects because they had to have food and, of course, the animals could not live on the land if there was no food. Once the first animals came onto the land, other animals came forth to eat them. This is always what happens. Before long, there were animals that ate amphibians as well as eating other living things.

As the drying continued, some new animals appeared: reptiles. Reptiles are animals that don't need to live by the water—in fact, they can live far from it. Reptiles have a dry and scaly skin, but amphibians are moist. Reptiles lay their eggs out in other places, but amphibians have to be close to water. These first reptiles could go all over the world, and they did. They took over. The dinosaurs are reptile relatives. On our mural, we can see huge animals thundering across the Earth—dinosaurs. Big, strong, dangerous, frightening. You might think you would want to be there, but this would be very frightening.

Dinosaurs were the most important animals of the time. They were the predominant animals that covered all sorts of areas. We don't know for sure what happened to the dinosaurs, but I'll tell you three ideas that people have. One idea is that something very small—see this little thing right here? Something very small had come into existence. It probably was no bigger than a few inches and it was furry. How could that threaten a big dinosaur?

Point to a very small mammal in the lower right part of the Mural of Life.

This tiny animal was probably beneath his notice. A huge dinosaur might not even be able to see it from his height. Because it was so insignificant, it could sneak around without being spotted, and for safety, it could scamper up a tree. These little creatures could go to the Tyrannosaurus or the Apatosaurus, or whichever dinosaur lived nearby, and invade its nests and eat its eggs. These little furry things are called *mammals*. These tiny animals were among the very first of their kind and they preyed on the young and the eggs of dinosaurs, among other things. They ate these young and they ate the eggs, but they were so small, they weren't worth paying too much attention to.

Another thing that probably happened, and that most scientists think happened, is that maybe some great object from outer space smashed into the Earth and threw up a great cloud of dust that blocked the Sun for many, many, many, many years and changed the climate so that dinosaurs couldn't live. That's an idea that is shown by this meteor coming from outer space, right here on the mural, that's suggesting that something crashed and caused a great explosion, filling the air with dust. This event is called the K–T extinction, and it harmed many plants and animals as well as the dinosaurs.

What a terrible thing it was for the dinosaurs. Because they were so adapted to their place and their time, they couldn't change rapidly to live there, but the mammals were able to adapt. We know that there was an object from outer space that did hit the Earth—we don't know for sure that that was the only thing that caused the dinosaurs to die out, but it was certainly a problem.

Point to the primitive bird on the Mural of Life.

Then there's a third possibility. Here it is—right here. They evolved into birds! Maybe the dinosaurs are still around us, except they have feathers, and they chirp. Birds began to appear, and we know that birds are descendants of reptiles. Birds are, in fact, reptiles that have changed in one way—mainly, their scales have become feathers, although they may still have scales on their legs and feet.

Probably all three of these things happened. Probably mammals began to rise and threaten dinosaurs. Probably an asteroid from outer space struck Earth, and the dinosaurs that had characteristics that are more birdlike survived better. So the next time you see a bird outside, you can think, "I just saw a dinosaur flying around in my front yard." Maybe instead of a bird feeder this winter, you might set out a dinosaur feeder and feed the flying dinosaur. Be aware, a small mammal may come to that same feeder just as they did way back then—mammals are still stealing the food from the dinosaurs!

Oh, and then came the time of great mammals. With the great dinosaurs out of the way, the mammals got bigger and bigger. They thundered across the Earth as well. A mighty rhinoceros was over twelve feet tall! A great wolf, the dire wolf, was over six feet at the shoulder. The mammoth and mastodon, elephant-like beings with great coats of fur, trampled across northern climates.

The giant beaver grew to over eight feet long! Most people call these giants *megafauna*. The giant mammals did not last as long as the dinosaurs because of dangers that they faced. The climate was changing and competition was increasing.

They also had to cope with a new challenge—a new predator that they had to deal with. This was a small animal, probably not very attractive, that appeared first in Africa. Eventually, some of these started to stand up just on two legs. They were very good at hunting mammals. They even became very good at hunting the large mammals. They may have been part of the reason the large mammals became extinct. Of course, there are still millions of mammals today, but the megafauna disappeared.

These new creatures, we know, liked to chatter a lot among one another, somewhat like monkeys in trees. They liked to prattle with each other, and perhaps they communicated in different ways.

We know that these creatures are still around, or at least their descendants are, because these were our first ancestors: early people. Early people were great hunters, and they were also great scavengers. Even when they found dead animals that some other animal had killed, they would eat whatever scraps or remains they could get. Eventually, as the giant mammals disappeared, our story turns to a new story.

Our story now turns to a tale all about one thing. It is the story of people. What happened to people? How did they get to be the way they are? How did they turn from small, chattering animals that raced around, not too attractive, and looking something like apes—how did they change from that into what we are now? Well that's another story, so we have to wait for yet another time to hear the answers to those questions.

For now, you can think about the story of life. Think about where you are in this great story. Think about where this story is in you. There will be more of this story to come, and you are in it!

The Creatures on a Quest

INTRODUCTION

When I took Montessori training in Bergamo, Italy, one of the key lessons to which I was exposed was called *The Story of the Drop of Water*. This story was meant to accompany or parallel the second Great Lesson, or possibly come after that lesson. According to *The Story of the Drop of Water*, there was a danger facing ancient life, which lived only in the ocean at this time. The danger was increasing calcium levels in the water.

In the story, it seems that water rushing across the surfaces of the Earth was dissolving calcium and bringing that into the ocean. This posed a threat to life. As a result, the story says, the various living things went on a quest. They formed a team to go to the wind, to the rain, and ultimately even the Sun to ask for help. Eventually, they got the help they needed from the lowly corals who cleared the water. This saved life in the oceans and ultimately, saved all of us.

This story was very popular with the children whom I taught. They liked it because when I mentioned wind or rain or the Sun or other characters in the story, they could participate with engaging hand motions or sounds.

Several years later, I had the opportunity to work extensively with Dr. Priscilla Spears. Priscilla is a consultant to Montessori schools, a science educator, and the proprietor of Big Picture Science, which provides science materials for elementary and middle schools. Naturally, our discussion turned to science.

I ended up telling Priscilla *The Story of the Drop of Water*, with interesting results. Priscilla told me that the story was misleading, and that it was not, in fact, supported by science. Because life requires calcium, she explained that the story could be confusing.

She verified for me that the problem was not with anthropomorphizing the living things (having them form a committee and going to the Sun or to the rain or to the rivers), nor with the quest they undertook, but with the fact that the science was at fault: life needed the calcium and the minerals.

Therefore, instead of trying to tweak the old story, I undertook to write a completely new story to replace it. My new story uses many of the same characters from *The Story of the Drop of Water,* and I also utilized the concept of the quest that the creatures undertake. However, I endeavored to give the new story an entirely different direction and emphasis.

The good news is that coral still plays an important role, and so does calcium, but calcium's role is now a positive one. Beyond the science, this new story is at heart a story of cooperation, of purpose, of unselfishness, and finally, what Dr. Montessori called a cosmic task.

This new story is a more valid presentation. It can help Montessorians to realize, I hope, the benefits of connecting with the greater scientific and academic world. Then, our stories can evolve with changing knowledge.

Both Priscilla and I believe that this would be Maria Montessori's approach if she were still alive. She did, after all, base her stories on the latest and most exciting theories of her day.

When I shared my new story with Priscilla, she gave me her seal of approval, noting, "The story is good scientifically. I realize that this type of storytelling is invaluable to young children, and I'm glad that you can do it." (Priscilla Spears, e-mail message to author, November 19, 2015) I hope you like it and find it both entertaining and helpful scientifically as an up-to-date approach to the drama of the early oceans.

Source: *The Creatures on a Quest* is an original story written by me, with input from Priscilla Spears.

Story

Long, long ago, back in the mists of time, when the world was very young, back in the days when all of the creatures lived in the sea's shallow, warm, clear waters, there was a problem. The creatures found that they had no homes and they had no food.

They needed somewhere to live and they needed something to use to build their homes—something that wouldn't dissolve in water, since that is where they all lived. They also needed to grow food. They knew they couldn't do all of this by themselves;

they would need to have help. Because they could talk, they got together and they thought and discussed what to do, and they decided something: they decided to go to the wind to ask for help.

So the creatures all went to the wind for help and they said, "Wind, wind, we need your help. We need something to use to build our homes and we need to grow food. Can you help us?" The wind smiled upon them in a kindly way and said, "I really can't do much to help, but there is one thing I can do. I can blow the clouds around."

All of the creatures thought that was a good idea, but it didn't solve their whole problem. So the wind said, "Why don't you go speak to the clouds? Maybe the clouds can help you." The creatures all looked at each other and then made a decision to go speak to the clouds.

They looked up and saw the clouds above and they said, "Clouds, clouds, can you help us? We need something to use to build our home and we need to grow food. We went to the wind to ask for help and he said that he can blow you around but he can't build our houses or make us food. Can you help?"

The clouds answered, "We can bring rain over the land, that we can do! But we can't make homes for you and we can't make food for you or deliver it to you. Maybe you should go speak to the rain. The rain might be able to help you."

So, they did go to the rain. They said, "Rain, rain, can you help us? We need houses to live in and we need food to eat because we're hungry. We can't do it all by ourselves. We need some help. We went to the wind and asked for help and the wind was able to blow clouds around but that's all. Then we went to the clouds for help and the clouds can bring rain but that's all. Rain, when you fall, can you bring us help?"

The rain replied, "There is just one thing I can do: I can fall. When I fall on the land I can dissolve minerals, but I'm not able to take the minerals to the sea. I don't know how to do that. I know you need the minerals because minerals like calcium can be used to build your homes. I think you should talk to someone else. Why don't you go talk to the rivers?"

So they did. And they cried, "Rivers, rivers, we need help. We need something to use to build our homes and we need to grow food. We've gone to the wind to ask for help and the wind can blow clouds but that's all. Then we asked the clouds for help and they said they can bring rain but that's all. Then we went to the rain and it said it can fall on the land and dissolve minerals but that's all. Can you help us?"

The rivers smiled at them and said, "We can bring minerals to the ocean once the rain has dissolved them. We can run over the rocks and dissolve more minerals and carry them to you. But we can't build homes for you and we can't feed you. We think that you should go speak to somebody else. Why don't you go talk to the seawater itself where you live?"

So the creatures went to the seawater and they said, "Seawater, seawater, can you please help us? We have a problem. We need something to use to build our homes and we need to grow food. We've gone to the wind to ask for help and the wind said it can blow clouds but that's all. Then we went to the clouds and the clouds said they can bring rain but that's all. They can't build our homes or raise food for us. Then we went to the rain and we asked the rain for help. The rain told us it can fall on the land and dissolve minerals but that's all. We need more help than that. Next, we went to the rivers and the rivers said they could bring minerals to the ocean but they can't build our homes or raise our food. Now we're asking you for help, seawater. What can you do to help us?"

The seawater responded, "I can spread the minerals and other nutrients all around throughout all my watery oceans so that they go everywhere and I know that will help you. However, I cannot turn those minerals into food and I can't turn them into homes. I think maybe you need to go the very top. You need to go to the Sun and see if the Sun can help you."

Now that was a little bit frightening, to go all the way to the Sun, but the creatures were so desperate that they looked at each other and decided they had better do it.

So the creatures all went to the Sun and they said, "Sun, Sun, can you help us? We need something to build our homes in the sea and we need to grow food. We've gone to the wind to ask for help and the wind said it can blow clouds but that's all. We asked the clouds for help and the clouds said they can bring rain but that's all. They can't build our homes or raise food for us.

We went to the rain and asked it for help and it told us it can fall on the land and dissolve minerals but that's all. Next, we went to the rivers and the rivers said they could bring minerals to the ocean but they can't build our homes or raise our food. Finally, we went to the seawater to ask for help and the seawater said that it would spread the minerals and other nutrients all around throughout all the watery oceans so that they go everywhere but that's all it can do and then the seawater told us to come to you. Oh, Sun, can you help us?"

The Sun smiled graciously and said, "I can send my warm rays to you. I can warm the oceans and all of the waters of the Earth and I can even warm the land itself. But you must capture my rays and make food. My warm rays are there for you to use, but I can't build houses for you and I can't make food for you. You'll have to do that yourselves."

But then the humble algae stood up and they said, "We can do this, at least part of it. We can make food using the rays of the Sun. We'd like to get started making food right away but we have no homes and so we're afraid we'll get washed away by the oceans." Then everybody looked at each other in confusion and thought, "Now what can we do?"

While all this was happening, there was somebody left behind. You see, all of the creatures had ignored the corals and had left them behind in the water. The corals were there by themselves. They looked around and they saw that they could actually do something. They started to take the calcium out of the water along with other minerals and they built structures with it, structures they called *reefs*. Those reefs could serve as a home.

What a beautiful idea, to use the very calcium in the seawater to build a structure. Then the corals invited some of the littlest algae to live inside their very own bodies and make food. And they did. Those little algae went inside and began to make food. That seemed to solve, or at least it helped to solve, the problem of food and housing, but not for everyone.

Luckily, there were some other algae who found that they could live on the outside of the coral reef, but the corals said, "Now, we're worried. We're worried that you will block the light and not let our own algae grow. Maybe we can find a way to solve that."

So the corals went to the fish and they said, "Fish, fish, come to us and you can graze on those algae to keep them from growing too thick." And the fish were happy. They said, "We will do exactly that." Then the fish came and began to graze on the algae. They liked the food, and you know what? They also found shelter in those coral skeletons in the reefs. And many other creatures from tiny plankton to great big fish found their homes there, too.

All of the creatures were happy that the tiny ignored corals had been able to do something wonderful. They had been able to build homes, which everyone benefited from, and they were able to play a part in getting food for everyone. But there was still one big problem: it was the ocean itself.

The ocean was crashing against the coral reef and if some other help didn't arrive, it could very well be that the reef itself would be broken down faster than the corals could build it up. This made the corals and all of the other creatures very worried. They were worried that the energetic, active ocean might destroy all of their work.

So, the creatures went to another form of algae. This was a form of algae called *coralline algae,* and they said, "Coralline, coralline, can you help us?" And the coralline said, "We can. We know how to take calcium out of the water, too, just like you do. We know how to put it in our cell walls." Because of this, those coralline algae were very strong, so they said, "With our strength we can help protect you. We will grow on the reef." And they did. They began to grow on the outside of the reef where the ocean waves were breaking and they made it strong and helped build up the reef.

The coral was very happy and said, "Thank you. We now have a secure home."

Now, did you notice that during this whole story, everyone worked together? Everybody, everybody had a part. The wind had a part. The clouds had a part. The rain had a part. The rivers had a part. The seawater had a part, and even the Sun itself had a part in helping them.

And what about the creatures? They all helped, too. It wasn't just the corals; it was the algae, and all of the other living things that began to grow. The fish that came showed up and began to help; the coralline algae that were so strong began to help. All of these creatures needed to work together, and as those fish and algae and corals worked together, they lived on the nutrients and enjoyed the place to live in, which now had become a thriving coral reef.

What do you think happened to all of them? They're still there. The corals are so important in reefs that even today, we call them a keystone species. That means they're one of the most important species for us; they have a crucial role. They are one of the most important kinds of creature in the whole ocean, and probably even in the whole world. Just think, without them, many other creatures would have had no homes and no food. That would even affect our lives. I think we need to say "thank you" to the corals and to everybody else who helped solve this problem.

And this was a story of how it all happened.

The Great Invasion

INTRODUCTION

The Great Invasion is another component of the second Great Lesson, *The Coming of Life.* Dr. Lawrence Schaefer, a renowned Montessori guide and teacher educator, wrote this important story supporting the second Great Lesson. A well-known storyteller with a Ph.D. in Modern European and American History, Dr. Schaefer has written nearly one hundred short history stories for Montessori children.

I am proud to count Larry among my friends and to offer this story, with his permission. Over the years, the topics Larry has explored in his work have included a range of all aspects of *Big History*.

Big History is a multidisciplinary and holistic way of approaching the entirety of history. It was first developed by David Christian of Macquarie University in Australia (2004). Big History incorporates the nearly fourteen billion years of the story of the universe with the history of the Earth, people geography, geology, and all other life.

The Great Invasion dramatizes that moment in time when life changed dramatically for all subsequent time—when life moved from the sea onto the land and adapted to its harsh conditions. It was a truly creative and epic moment for us land creatures.

Source: *The Great Invasion* is an original story written by Larry Schaefer.

Story

Millions and millions of years ago, before there were trees and flowers, before there were frogs and salamanders, before there were insects, life existed only in the oceans and seas.

The land was barren and empty.

Within the warm and secure embrace of the seas, plants flourished—the algae, the bacteria, the fungi, and thousands of kinds of seaweed; and the animals flourished—from primitive, one-celled protozoa to the multi-celled sponges, corals, sea urchins, sand dollars, crabs and lobsters, trilobites and anemones, ammonites, and hundreds of kinds of fishes. Life flourished in the comfort and security of the oceans.

But the land was barren and empty.

The mountains and hills were barren, as were the valleys and plains. Everywhere there were barren rocks, dry sand, and clay, and the wind blew dust everywhere.

When the Sun shone hot, it burned and boiled and scorched the land so that the earth cracked and split. There was no shade.

When the rain fell hard, it tore up the sand and clay and washed them away in countless swirling rivulets and streams. There were no plants to hold the sand and clay in place. There was no living dirt.

But as the plant life looked out from the comfort and warmth and security of the seas, they saw a fantastic treasure—golden sunlight everywhere and oceans of carbon dioxide.

Their eyes swam and their heads swirled with the wonder and enchantment of it. Plant life yearned and dreamed of this great treasure.

There was no life on the land, although the algae coated the rims of streams and ponds for a few inches where the splash of waves and the tides kept them moist. Without water, the sun would fry them even a few feet from the water.

The great leaders of the plant kingdom summoned their generals and business leaders, their poets and scientists, their best minds in every field, to a grand council.

"There is great opportunity," they said, "a price beyond compare for those inventive and courageous enough to see it. There is a chance to gain endless sunlight and carbon dioxide in countless buckets and the gratitude of the whole plant world forever."

"Where? Let's go. Let me try. I can't wait!" was the general reply from those assembled.

The plant leaders pointed out of the water. "Look to the land. See what is there—sunlight and carbon dioxide in endless supply."

Dark despair descended on the council. The giant seaweed—some that grew to over one hundred feet, whom you would have expected to take the lead and be most courageous—were, in fact, the most timid and negative. "No way! It's suicide. It's crazy! You won't find us doing anything so stupid! It can't be done—EVER." And away they marched.

But it was the tiny green algae who, in the end, came up with a plan. I suppose we should have expected it, because they were the ones brave enough to live out of the water on the edges of the seas.

"Suppose," they said, "we were to lie on our sides and half of our filaments grew down into the ground and half grew up toward the light. The filaments growing down could hold us tight and seek out nourishment. And if we all stayed close together and protected each other, and if we could reproduce by means of little seeds wrapped in a tight, protective casing, then it might work. Anyway, it's worth a try."

The plant leaders had very little choice but to give the tiny algae a chance. So the green algae organized themselves, made two or three small adaptations, and marched out of the water in tight little regiments to begin the great experiment.

Did it work? Well, look on the forest floor, look in the damp places, look on rocks and boulders, and you will find tiny little mosses. These mosses are the adapted algae, and they were the first plants ever to live on the land.

Imagine now a barren landscape with wrinkles of green fuzz wherever water collected. These green fuzzy areas were the beachheads of the great invasion of the land.

But these tiny algae were not finished. They soon solved a greater problem. To move away from the shore and other wet places, and to survive when water dried up, plants needed to keep a reservoir inside their stems to use when no other water was available. There soon appeared a tiny plant, only inches high, bare of leaves, stuck in the ground without roots, but inside its stem and skinny branches was the life-preserving reservoir of water. These were the world's first vascular plants. We call them *psilopsids.*

Then, in a blink of geological time—ten million years—club mosses and horsetails, plants with genuine roots and needle-like leaves, appeared. From regiments of mosses and psilopsids, the plant kingdom had now a whole army corps of club mosses and horsetails.

Then, the first forest appeared, still tentative and highly dependent on moist and swampy ground. Into and onto the green carpets that began to spread in damp and watery areas came worms and spiders and millipedes and slugs and a multitude of tiny animals.

THE TIMELINE OF LIFE

The Timeline of Life, (Figure 7, pictured below) is used after the Second Great Lesson to begin the introduction of more detail into the history of life. It is similar to the Mural of Life, but with greater detail, and text as a part of it. When this timeline is used, the story of *The Coming of Life* should already have been told and the children should already be familiar with the Mural of Life.

Like the Mural of Life, this timeline is a long chart or poster, usually measuring from eight to ten feet in length. Do not substitute a smaller or "tabletop" timeline. The impressive size of this material is important in striking the imagination of the children.

The Timeline of Life is divided into three eras—*Paleozoic Era*, the *Mesozoic Era*, and the *Cenozoic Era*. Paleozoic means "old animals," Mesozoic "middle animals," and Cenozoic "new animals."

Montessorians separate a part of the Cenozoic Era to create a fourth era, the *Neozoic Era*. The Neozoic Era is brightly colored in red to indicate the importance of the appearance of humanity on Earth, and the role of love in humanity. Most scientists do not separate out the Neozoic in this way.

The Timeline of Life represents the entire time of the Earth's history after the Proterozoic Era. A small pink strip on the extreme left of the Timeline shows a small part of the

Figure 7. The Time Line of Life.

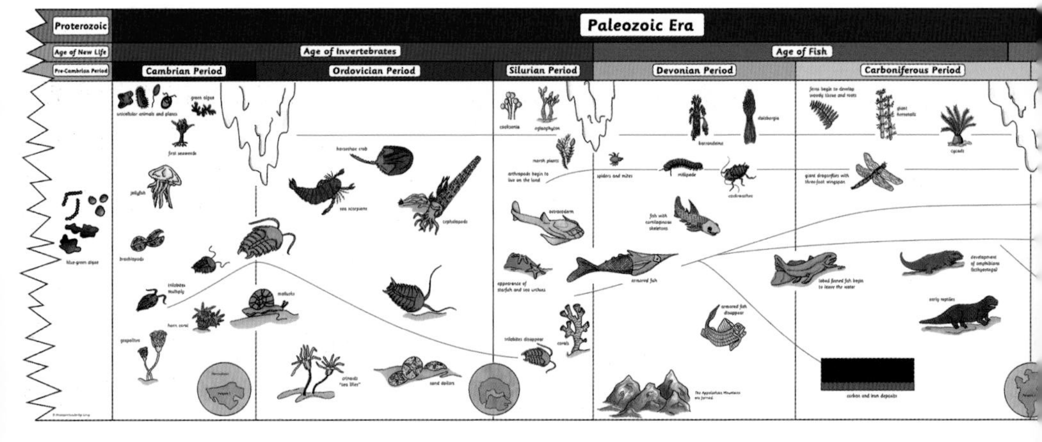

Proterozoic Era. Its jagged edge indicates that the Proterozoic Era had already been going on for a long time before this Timeline.

Each era is divided into different periods. Each period is remarkable for certain climactic conditions and certain animal and plant ascendancies.

At the top of each section is listed certain forms of life that were significant during the era involved. For instance, the first time period during the Paleozoic era is called the "*Age of Invertebrates.*"

The duration of the different eras and periods is not entirely agreed upon by all scientists. In addition, different names for the periods are sometimes used. This is because new fossils are continually being discovered, adding to our knowledge of what life was like during these periods.

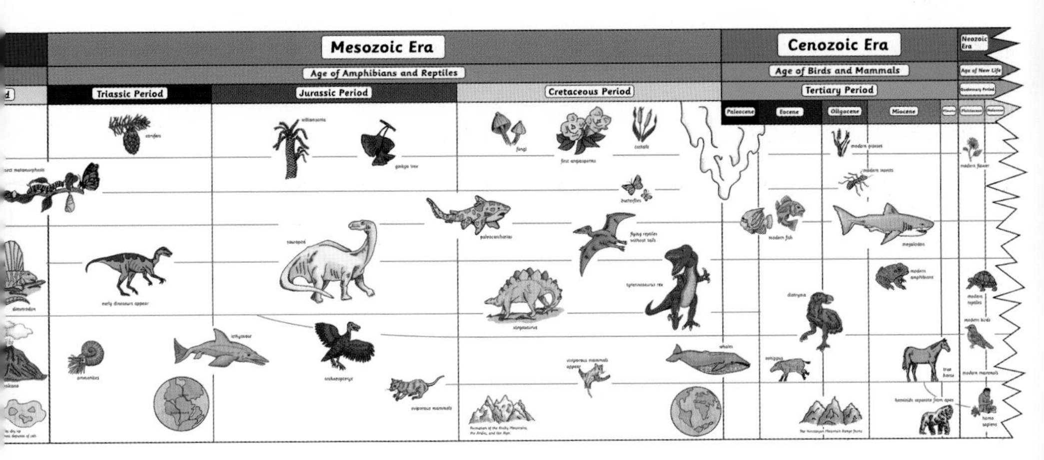

The Third Great Lesson: *The Coming of Humans*

(Elementary Levels)

Introduction

The story *The Coming of Humans* is the third Great Lesson in Montessori schools. It is usually presented with a very long chart or poster called the *Timeline of Humans*. This timeline shows images of a variety of prehistoric humans including *Homo habilis*, *Homo erectus*, *Homo neanderthalensis*, and *Homo sapiens*. It also depicts the tools and art developed by these early people.

If you do not own a Timeline of Humans, there is an alternative. The story could also be presented with a series of pictures that could be shown to the children as the different human groups are discussed. Then, simply lay the pictures out in order of chronological time.

Like all Great Lessons, it is generally presented to the entire class.

At the end of the story, there is a suggestion of what will come next. In fact, in Montessori classes, this next part is a full-year study of early people that is usually undertaken in the third year of the elementary program, which corresponds generally to third grade. It is frequently revisited in greater depth in the first year of upper elementary, the 9 to-12-year old program, or grade four.

Source: *The Coming of Humans* is based on traditional Montessori ideas that I have very significantly updated and reworked in a narrative form.

STORY

Display the Timeline of Life. Point to the picture of a human being at the extreme right end of the timeline.

Do you remember when we looked at the Timeline of Life? Let's go back and think about it again. Here, far at the end of the timeline, all the way at the very far end, is a picture of a person, a small picture of a person. We are going to take that time and stretch it all out so that we can talk about it in detail. We are going to talk about people. And in particular, we're going to talk today about four different kinds of people, as well as somebody else who doesn't quite fit the category of being a person, because our earliest ancestors were probably very, very, very different than you and me.

Our early ancestors were probably much shorter than we are, and they didn't stand up straight. They probably made many noises, much like we do today, to communicate, but their noises probably weren't languages we know now. Our earliest ancestors almost certainly lived in the land that today we call Africa, though they didn't use that name for it. But today, we call it Africa, and that's where they lived.

Now, bring out and display the Timeline of Humans.

About three million years ago, or more, way off the edge of this timeline, before this timeline even begins, those early ancestors that we call *Australopithecus* lived. There were even earlier ones, but this is the earliest one that we are going to talk about.

Australopithecus was an ape that is related to us; we are its descendants. However, we won't use the word *human* yet. That is yet to come.

What was unique about *Australopithecus*, I wonder? *Austra* means "southern," so they lived in a southern region. What was the special thing about this ancestor that makes him so important? He could stand up, and he did stand up. One thing that is so very important about that is that the hands were free. Standing up on two legs frees the hands—and the thumbs. Because the hands are no longer used for moving, they are freed. This is a very important thing.

We are going to learn now that human beings are notable—and different from all other kinds of life—because of three great gifts that we have received. These three gifts will define all of our ancestors that come after.

The three great gifts have to do with the hands, the heart, and the head, and we do call them gifts, these three characteristics of humans. These three things set human beings apart, and they have something to do with our hands, something to do with our hearts, and something to do with our heads.

The time that we are talking about is called the Stone Age. This is because the tools that these very early people created were made of stone. Living in the Stone Age was dangerous. Early people did not have long sharp fangs or claws for fighting. They were also not the fastest animals. They had to use other gifts to be able to survive, so they used their hands to make very sharp tools. They also used their heads, and they grew smarter than other animals.

Let's talk about someone specific. Let's talk about *Homo habilis*. *Homo habilis* is all the way back here on our timeline, about two million years ago to one million six hundred thousand years ago. *Homo habilis* lived in Africa as an early kind of person. When we say the word "homo" at the beginning of his name, we mean "belonging to the human family." The *Homo habilis* is the first of the true human people.

Point to each hominid species on the timeline as it is mentioned.

We know that *Homo habilis* made tools, and in making the tools this early person used one of those three gifts: his hands. Because of this, these early people were named *Homo habilis*, meaning "handy human."

If you take your hands and you rub your fingers and your thumb altogether, you will find you can touch all of them together easily. That ability makes it possible for you to grab a pencil, or a pen, or a paintbrush, and be very, very precise with it. If you were *Homo habilis*, you could grab a rock and use it as a tool. Or you might use another rock to chip away at another, so that it could become sharp and pointed.

We know that *Homo habilis*, all the way back at this time, was a toolmaker. That's why we see the picture right here, of a person chipping and flaking a large rock into sharp flakes, or tools. These can be used for what's in the other picture—cutting up pieces of an animal. They're not cooking it; they're going to eat it. We don't know if they hunted it or if they found it after it was

At moments like this, where the story says something like, "And that's why we see

contuned on next page

contuned from last page

the picture right here...," point to the corresponding image on the Timeline of Humans. If you do not have a Timeline of Humans then prepare pictures that you can show to your class as you tell the story. Excellent pictures are available in many books and online.

killed by something else. Most likely it was something left over, because *Homo habilis* probably did not hunt large animals very often. Maybe another animal had come and killed it first. After eating it, that other animal may have run off for some reason. Then *Homo habilis* could have decided, "There's something left here for me, I would like to get some of it, too." They scavenged for scraps and bones with marrow in them.

We can also see that there's a picture here of people in the background finding other kinds of vegetable material to eat, maybe fruit or stems or other plant parts. Some of those plants may have had insects or grubs on them. That was all right, too. Mostly, they probably ate fruits, roots, nuts, and plant parts that they found. They were not able to use fire to cook at that time.

I want to talk to you now about another human that's going to come along. This one is right here, and is called *Homo erectus*. You still hear the word *homo*, meaning that this is a human, but *erectus* means upright, to stand up, so *Homo erectus* is upright human. *Homo erectus* lived in Africa, but moved out of that continent to places as far away as Java. They lived from about one million seven hundred thousand years ago to about one hundred thousand years ago.

Homo erectus was much more advanced than *Homo habilis*, although they both lived for some of the same time. *Homo erectus* had tool-making skills that were much improved over *Homo habilis*. They even made weapons like knives and stone axes. Instead of simply scavenging, *Homo erectus* probably actually hunted—they were the first real hunters.

Another great advancement for *Homo erectus* is that he had fire-making skills, a simple act that completely changed human life forever.

We don't know exactly how fire came to be mastered by humans. We really don't. It's possible that there was an electric storm, and lightning may have started the first fire. Perhaps there could be other things that helped humans to control fire.

Point out the person staring at the fire.

In the background of our timeline, we see fire being tamed. Here is one person standing and looking at the fire as though he's worshipping. Perhaps this person thinks the fire has power and should be worshipped. Here is another person running away in fright. He's terrified. Maybe he is fearful because fire does burn and can kill. In the foreground, somebody has actually grabbed a flaming stick and is bringing it with him while the fire still burns on it. Here is a last person, watching in wonder, or awe, that this other person is actually carrying fire.

Fire was a great help in helping humans stay safe, too, since most animals are afraid of fire. Now, humans could make a fire to keep predators away. Fire was a very, very important tool for protection.

Fire can be a frightening thing, but the use of it meant that people could cook their food, which automatically allowed them to live longer. Cooking softens food and makes it edible and digestible by older people who may have no teeth, which they often didn't, since they didn't have dentists! With softer food, they could live longer. Cooking can also soften food for very young children who might not otherwise survive. Cooking also helps to kill things that might be in food that can cause disease, like parasites. This makes *Homo erectus* the world's first cook.

What do you think that they ate? *Homo erectus* probably still scavenged for scraps and marrow bones, but he also ate meat, roots, plant stems and leaves, fruit, nuts, insects and grubs, honey, and birds' eggs. Delicious!

Now let's move down the timeline to the next human group. Here is another picture. Somewhere around three hundred thousand years ago to around thirty thousand years ago there lived a people called *Homo neanderthalensis*, or Neanderthals. Although as a group, Neanderthals are not directly ancestral to us, they are very like us. They are called Neanderthal because their bones were first discovered in the valley of the Neander River in Germany, though they, too, also originally came from Africa. Neander is the river, and Tal means "valley."

Here, on the timeline, is a picture showing a family grouping of the Neanderthals. It shows different people doing different things. When I told you that we have three great gifts, one of the gifts I mentioned had to do with the heart, and that is love.

Point to the family of Neanderthals on the timeline.

Point again to the family of Neanderthals on the timeline.

Here, when we see the human holding a child, and when we see them working together, these are our first examples of love on the timeline.

Human beings have a different kind of love than other animals. Other animals can love as well, but humans don't only have one kind of it. We have the kind of love that two people share—the kind where people may be in love with each other—but we also have a different sort of love. Humans have love at a distance. We can even love someone we may never see. We may help others that we hardly ever know, just because they're human beings. This love has an origin, and the origin is in the depths of time, way back here, when at some point in the past, people began to care for one another in a way that went beyond what other animals do.

Our capability to love is our second great gift. You and I and any other human can show our love for others. When something terrible happens to other people, we can support them in some way by giving them something—even if it may be that we will never know them, never know who they are, never meet them. We can do this without ever even expecting thanks. That's a kind of a love for others that other animals don't have. We have that transcendent kind of love, when we choose to use it.

The capacity for a uniquely human kind of love was one of the most special things about Neanderthals. Neanderthals also had several other interesting and unique characteristics. The Neanderthal people may have had variations in skin color. It seems that many of them may have been red-haired. Most likely, they had some kind of language abilities.

What kinds of food did they eat? It seems that to a huge extent, the Neanderthals ate meat. They may have added some plant foods, but meat was prominent. They got their meat by hunting, although they may also have scavenged. They were very skilled hunters, and they used stone-tipped spears. Their favorite meats included mammoth, deer, and horse. The Neanderthals were talented fire-makers, and they usually cooked their food.

These people were very able. They often used caves as their homes. They may also have built temporary shelters from animal bones or tusks or used tree branches covered with animal skins.

Neanderthal people buried their dead with ceremony. We call this the Birth of Religion, since it suggests that they believed that humans were different from animals, and they may have believed that there was an afterlife. On the timeline, we see a burial ceremony in progress. They are decorating the dead person with flowers and possibly pollen as well as a weapon.

The next thing I want to show you is down on this end of the timeline where there are people very like us. We call these people *Homo sapiens*, or *Early Modern Humans. Homo sapiens* appeared around one hundred fifty thousand years ago in Africa. They seem to have moved beyond Africa by one hundred thousand years ago, and by about fifty thousand years ago, they reached Europe.

The appearance of *Homo sapiens* may have marked the end for the Neanderthal people, who were not able to successfully compete with the more advanced Early Modern Humans (also called EMH).

These *Homo sapiens* are people that are very much like us. After all, that is what we are called, too. We are also called *Homo sapiens.*

Here they are on the timeline. Look at some of the things they have. Here is a bow and arrow—those are things from the EMH people that we still have today. Here are some very sophisticated shelters that they made to live in.

Point to the early human shelters on the timeline, or show a picture that you have collected.

EMH people also developed exquisite art. Look at this small statue that they carved from ivory. They made magnificent paintings on the walls of caves. They even developed lamps that burned animal tallow or oil. They're very like us.

Now let's talk about our third gift, the head. Human intelligence is something really special. We have what we call a reasoning mind, and so did the EMH people. You have the ability to think things through. You have a mind that doesn't just react to things, but can actually work things out, solve problems. It's true. That's a very important gift, a great gift.

Homo sapiens did make stone tools, but that's not all. They also used other materials, like bone, to make fish hooks and sewing needles. They made warm boots from leather or bark, lined with fur or grasses.

Point to the Homo sapiens at work or show a picture that you have collected.

Here, in this picture on the timeline, we see people doing two simple things that are interesting. An early artist is painting something. He's using his head, using his mind, to envision something and bring it into being. These other people are drying meats over a fire; if you look closely, you'll see that their clothes, their leather clothes, are stitched, sewn together with bone needles and thread made from other parts of animals.

This picture shows three very, very important things. The first thing is pottery. The EMH people used their minds to develop a natural resource, clay, into an indispensible part of life, pottery. With pottery, you can cook liquids in a pot. It is possible that *Homo sapiens* began working with clay as long ago as thirty-five thousand years ago. The earliest fired pot that has been found dates back to about twelve thousand years ago and appears to have been fired in an open fire. *Homo sapiens* was the first potter.

The second great thing to see in this picture is a domesticated animal. Here on the timeline, they're milking a goat. Take a look at the little boy standing there by the goat with his mother. This is an example of love.

By about eleven thousand years ago, *Homo sapiens* in western Asia had domesticated sheep and, soon after, goats, which were raised both for milk and meat. *Homo sapiens* also used hides, hair, and wool for clothing and for tools.

Homo sapiens was the first to care for livestock. By about ten thousand years ago, people were raising domesticated pigs in the Near East. By eight thousand years ago, cattle were domesticated in the Fertile Crescent region. People were on their way to animal husbandry, breeding and raising farm animals.

Point to the picture of an early farmer or show a picture that you have collected.

In the background right here, we see a person dragging a forked stick through the earth. This demonstrates the third great thing in this picture: the birth of agriculture—planting. Agriculture is one of the most important discoveries of the EMH people, and it led to deep social changes. Agriculture is the basis for civilizations.

Agriculture started as gathering. Wild cereal grains—grass seeds, really—were being gathered and eaten as far back as twenty-three thousand years ago. Agriculture changed this by allowing people to plant and raise what they needed, becoming farmers instead of continually being on the move to look for food. By about nine thousand five hundred years ago, humans began to cultivate the first crops in the Middle East. These crops—all grasses—were barley, and two early types of wheat: emmer and einkorn.

The early farmers used sticks with sharp ends to break up the ground for planting. These digging sticks led to the development of the hoe. The first hoe was probably a forked stick. *Homo sapiens* was the first farmer.

These three things are huge works of the mind. They are great inventions of human beings: making pottery, domesticating animals, and becoming farmers.

Let's talk one last time about the three gifts that humans have that make us unique, special, and different. It's not just that we are alive, because many things are alive. It's not just that we are animals, because many other animals exist. It's not just that we can be friendly, because many animals can be friendly.

Three very special gifts are what I call the hand, the head, and the heart. The gift of the hand—the use of our thumb and fingers—makes it possible for us to be tool users. The gift of the head—our mind—allows us to reason, think, solve problems, and imagine. The gift of the heart—love—makes all of the other gifts worthwhile. Love is transcendent in its own way because it makes us care deeply, and that's why we're together today, because we love and care for one another.

For the rest of this year, we are going to spend lots of time looking at all of the vignettes on this chart. We are going to look at each one and tell a story with each vignette. We will read about the people from each area. We will learn about what early people did in different places, and we're going to learn about where they lived.

During the entire time, I want you to be thinking of three things: their hands, their heads, and their hearts, and think about how you use your three gifts. In this way, you can find yourself in the story and find where this story is in you.

Think again about all of our ancient ancestors. The long-ago early people gave us such wonderful gifts. I hope we are all grateful for them.

This is the story of humans. It is our story. Think about where you are in this story. Think about where this story is in you. Everybody on that timeline is one of our cousins or ancestors.

This story is your own story and it's a continuing, ongoing story. Yes, you are in this story too, every one of you. Soon we will see what is in the next chapter of our story.

The Fourth Great Lesson: *The Story of Language*

(Elementary Levels)

The Fourth Great Lesson is a Montessori introduction to human language. It is actually not a single narrative, but is divided into three parts, each with an accompanying story. The three stories are *The First Word* (p. 111), *The Ox and the House* (p. 114), and *The Piece of Paper that Sees and Speaks* (p. 118). As its name suggests, *The First Word* is an origin story about the birth of human speech. *The Ox and the House* looks at the beginnings of the alphabet, thus its focus is writing. Reading is the subject of *The Piece of Paper that Sees and Speaks*. By using these three stories, all three of the components of language—speaking, writing, and reading—are introduced in a narrative way. They should be presented in the order in which they appear in this book.

The First Word

Introduction

Have you ever wondered what might have been the first human word? Certainly there once was a first word, the very first word ever spoken. At some time in the distant past, someone spoke, and humans have not been silent since. This is a part of the Fourth Great Lesson, *The Story of Language*.

The story, called *The First Word*, takes the position that the first human word was *mama* (or *mamma*), a word uttered by a child. *Mama* is a powerful and meaningful word to which all children can relate. Children know how important a mother is; certainly the word is important as well. It carries strong emotional content.

We also say that while *mama* is the first word of humanity, it has also been the first word of most humans. Of course, the word is a noun. This gives some credence to the theory that nouns may have been our first part of speech.

Source: *The First Word* is an entirely original story, which I wrote.

STORY

She was very, very excited.

She was very happy and excited about what might be happening. She lived in a time before people spoke. She lived in a time before there were names. She lived in a time when people communicated with gesture and with movement, and even with grimaces. In this time, people communicated with sounds, but not words or language.

She was excited because something was stirring inside of her and she could feel inside of her the stirring and the moving, the changing that was growing inside of her. She knew, from having seen others in her clan, that the stirring and moving inside of her meant that a new one would join them soon.

As she grew and expanded, she could feel the new one. Sometimes there would be little changes. There would be things that would make her think "it lives," or "there's something in me." Sometimes she felt a movement, sometimes even an inner bump or a kick.

She was so very happy that this new one might be among them at some time soon. As every day went by she would put her hands on her belly in this way and feel the young new one as it moved around inside of her. She wondered how it got there. What caused it to be there? What had happened that made it be there? And what would it be like?

Place your hands upon your abdomen and feel around.

But she couldn't express those wonderings. She couldn't

voice those questions, because there weren't any words to express them yet. There simply were no words. Nobody had ever used words yet.

Then, at some point, the young one came. One day, as she lay there in her bed, there was a spreading wetness and she knew that soon the young one would be joining her, soon something would happen. Some of the other women in the tribe came to help, because they always helped when a new one joined the tribe, when a new one showed up.

Soon, then, there was a squalling sound. It was a sound of crying, but it was a wondrous crying. It was the sound of a new one joining the Earth. Joining. Coming.

It was red and wrinkled. It was purplish in places. It had some sort of substance on it that came off a bit when they rubbed it with a fur. And the wise women showed it to her.

The new one's eyes opened and she knew "this little one has joined me." "This new one is mine." She felt such happiness, such joy that the new one was there. And they gave it to her. And she put it to her breast and she began to feed it.

This new one lived with her and added to the tribe. Over the days and over the weeks, she was thrilled and happy as she felt its little life pulse within it, as she held it to her and could feel it in its warmth. She could see it grow. She could see the thick patch of dark hair that began to emerge from its little head. She could feel the softness in the top of its head begin to change. And she saw its face as it changed over time.

One day, as she held the new one in her hands, it looked up at her, as it always did. It looked her in the face as she made warm and cooing sounds. And then it made a sound. It sounded like "Ma ma. Ma."

She thought, "That's me. I have a name. For the first time. Mama. That's me."

So, for the first time, the notion that someone could have a name, that someone could be called something, emerged on Earth. Ma ma. *Mama.* This word was the first word. This word was the word that was the first word to be recognized as having the power of a name, having the power of a word. Ma ma. *Mama.*

And do you know what? It is still the first word. It was the first word, and today, it's still the first word. It's the word that has the most power. It's a word with energy and strength. It's a word with beauty. All languages start with a word—they must start somewhere. Our own words can start with something as powerful as "mama." Maybe that was your very first word!

The Ox and the House

Introduction

The Ox and the House is an origin story that addresses the development of the alphabet. The title comes from the Proto-Canaanite and Semitic alphabet. The first letter of that alphabet was *aleph* or *alif.*

It is generally thought that the original letter *aleph* comes from an early Semitic word, which means, "bull" or "ox." The earliest letter was actually a pictograph shaped like the head of an ox. This eventually led to the Greek letter *alpha* (α) and to our present letter *A*. This accounts for the ox in the title of the story.

The word *house* in the title comes from the second letter of early Semitic alphabets, which was *bet* or *beth*, meaning "house," which was also originally a picture (of a simple house). This early letter evolved into the Greek letter beta (β) and is now our present letter *B*.

The story tells of a boy named *Alim*, whose name in Arabic means "wise," "learned," or "scholar." Alim makes a great discovery about letters. He and his family have been using pictographic images to depict things, such as an ox, a house, a finger, or water. As he thinks about his name, he realizes that it starts with the same sound as *aleph* the ox, which is a source of pride to him. As he thinks about each sound of his name, he idly sketches the pictures that are linked with each sound. Suddenly he has written four pictures in order and has in fact discovered the alphabetic principle that a symbol can stand for a sound, not just for a thing.

When offering this story, I write or draw each symbol as Alim thinks about it. Eventually, the four letters together create his name. Be sure to write from right to left, as most Semitic languages are written.

Source: *The Ox and the House* is based on a traditional Montessori concept, from which I wrote this original story.

STORY

There was once a young boy named Alim. Alim lived in a place called Phoenicia, in an area close to the Mediterranean Sea. This story takes place very long ago, thousands of years ago.

Show a globe or map at this time, locating ancient Phoenicia on the eastern end of the Mediterranean Sea.

Alim's father herded a large group of oxen, which are big, strong cattle. Of course, Alim himself wanted someday to herd oxen. He wanted to follow his father.

Alim had been named *Alim* because it means "wise one," and his parents had hoped that with that name he would become wise and strong and know so much that he would be all-knowing. We will be the judges, as we listen to this story, as to whether their great wishes came true.

Alim lived in a house—really a hut—that in their language was called *beth*. Beth meant hut or maybe house. In those days, they could draw a picture, also called *beth*, which showed the house where they lived. Using a picture to show something was the only way that they could write.

Draw a picture of the Proto-Sinaitic symbol *beth*, as in Figure 8.

Figure 8: This is the Proto-Sinaitic *beth*.

If Alim wanted to show his family that he had gone to his house and he was not there to tell them he could just draw this picture, *beth*, and they would know, "Oh, Alim is in the house, he's gone to the house. He's taken the oxen back. He's in the *beth*, the house." The picture or symbol meant house.

One day, Alim left his house to go out with the oxen and take them to a grassy pasture. Now the name for an ox in those days was *aleph*.

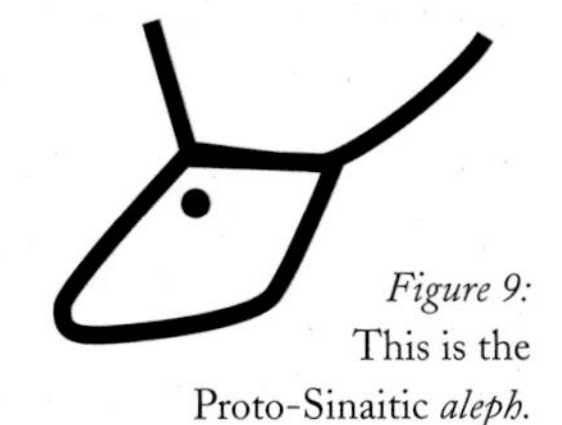

Figure 9: This is the Proto-Sinaitic *aleph*.

Draw a picture of the Proto-Sinaitic symbol *aleph*, the head of an ox, as in Figure 9.

Aleph is the ox, and the symbol or *pictograph* of *aleph* that they used

As each letter is named you should show a card with that Phoenician symbol on it, or you may draw the symbols yourself.

was this. The ox. Alim was walking with the oxen when he realized something amazing. The name *Alim* and the word *aleph* start with the same sound. "Isn't that interesting?" he thought to himself. "I'm something like an ox myself. I am strong, like an ox."

"Alim. *Aleph*. I am Alim, *aleph*. I am an ox."

And Alim walked with strength and power in his walk—like an ox might walk—as he thought to himself how strong he was. He was proud to be like an ox, so strong.

Now, Alim had a *goad* for the oxen. A goad is a pointed stick that he used to prod and move the oxen. Sometimes he used the goad to pull on the oxen, or to poke them to make them go where he wanted. A goad helped to direct the oxen. The Phoenician word for goad was *lamedh*. With the goad, *lamedh*, he was moving the oxen along, and this is the symbol that means the goad, the ox goad or the ox stick, that helps to move the oxen.

Draw a picture of the Proto-Sinaitic symbol *lamedh* as in Figure 10.

Figure 10. This is the Proto-Sinaitic *lamedh*.

Alim was moving them along when he thought that *lamedh* and *Alim* both share something. His name, Alim, and the goad, *lamedh*, both have the "lll" sound in them. Alim thought, "Well, in a way that works, because Alim has the goad. Alim, *lamedh*, that's interesting."

Alim had never thought about sounds and words before—that words could have a sound or maybe more than one sound. Because in those days each symbol always meant a complete word. *Lamedh* was simply the goad, the thing that moved the ox along. This was something worth thinking about.

As Alim walked with the oxen and his goad, he pointed forward to water where he was taking the oxen, and he extended his arm to point, and he thought "that's interesting, because the word for arm is *yodh*." And as his arm came forth, he thought again, "*yodh* is like the 'y' sound in Alim. *Yodh*, Alim. Y. Y."

Here, do not say the name of the letter *y*, like *wye*. Instead, try to say its sound like *yuh*.

So Alim drew a picture in the sand that shows the symbol for the arm, *yodh*. This is the symbol that he drew, and it means *yodh*, arm.

Draw a picture of the Proto-Sinaitic symbol *yodh* as in Figure 11.

Figure 11. This is the Proto-Sinaitic *yodh*.

Alim said to himself, "Alim, strong like the ox, *aleph*. Powerful with the goad, *lamedh*. With his strong arm, *yodh*." As he said each sound he acted it out a bit, stomping like an ox when he said *aleph*, swinging the goad when he said *lamedh*, and flexing his arm as he said *yodh*. These sounds are interesting, and they are all about me!

At that moment, they arrived at the pool of water where the oxen were about to drink, *mem*. The water is called *mem*. This is the symbol for *mem*, water. Alim thought, "Isn't that interesting? I hear that 'mmmm' in my name, too. At the end, *mem* is like Alim." He said it again, stretching out the last sound, "Alimmmm ..."

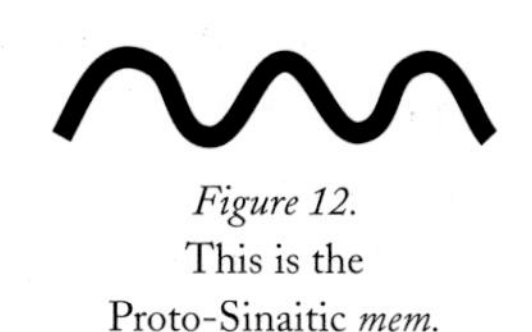

Figure 12. This is the Proto-Sinaitic *mem*.

Draw a picture of the Proto-Sinaitic symbol *mem*, as in Figure 12.

Alim thought to himself, "Alim, strong like the ox, *aleph*. Powerful with the goad, *lamedh*. With the strong arm, *yodh*. Vital like water, *mem*." Now, once again, as he said each sound, he acted it out a bit, stomping again like an ox when he said *aleph*, swinging the goad once more when he said *lamedh*, flexing both of his arms as he said *yodh,* and making wave motions with his hands as he said *mem*.

Alim drew all four of these pictures, he drew the picture of the ox, *aleph*; the picture of the goad, *lamedh*; the picture of the arm reaching out, *yodh*; and the picture of the water, *mem*.

Put the four Proto-Sinaitic pictures that you have drawn to form *Alim,* but arrange the letters right to left so that they seem to spell *mila,* as in Figure 13.

Figure 13. This is *Alim* spelled in right to left Proto-Sinaitic script.

Then a most miraculous thing happened, something that had never happened before, something that changed human life for all time. Not just for Alim, but for all of us. For Alim suddenly thought that this first picture, *aleph, lamedh, yodh* and *mem*, had four sounds. They were the four sounds that started each word. If Alim said the sounds, they could make his name, Alim, Alim. Alim. "My name Alim."

While saying Alim, stretch it out, emphasizing each initial sound. Point to the four symbols in right to left order as you pronounce them: *aleph, lamedh, yodh, mem.*

Before this there was no symbol for Alim, but now Alim felt like he'd literally written a word—with four pictures, he could actually make his name. There's no single picture for Alim, like there is for water, like there is for the arm, like there is for the goad, like there is for the ox. By drawing these four pictures together he could write *Alim*. So, he wrote it over and over and over and over again. Then he scratched it in the rock where it still could still be seen today, Alim.

Once again, display the Proto-Sinaitic *beth* card, as in Figure 14.

Figure 14. This is the Proto-Sinaitic *beth.*

At the end of the day, Alim took his oxen back to the house, *beth*. He was so excited that he drew the picture for the house as well, even though it didn't fit in his name.

When Alim got to his house, he told his family the story of the ox, the goad, the arm, and the water, and he showed them his name, and the symbol of the house. Alim even wrote his name on the house itself.

Today, many, many years later, Alim is no longer alive. But we still do have the ox and the house as well as the goad, the arm, and the water. We actually have them right here.

Show the Greek letters *alpha* and *beta*.

Figure 15. These are the Greek letters *alpha* and *beta*.

It's true! The ox, *aleph*, and the house, *beth*, have changed a lot over all these thousands of years, but finally they were renamed by the Greeks as *alpha* and *beta*. Those two symbols, especially, have come down to us in a unique way, because, put together, they made our word *alphabet*. The ox and the house became the beginning of our alphabet, the first two letters. This is the story of the Ox and the House, how our alphabet came to be.

So the story is told, and here it ends.

The Piece of Paper that Sees and Speaks

INTRODUCTION

This story is another part of the Fourth Great Lesson, the Story of Language. It tells the children about the importance of reading, which makes *The Piece of Paper that Sees and Speaks* a curriculum story as well.

The story tells of a master gardener, Phyllis, who wants to send some fruit to a friend named Albert. To do this, she employs a young lad from a nearby village. The child cannot read, so he does not know why Phyllis includes a piece of paper along with the fruit. Eventually the fruit is delivered (twice), and the use of reading is revealed.

The Piece of Paper that Sees and Speaks makes use of dramatic irony. The children in the class realize what is going on even when the child in the story does not. The audience relishes this knowledge. Sometimes they may even want to say what is going on, as if to tell the character what is happening.

This story is a traditional Montessori story that goes back many years. No one seems to be certain who it was that first told the story, but it has changed extensively. My version has had very substantive rewrites and changes; even the characters Phyllis and Albert have specially chosen names.

I never reveal the meanings of the names to the children, nor do I even hint that they have special meanings. However, it has happened that later, in some cases many years later, that some children have discovered that the names have meanings. I have had them come to me with eagerness to share their discovery. I will leave it to you to discover the meanings of the names, if you should like to.

This story is told early in the year, every year. The children love it.

Source: *The Piece of Paper that Sees and Speaks* is based on a traditional Montessori tale that I have very significantly altered, updated, and reworked in story form.

Story

Once upon a time in a faraway land, there lived a talented gardener. Now, her name was Phyllis, and Phyllis loved to garden. Oh, she had the most beautiful gardens. Phyllis had flowers that were impressive, with lovely blossoms. They were wonderful. And the delightful scent, ahhhh, the beauty.

Phyllis had vegetables that were luscious and delicious. They were beautiful as well. She had asparagus with great feathery fronds, and beans that climbed high poles. There were tubers, roots, and stems of all sorts that were wondrously edible.

Of all of her plants, Phyllis was most famous for her fruits. She had fruits that made people come from miles around just to see them. Deep-red strawberries, luscious plums, dark-green melons, tasty pears. But most of all, Phyllis had delicious peaches.

Phyllis grew peaches that were unheard of in any other garden anywhere nearby. Each beautiful golden globe carried a scent of heaven. The beauty of the peaches' shading and color was only exceeded by their magnificent taste.

Oh, these peaches were so wonderful, so huge, and so excellent; but they only came at a certain time of year. So, if one were there, perhaps if one were very, very lucky, Phyllis might share her peaches. She might give you a peach. Then you would be in heaven, for these were peaches beyond any that you have ever experienced.

One day, at the time when the peaches were ripening on the trees and they were laden with scent and they were heavy with fruit, Phyllis summoned a young boy in the village nearby. She said, "I have a gift. I have a gift for my friend, Albert, who lives some distance down the road. Can you please carry this gift to my friend for a small token of my friendship?" The child was happy to do so.

So, Phyllis took a basket out to her orchard where she carefully plucked twelve beautiful, perfect peaches. The bouquet arose like a scented perfume, an exotic aroma from the Orient that filled her nostrils with loveliness. Phyllis was also filled with happiness that her friend, Albert, would soon be receiving these magnificent peaches.

She carried the peaches back to her house in the basket and covered them completely with a clean, white, folded linen cloth. The boy was watching her as she did this. Then, at the last minute, she thought of something.

She thought of something, and she picked up a piece of papyrus, or paper and something like a crayon. On the paper, she made some sorts of marks. She made marks on the paper, folded it up closely, and put the paper under the cloth. Then she gave the basket with the peaches and the paper, covered by the cloth, to the child and he took them and off he went on his long journey to Albert's house.

As he walked along, it turned out that it became a very warm day and the heat of the sun beat down. He was strong and young, so he kept walking, but the heat of the sun also caused the basket of peaches to warm. As they warmed in the sun, they gave off the most exotic perfume. They gave off a scent that was irresistible. They gave off a smell of deliciousness. They gave off an indication of great taste and flavor that could be located inside that basket if only he could—well ... but ... but no, he couldn't do that.

Soon he came to a large rock by the side of the road, a great stone, casting a shadow, and he felt this might be a good place to sit for a while, rest in the shade, and cool a little bit.

As he sat there with the basket next to him, he thought, "Well, after all, who would know if I took just one peach? How would Albert even know? I mean, I can be very careful. Who would know? I can take just one."

And before his thinking was even over, he noticed that he had opened the linen cloth at the top so that he could admire the beauty of the peaches. Then he thought, "Well, it really wouldn't hurt to take one in my hand and just feel it for a little bit." As he reached to take a peach, he noticed the piece of paper, but he thought, "Who cares?" So, he took the peach, and you know what happened—he sunk his teeth into it.

Once that had happened, he thought he might as well eat the whole peach. So, he ate the peach, and it was indeed just as delicious, just as juicy, just as great as he had imagined. When he was done, he cleaned up, put the paper back in the basket, covered the basket with the linen cloth, and went on his way.

Now, when he reached Albert's house much later in the day, he presented Albert with the gift, saying, "From your friend, Phyllis, who has grown these beautiful peaches for you." Albert was so very delighted. He said, "Oh, thank you." Then he opened up the basket, took out the piece of paper, and looked at it. Then he looked at the peaches, and then he looked at the paper. Hmm. Finally, Albert looked at the child and he said, "I see you must have eaten one."

How did he know? How could he know? How could he know that? "There's only one way," thought the child, "that piece of paper must see and speak. It must have seen what I did and somehow it must speak to Albert." And he mulled this over all the way back to his home. How could a piece of paper see and speak?

Well, it was only a few days later when Phyllis called the boy one more time. It turns out she had another fine crop of peaches, and once again she had filled another basket that she wanted to send to Albert. "Would you again, for a small token of my appreciation, please carry this basket to my friend Albert, as you did before?" The child said, "Yes."

The same thing happened. She went to the orchard, she plucked the peaches, she put them in the basket, and she covered them with the beautiful white linen cloth. Once again, she took a piece of paper and made marks upon it, then she put that piece of paper, folded, into the basket.

Once again, the young boy started on the long walk, and once again the hot sun from above shone down so that, again, he was hot, tired, and a little bit hungry. Again, the smell of the peaches rose from the basket, assailing his senses with beauty and elegance.

As he walked, as he trudged along, he came to that same rock. And at that same rock, where he remembered that he had stopped before, he stopped once again. He looked at the basket of peaches and he thought, "Well, somehow the last time Albert knew." He thought about this. It was the piece of paper, he thought.

So, he opened up the basket and very carefully took the piece of paper out and set it over to the side. He put a big rock on top of it so that it couldn't see what he was about to do, and then he was ready. He carefully selected a beautiful ripe peach. It was perfect. He enjoyed that peach fully.

He cleaned up and covered the basket back up. Only then, he took the piece of paper out from under the rock and slid it back inside the basket under the linen cloth. It had not been able to see a thing! With a great deal of joy in his heart, he went on, all the way to Albert's house, knowing that the piece of paper had not seen what he had done.

When he arrived at Albert's house, Albert happily opened up the package, looked under the linen, took out the piece of paper, and looked at it. Then he said again, "I see that you've eaten another peach. I hope it was delicious."

How could he know? How could he know? The piece of paper couldn't see; it was covered up. All the way home, he troubled himself with this question until he got back to the village and he spoke to his father.

The next day, the boy and his father went to see Phyllis and they said, "Please, wise lady, you have a magic gift. You have a mysterious gift. You teach paper to see and speak. Can we buy the secret from you? Can we somehow pay you to teach us the magic, to teach us this wonderful gift?"

As the boy and his father explained what had happened and as they told her about the piece of paper that sees and speaks, she smiled at them and said, "This gift is beyond any price that I could name. This is a gift that I shall not sell, but I shall give for free. Because all people should have this gift, for it allows you to make papers around the world speak to you. This is the gift called *reading*. And that gift I shall give to you, your village, and your people without charge, fully from my heart, for it's something that all of us should have and will give us all great pleasure. It will give you pleasure just as it has me." And you know what? That's exactly what she did. And all learned to write and read, just as you shall in this class.

And this is a true story. And if it isn't, it should be.

The Fifth Great Lesson: *The Story of Mathematics*

(Elementary Levels)

The Fifth Great Lesson tells *The Story of Mathematics*. I divide it into two parts. I wrote the first story, *Dawn Child*, to address underlying motivations for counting in a pre-numeric, pre-counting human era. The second narrative, *Our Numbers* (p. 129), is an adaptation of how our number symbols came to be. Syneva Barrett, a wonderful teacher who loves the Great Lessons, wrote this adaptation (more on Syneva on p. 129). There is certainly room for more in this area. Rich areas for new story writing include topics such as shapes and the origins of geometry or the origins of other mathematical disciplines such as algebra.

Dawn Child

Introduction

As mentioned above, I wrote *Dawn Child* to be used as a part of the Fifth Great Lesson, *The Story of Mathematics*. It tells a tale of a girl in prehistoric times who likes to hunt but finds it helpful to her hunting to be able to count.

Before counting began, it is believed that one-to-one matching, or pairing, occurred. In today's world, a simple example of pairing would be matching yourself to an empty seat at a concert, or your car to a parking place. In ancient times, it may have meant matching a notch on a stick to something—it would have been like counting by ones only. One, one, one, one, one, etc. This is not really counting as we understand it, but it was, and remains, an essential first step in human counting ability.

Source: *Dawn Child* is a completely original story, which I wrote.

STORY

Let's take a trip far back in time, to a time so long ago that that we have lost count when. Back when people were living in caves—when there were no houses.

One group of people lived in a cave overlooking a beautiful, beautiful valley. They could look out and see green grass, many trees, a watery stream, and the lovely valley beneath, frequently traversed by many different types of animals.

This story is about one person, one special person, that lived in that tribe, a girl whose name was Dawn Child.

The girl was called Dawn Child because she rose early every morning, at the time of the dawn, to see the animals and the warm light that illuminated the sky at that time. Dawn Child loved so much to go down into the valley, close to the river. There, she would see birds and fish. She would see amphibians and animals in the trees, and she would see large animals that had come to drink. She loved to follow the hunters and watch them when they went out to chase animals great or small.

Sometimes, the hunters chased animals as small as the hare or the squirrel, and other times, they were able to find large animals like deer or caribou. The wise woman in the tribe frequently told her, "Dawn Child, hunting is not for you. Hunting is for the men of the tribe. You are not to go with them."

But Dawn Child wanted to go, and she loved to watch the hunters when they practiced by putting a stone into a sling and whirling it around their heads again and again until they released it forcefully at a tree. In this way, they perfected their technique so that when they were out hunting, they could throw the stone to easily catch a rabbit.

Dawn Child also loved to watch them when they made a

spear. The hunters made the head of the spear very carefully from flint, and they would take this spear and put it into a wooden spear thrower called an *atlatl*. She watched them practice throwing. The spear would go a tremendous speed, and very accurately, toward the target.

Over time, Dawn Child learned how to do these things, too. She watched and she learned how to whip the stones, and she watched and she learned how to throw the spear. She became an expert at using these things. She learned to knap flint and make sharp knives and spearheads, and eventually, she became a hunter. Even though people had warned her not to do this, she was respected because she could do these things.

When they went on a great hunt, they needed to consider how they would carry back the food, for one person could only carry so much. If one person went far away and found many, many caribou, it would be impossible to bring all the meat and hides back. When they went on a long hunt, there was always a question of who should go. Should everyone go? How many people were really needed? Answering these questions was always very difficult—because in these days, no one knew numbers. There were no numbers and counting had not been invented. The only thing that could be counted was one thing—something by itself.

One day, Dawn Child went quite a ways away from the tribe's area. She went about as far as she could run in two whole days. She ran and she ran until she came to a high ridge that overlooked a broad plateau, and in that plateau was a beautiful set of pools, maybe just right for animals to come and drink, she thought. She stayed there through the night, until the next morning. Then she could watch at her favorite time, the dawn, to see if animals would come to drink.

And they did. There were many caribou—enough to feed her tribe for the winter. She knew that her tribe could eat well and live if they could only kill all of those caribou, but she also knew that she could not carry them all back by herself. She was frustrated because she feared that she wouldn't be able to tell people how many hunters were needed to come back to help.

As Dawn Child sat there thinking and looking over the plateau, she happened to be holding a stone in one hand. In her other hand she held a stick. She was idly scratching at the stick as she was thinking—just sort of absentmindedly scratching away at the stick, "What to do, what to do?" Scratching and chipping away at the stick kind of helped her to think. When she looked down at the stick, suddenly a great idea came to her.

She made a sort of mark on the stick, and she stared at it, with her forehead furrowed in concentration. For some reason it occurred to Dawn Child that her mark was like a caribou. Just a lone caribou, not a herd.

She made another mark on the stick. Dawn Child looked and she thought, "Hmm, and this mark is also like one caribou." And she scratched another mark, and thought, "This is also like one caribou." Dawn Child kept marking one and one and one and one and one until she made one mark for every caribou that was there. One and one and one and one and one and one and one and one—a mark for every caribou she saw. Many caribou, many marks on Dawn Child's stick.

Dawn Child picked up her stick and began to run. She ran the long way all through the day and most of the night. She ran all the way back to her village, to her cave, to her tribe. They were hungry, but her people would not be hungry for long. For when she reached them, she also thought something: that one mark is like one hunter. One and one and one and one and one and one and one and one were needed to go find the caribou and bring them back.

Dawn Child's idea worked. The hunters were very successful. They had exactly the right number of people to carry exactly the right amount of meat back to her tribe, and they ate very well that year because of Dawn Child.

Now, Dawn Child really wasn't counting because she could only count "one," but she could count one many times, so that is what she did. Today, we call the stick that she used a *tally stick*, and the scratches that she made we call *tally marks*. By making those tally marks, Dawn Child started something wonderful, which was the beginning of counting—the first step leading to humans being able to count.

People discover things when there is a need. Those early people had a need, and Dawn Child discovered it. This probably happened more than twenty-five thousand years ago.

I guess I should say that the wise woman never again told Dawn Child that she should not hunt, because Dawn Child had proven that she could do just that. Dawn Child showed that she was not only a person who loved the dawn but she was also a great hunter, and an inventor.

Our Numbers

INTRODUCTION

The story that follows, *Our Numbers*, is a reworking of a traditional Montessori tale. This adaptation was authored by Syneva Barrett, an experienced Montessorian who has focused upon the elementary school years. She has also worked for many years as a Montessori teacher educator. Among her areas of special expertise are the Great Lessons.

Source: *Our Numbers* is an adaptation of a traditional Montessori presentation on how our number symbols came to be. Syneva Barrett wrote this creative adaptation; I edited and revised it.

STORY

The story I have for you today is the story of *Our Numbers*. This story is going to take us throughout the time of humanity and show us many gifts that we have been given, by many different people around the world, that have allowed us to have the number system that we have today.

For this story to start, we have to think way back to the Timeline of Humans. Close to the very end of that timeline, do you remember that there's a picture showing a person milking a goat? That's meant to symbolize the time when humans learned to domesticate animals, which greatly changed the animals from their wild ancestors. Domestication of animals revolutionized humanity, too, because humans no longer had to travel from place to place following a herd. Instead, they could stay in one place, and staying in one place meant that they were better able to meet their physical needs of food, shelter, and clothing. Now they could work on other needs. This allowed other human inventions, such as mathematics, to flourish—even though those inventions or discoveries came from very simple beginnings.

During this ancient, long-ago time, about 6,000 years ago, there was a shepherd, called Aapeli. His name meant *meadow*, and he had been named that to honor his future work, which would be as a shepherd, herding his flocks in beautiful meadows.

Aapeli would let his sheep out to graze in a meadow during the day and bring them back into his pen at night. Aapeli could not count, but it was very important to his livelihood and to his family that he keep track of those sheep very closely. He could not afford to lose even one sheep, for his family depended on them.

When he would let his sheep out of the fold in the morning, Aapeli would put a stone in a pile for each sheep that passed through the gate. Then he went off for the day and worked, and at the end of the day, when he called the sheep back in for the night, he would take a stone out of the pile for every sheep that returned. This way, if there was a stone left, he knew that there was a sheep missing and he needed to go and search for it.

Even though Aapeli didn't know how to count, he knew how many sheep he had by using the stones in a one-to-one match to represent the sheep. That was one of the earliest forms of counting, and it was very similar to Dawn Child and her notched counting stick. So other people were learning to count in this way, too: some of them made notches on sticks or antlers; some would use stones. And some of them would even carry along a rope into which they could tie and untie little knots as they counted. Can you imagine a shepherd tying a knot in a rope for every sheep that he let out, and then untying each knot when the sheep came back in for the day? Well, that's how people started to keep track of their things!

Eventually, people invented words for numbers, and those have led to the number names we still use today. No one knows for sure where those words first came from.

Humans have only ever invented numbers for the amounts of things that they needed to count—for the things that they had in their environment. And so, it has taken a great time for numbers to grow as high as we can count today. First, people just needed numbers in the units and tens; then into the hundreds, and then the thousands. Today, we have a googol!

Now let me tell you another number story. The people of ancient Egypt were blessed with having a great river, the Nile, that flowed northward through their country. The Nile also flooded almost every year. This made the land around the Nile very fertile for farming. The Egyptians were lucky, because meeting their basic needs of food and clothing and shelter was helped by the Nile River. Just like the Babylonians, the Egyptians, with their fundamental needs met, were able to develop more things, and both numbers and writing flourished there. In fact, ancient Egypt is considered one of the greatest civilizations of all time.

The Egyptian king was called the *pharaoh*. So, the pharaoh was responsible for everything and he owned everything. Of course, as the owner of all things in Egypt, he wanted to keep track of all the things that he owned. He wanted very precise records kept. And the Egyptians had a special way of writing. We call their writing *hieroglyphic*—it was actually the Greeks that named it that; *hiero* meant *sacred* and *glyph* meant *carving*, thus *sacred carvings*. Yes, the Egyptians actually carved their writing in stone. Imagine how precise those stonecutters had to be to keep these precise records and carve them into stone! We still have evidence today of their stone-carved records, and this is why we have been able to study and learn so much about Egyptian numbers.

Now, their first numbers were very simple. They were just strokes, like you could imagine tally marks. One stroke for one,

Display the illustration of the Egyptian one, two, and three as in Figure 16.

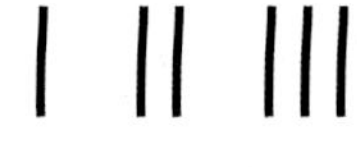

Figure 16. These are the the Egyptian numerals 1, 2, and 3.

two strokes for two, three strokes for three, and so on. That system didn't work very well when they started to get into higher numbers—it would take too long to count so many strokes. So, the Egyptians invented special symbols to represent certain numbers, and then they would put together multiples of those symbols to make other numbers. And so, a ten looked like this. Many people believe that it is a symbol of the *hobble*, a special device that would go over the neck of their oxen, so that the oxen could pull heavy loads. Others believe that it represented a heel bone, or even a twist of rope.

Display the illustration of the Egyptian ten, as in Figure 17.

Figure 17. This is the Egyptian 10.

The symbol they used for one hundred looked like this—it was a coiled rope. The symbol for one thousand was a lotus flower. The symbol for ten thousand was a crooked finger. The symbol for one hundred thousand was a tadpole. And the symbol for one million was a god or an astonished man with his arms raised toward the heavens. The Egyptians carved and used these symbols to keep track of the things in the pharaoh's kingdom.

Display the illustration of the Egyptian 100, as in Figure 18.

Figure 18. This is the Egyptian 100.

Display pictures of the Egyptian symbols for one hundred, one thousand, ten thousand, one hundred thousand, and one million, as in Figure 19.

Figure 19. These are the Egyptian 1,000, 10,000, 100,000, and 1,000,000.

Now, the counting system that we use is based on ten. It's called the decimal system because it's named after the Latin word for ten: *decem*. Not all people use a base ten system, and in the past, other systems were used as well.

Some of the oldest numerals known were used by very ancient civilizations, such as Sumeria. The Sumerian numerals existed as early as nearly 8,000 years ago.

Show a chart of Sumerian numerals for 1, 2, 3, 10, and 100, as in Figure 20.

Figure 20. These are the Sumerian numerals for 1, 2, 3, 10, and 100.

Later, the Babylonian number system emerged. It is very ancient. It started possibly as early as 2000 BCE. By 2100 BCE, the Babylonians had their own system of counting based on the number sixty. The Babylonian system is credited as being the first known positional, or place-value, numeral system.

Show a chart of Babylonian numerals for 1, 10, 100, and 1,000, as in Figure 21.

Figure 21. These are the Babylonian numerals for 1, 10, 100, and 1,000.

Farmers at that time were trying to figure out when to plant their crops. Because there was a time of year when it would always flood, they realized that it was necessary to consider this for their plans.

As they tried to solve this problem, they formed a belief that whenever the brightest star rose before dawn, it always began to flood immediately after. And so they started counting. How many days passed until the next time that brightest star rose in that exact spot in the sky before dawn? They counted 360 days. Were they right? Now, we know there are 365 and one-quarter days in a year. They were close, weren't they? Yes, they were very, very close.

Well, they took that cycle of the year, and they divided it into 360 parts, and we still divide our circles into 360 parts and we call them degrees; that is all based on the Babylonians and their cycle of the year. Can you think of other things that we still use today that are based on the number sixty? Of course! It is our time, our clocks. We have sixty seconds in one minute and sixty minutes in one hour. So we can also, here in our time, see the Babylonians' influence on us.

The city of Babylon was built upon the Euphrates River and divided in equal parts along its left and right banks. This was not too far north from where the Tigris and the Euphrates rivers met.

Display a picture of a Babylonian 3, as in Figure 22

The Babylonians used *cuneiform writing*. Cuneiform is a type of writing made with wedge-shaped marks that are pressed into clay tablets with a blunt reed.

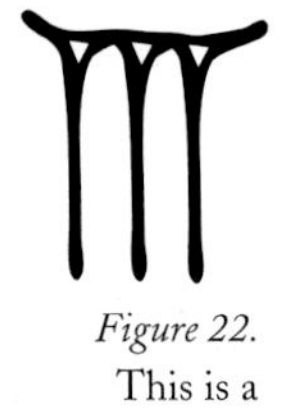

Figure 22. This is a Babylonian 3.

The people were able to dig clay from the riverbanks, and they harvested reeds that naturally grew there. When they would cut a reed in a particular way, they were able to make a triangular-shaped stylus, a writing tool that they could press into the clay. When they did this, it made Ú-shaped imprints that they could make either small or large. They could also give the impressions different orientations in the clay by changing the direction that they held the stylus.

Display a picture of a Babylonian 10, as in Figure 23

Figure 23. This is a Babylonian 10.

So, a Babylonian three in cuneiform looked like this—they pressed their stylus in three times. A ten looked like this—they would turn the stylus and press it in. A sixty, of course, had its own larger special symbol because their numbers were based on sixty.

Now, the Babylonians traded with many people in the area around the Mediterranean, and they kept track of their trades. If, for example, they sold three bowls, they would make their symbol for bowl and then put three tally marks underneath it to keep track of that. Because they were doing this on clay tablets, they were able to bake those in the sun so that they hardened—these tablets were like the first form of receipts, where they were able to preserve a record of their transactions. Some of those were very basic transactions of traders at markets, but archaeologists have also found great stores of these clay tablets that have been kept. By studying these, we know that the Babylonians were able to do some very complex mathematics. Some tablets use fractions, algebraic formulas, and even the Pythagorean theorem! The Babylonians were actually doing some very advanced math.

The Hindu people of India developed numerals that led to our numerals today. Their numbers one, two, and three looked like this.

Display Indian numerals 1, 2, and 3 in Brahmi style, as in Figure 24.

Figure 24. These are Indian numerals 1, 2, and 3 in Brahmi style.

Their numeral for ten was quite different.

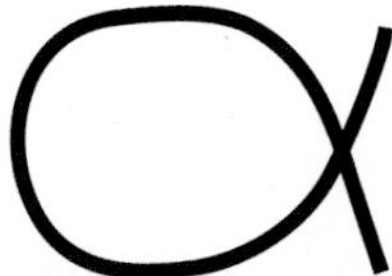

Display a numeral 10 in Brahmi style, as in Figure 25.

Figure 25. This is an Indian numeral 10, in Brahmi style.

The Hindu people of India also left us another great gift—a huge gift. We are so lucky that the Indians left behind this wonderful, incredible, glorious gift. Can you imagine what this great gift was? Do you know? Guess what? It was nothing! Nada! Zilch! Nulla! Zero! That's right, zero!

After all, somebody had to invent the idea of zero, and it was the Indians. Around 600 AD, in the Indian language of Sanskrit, zero was *schunya*, which meant "void," or "empty." Now, the zero carried incredible power, because then, in their language, they were able to create large numbers by simply adding a zero.

That very first zero was just a small dot, and this powerful, wonderful, almost unbelievable idea that the Indians invented worked so incredibly well that the Arabs, who were trading with the Indians, picked up on it. Yes, eventually, although it took hundreds of years, the Arabs caught on and they started using the zero, too! They saw how quickly the Indians were able to calculate things when they were doing trades—because of the great and powerful zero.

Some people still argued against having a zero. They said,

"Zero is not a real number. How can you have a number that means nothing? If zero means nothing, then it's not a number. The whole point of numbers is to count things, and if you have nothing, then you're not counting! If zero was a real number, you should be able to divide by it." All of those were their arguments against zero.

But the Arabs had their own arguments. They had a powerful one, which was that zero actually worked for calculations, and you no longer had to use an abacus to calculate things if you had zero. The Arabs became the real inheritors of the Indian system of numerals, including the zero. The numerals they developed look a lot like our numerals today.

In Europe, the Romans had developed their own system of keeping track of numbers. You may be familiar with these—they are called *Roman numerals*. They were based on seven signs. The "I" was one. The "V" was five. The "X" was ten. The "L" was fifty. The "C" was one hundred, because the C stood for *centi*, which meant a hundred. You'll see that root used in many Latin words, like a centurion, the leader of a hundred army troops. A "D" was five hundred. An "M" was one thousand.

Show the basic chart of Roman numerals, as in Figure 26.

I V X L C D M

Figure 26. A basic chart of Roman Numerals.
They represent 1, 5, 10, 50, 100, 500, and 1,000.

The Romans made a rule that the order in which you arranged the letters indicated whether you were to add or subtract: if the smaller number came second, you were to add. So, XI equaled eleven. If the smaller number came first, you were to subtract; so, IX equals nine. Where have you seen Roman numerals? Sometimes, we find in our books that the chapters are counted in Roman numerals. Often, on important buildings, you will see that the date it was built is recorded in Roman numerals, often etched in the stone. Today, even our Super Bowl always has the year recorded out in Roman numerals.

Why do you think that we use Roman numerals for these

things? It's a system that works very well for counting. But, it isn't very good for calculations. Imagine trying to do a multiplication problem that looked like this:

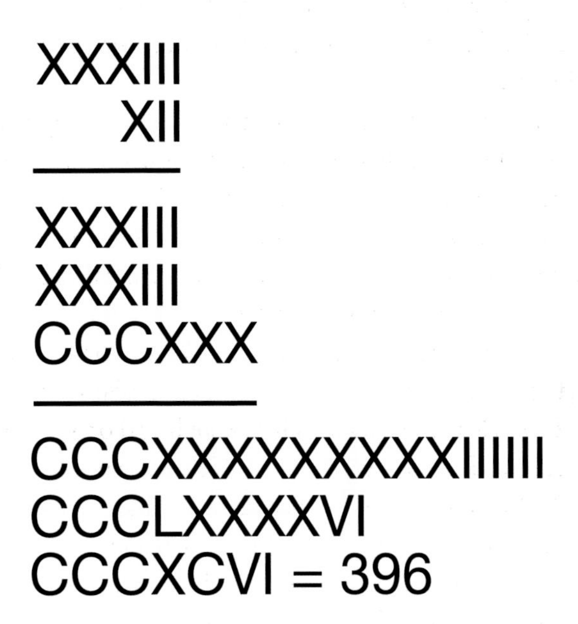

Show a multiplication problem in Roman numerals, such as Figure 27.

Figure 27. This is a multiplication problem in Roman numerals, 33 x 12 = 396.

So, the Romans, instead of doing their calculation in numerals, had a special device called an abacus. You can think of an abacus as being a little like our bead frames, where beads represent numbers and you can manipulate them with a stylus to calculate. When they finished their calculations, they wrote out their answers in Roman numerals.

Meanwhile, the Arabs were trading with people in Europe. Of course, they used their numerals to keep track of buying and selling. The idea of Arabic numerals had simply traveled with the Arabs and spread over to Europe. They brought that system to Europe around 1000 AD, but—can you believe this?—the Europeans did not want it!

No, the Europeans did not want the Arabic numerals. They did not want an Arab idea to spread. However, those numerals were such a good idea that they did spread anyway, especially with merchants, traders, and sellers. They liked the Arabic numerals because they could easily use them for math.

Although it took centuries, the transition from Roman numerals to Arabic numerals was finally accepted. Our numerals and our way of calculating today are based on the Arabic numerals. In fact, that is why, when we add up our columns of numbers, we go from right to left, just like the Arabs read.

It would be ideal for the storyteller to have an actual copy of the book or a page from the book to share, such as Figure 28. This may be available from a library or on the Internet.

Figure 28.
This is a page from the book *The Algebra of Mohammad ben Musa* (Arabic) by Muhammad ibn Mūsā al-Khwārizmī.

The Arabs had many other great gifts to give to us. In approximately 830 CE, a Muslim scholar called Muhammad ibn Mūsā al-Khwārizmī wrote a book about calculation. In his book, he discusses an operation that he called *al-jabr*, which meant *completion*.

What does al-jabr sound like? It sounds a lot like *algebra* doesn't it? Well, that's because *al-jabr* is where the word *algebra* comes from!

I have another important discovery to tell you about! In the seventeenth century, there was a German mathematician named Gottfried Wilhelm von Leibniz who made a system where it was possible to count using only two digits. Now, at the time, everyone thought he was just crazy. They laughed at him because his system looked so strange compared to the numbers that everyone was used to at that time. The idea that Leibniz had was that by only having two digits, you could have a switch that was either on or off. So, a one looked like a 1. A two was a 1 and a 0. A three was a 1 and a 1. A four was 100. A five 101. A six 110, and so on. People thought this was preposterous—they laughed at him and told him this was the craziest thing they had ever seen and that no one would ever use this system of counting.

Well, guess what? The system he invented way back then is now called the *binary number system*. It's true! He invented binary numbers. Leibniz's discovery wasn't used for three hundred years, but now, it powers every computer in the world. That's right—all computers use the binary system for their calculations. People may be laughing at new mathematicians, but who knows? Maybe their discoveries, too, will have a great future.

We must have gratitude for all of the past explorers that came before us and gave us the gifts of mathematics that we have today. Thank you to the early humans for their notched counting sticks. Thank you to the shepherds, like Aapeli, who counted with rocks and rope. Thank you to the Babylonians for counting our year, for dividing our circle, and for keeping time. Thank you to the Egyptians and their stonecutters for their precise hieroglyphics. Thank you to the Romans for the Roman numerals we still use today. Thank you to the Indians who came up with that great, stupendous idea of zero and gave us the power to calculate. Thank you to the Arabs, who believed in that great zero and who developed the numbers we use today and spread them around the world. Thank you to all the mathematicians of the world who've made mathematical discoveries. Thank you to all of those who came before us!

Just think about this … Perhaps you in this very class will be the future mathematics explorers who will also make great discoveries that help all people.

Curriculum Stories for Language Arts

"Storytelling is one of the most important tools of any educator because it engages children in learning."

—Brian Ellis, poet, storyteller, and writer
& Stephanie McAndrews, assistant professor
at Southern Illinois University

The Multitude

Introduction

This remarkable, traditional story is a grammar-based Montessori curriculum tale focused upon nouns. *The Multitude* is based on the idea that, in essence, we inherit words, especially nouns, from all of the people who have gone before us. Our predecessors invented words to identify concepts, just as we continue to do. After they are no longer with us, their words live on, so the words in our vocabulary are actually antiques—gifts from the past.

The Multitude is a brilliant story in that it links children to the past in a striking way. It demonstrates that history is not just a matter of dates and events, but instead, is something that lives within the very words we speak. Furthermore, when we use slang, colloquial speech, or neologisms that may live after us, we are all participants in creating history. Even our accents and intonations may eventually give rise to unique dialects, speech patterns, or even new languages.

This story leads children to explore etymology, the history of words. I suggest that every elementary classroom, Montessori or not, have at least two different etymological dictionaries easily accessible to the children. This will encourage children to investigate the story of many interesting words.

As an extension to this story, students may also enjoy compiling lists of words that they use, many of which may be of their own invention, or other new words like so-called slang words. Such words, which may be interesting, fun, or even distasteful, may not have come from the distant past, but they are words through which the children will participate in giving to the future. In this, children can become a part of someone else's past, or as I like to describe it, they can become architects of the future.

Source: *The Multitude* is my significant adaptation of a traditional Montessori lesson into a narrative story form.

STORY

So long ago that no one can quite say when, early people really had no names for anything. Do you remember the story of *The First Word*, when we learned that there was a time when there were very few names? Once the idea of names finally did occur, people made it their business to name everything; in fact, they named every single thing that they could!

The first thing that people decided to name was the most important thing: their families. They had to name their mothers, and we heard that story about *Mama. Madre. Matri. Ama. Eema.*

Of course, they had to name their fathers. *Papa. Daddy. Babbo. Abba.* And they had to name their uncles. *Zio. Oom. Tío. Seta.* And they had to name their aunts. *Néni. Tante. Amma. Zia.*

They had to name their sisters and brothers. *Ikhtee. Hermana. Bruder. Fratello.*

They had to name their children. *Child. Daughter. Son. Boy. Girl.*

A good plan is to replace these names with the names of students in your own class.

They named each special relationship—every person received a title. Every person had to receive another name as well—his or her own name. Jacob, Santiago, Emma, Sofia, Ethan, Kayoko.

Then they had to name their bodies, so they named all of

the parts. Hands. Head. Arms. Hands and feet. Fingers and toes.

Those ancient people are not with us anymore. They are gone now. This was thousands of years ago. But, all those names live on. Even though the people are gone, we still have the names. We have the names of the relationships, we have the names of the body, and we even have many of the same names that people called each other all those years ago. All those names certainly lived long beyond the people who first made them up.

Do you know what else? The people also named their food, because every single thing they ate needed a name. Whether it was a food that came from an animal or a food that came from a plant, everything got a name, one thing at a time. Meat. Fish. Cheese. Asparagus. Wheat. Rice. Every way in which they made the food had to be named, too. Boiled. Fried. Soup. Stew. Even the leftovers and the waste that was left when they were done had to have a name.

Even though those people aren't with us anymore, they are gone now, the names live on. Even though the people are gone, we still have the names. So, we still have names for every single kind of food, and all of the ways to make the food, and all of the places food was found, and even the waste left over when we're done with the food. Yes, all these names lived long beyond the people who came up with them.

Now those people also had to name places. They named places that were wet. They named places that were dry. They named places that were high, and they named places that were low. They named places that were cold, and places that were warm or hot. They named the places where they lived and the places where they hunted. They named places with trees. They named places with grass. They even named the trees and the grass that were in those places! They named the mountains that made places high and they named the valleys that made places low. They named the rain that made places wet, and they named the heat that made places hot. They even named places that only lived in their imaginations.

Today, those ancient people are no longer with us. They are long, long passed and gone. But the names live on. Even though the people are gone, we still have the names of places that have lived long beyond the people. The names come to us from the past.

People also named all of the animals. They named the animals that they ate and the animals that they hunted. They named the animals that gave them fear, and they named fear itself—even fear got a name. They named how they ran from an animal that gave them fear, and they named the running. They also named how they hunted an animal that gave them food. They named everything that could be named about an animal, including all of its parts, from its head to its tail—and everything in between.

Those people are also no longer with us today. They are no longer here. But the names live on. Even though the people are gone, we still have the names. We have the names of the animals that have lived long beyond the people. They come to us from the past.

Another thing that people named was the love that they felt for one another. They named the special love that they felt for their mothers and their fathers. They named the special love they felt for their children. They named the love they felt for their husbands and for their wives. They named the love that they felt for their grandparents, and for their cousins and their uncles and their aunts. They named all the loves that they had for all sorts of things, and those names stay with us even though those people aren't here.

Those people are also no longer with us today. They are gone now. But the names live on. Even though the people are gone, we still have the names. We have the names of love. These names lived long beyond the people. They come to us from the past.

These names are the multitude. All these many names, these millions of names, are the true multitude. They are gifts from the past, from the people who no longer live but give us the gift of the multitude. The multitude of names is the real multitude that we were given from the past. There are more names than there are people. And we can know all the names even though we may never know who it was that first named something. These gifts of the multitude are our nouns, and they will live on even after we are no longer here. This is one of the greatest gifts of the past. The multitude.

The Noun Family

INTRODUCTION

Many of the presentations in this book are, unabashedly, stories. They have a plot device and often have characters as well. There may be conflict and possible resolution. Of course, these stories are told as oral narratives.

Then there are other oral presentations, without plot or characters as such. Technically speaking, these should not be considered pure stories, but simply narratives. Essentially, they are lessons presented in a narrative format. An example of this type in language arts is *The Adjective Picnic* (p. 154).

The Noun Family is another example of this variety of oral presentation. These are simply any lessons presented in an oral, interactive setting, and they can be used just like the more traditional sorts of stories. There is no plot, there are no characters, and there is no conflict or resolution. These narratives do, however, use voice, gesture, expression, tone, and other elements of story. These elements and techniques bring the presentation to life.

The interesting thing is that children devour these narratives with the same enthusiasm as they do plot-driven stories. Even though they might not meet the technical definition, these narratives just feel like stories.

The Noun Family is part narrative and part lesson, with imaginative qualities, oral elements, and visual components using special charts or posters. Presentations like this engage children through their involvement and participation. They also have an easygoing, conversational, almost breezy style that feels story-like. To the children, it is received as a narrative. I include this presentation in this book as an example of how the oral quality can enrich almost any instruction. It should be clear that even though this is neither a story nor a narrative, its approach draws upon the oral qualities that have been and are being established in the classroom to make better lessons.

The Noun Family is a curriculum presentation about three parts of speech: the noun, adjective, and article. Using anthropomorphism, Montessori educators call these three the noun family. In Montessori schools, solid materials are used in which each part of speech is represented by a special symbol—a small, light-blue pyramid for the article; a medium-sized, darker-blue pyramid for the adjective; and a large, black pyramid for the noun. Ideally, these three shapes are actual solids—pyramids of wood, ceramic, or other material. It is generally best, when possible, to have initially presented each member of the noun family with three-dimensional solids. These pyramids can be purchased or made by folding paper.

The three pyramids that are shown while the story is told appear on three posters or charts that support the telling of *The Noun Family*. Each chart demonstrates a different aspect of the family. If you do not have these in your classroom, they are very easy to make. I would suggest using the traditional colors.

The first chart shows the three parts of speech as an actual family with a mother, a child, and a baby. A second chart shows the three pyramids in the desert, recalling the Great Pyramids of Egypt. The last chart depicts the three as flat triangles rather than pyramids. This is to prepare the children for a simpler way of drawing and symbolizing the parts of speech in a two-dimensional format.

Source: *The Noun Family* is my adaptation of a traditional Montessori idea into narrative story-like form.

STORY

Do you know what a family is? I do. A family might have many people in it, or sometimes just a few. Maybe it has a mother. Maybe it has a father. Maybe it has a grandma. There might be babies. There might be other people, too.

I belong to a family, and I'm the dad in that family. I also have a family where I have a mom, and in that family, I am the son! I wonder if you knew that words could have families too?

Isn't that interesting? Words can have families, and they do.

We have been learning about nouns, so I'm sure that you remember that they are naming words. Well, the noun has a family, and I have its picture right here. It's true; I have the picture, the actual picture of the noun and its family right here. Here it is. This is the family of the noun. The noun's family has three

Hold up the first chart, showing an actual family with a baby on the left, a child in the middle, and the mother on the right, as in Figure 29.

Figure 29. The Noun Family, shown as people.

members. The noun, itself, is the head of the family, the source of strength, and the leader, like this mother. It is in charge of the family and others look up to it, just as you probably look up to your mother, I hope.

Each of these parts of speech would have been presented separately before this story lesson, and in earlier presentations, etymologies such as this one would also have been given.

Here, holding hands with the noun, is the adjective. The adjective helps the noun. The adjective works with the noun. The adjective is like the child of the noun, and we learned its name means that it is thrown in, it's in the middle here. It's set in the center. The adjective is almost like a child to the noun, but, like you, it is a very helpful child.

Then at the very beginning is the baby, the article. What a cute little baby! The article is like an infant in the noun's family.

So there are only three members of this family. Guess what? There are only three possible articles, too. That means that there

This arrangement of article–adjective–noun works well for English. It will need to be altered for other languages that use a different word order.

aren't very many articles for us to learn, and that's good for the baby, the little baby of the noun family, the article.

This is the noun's family. The noun has only three members in its family, but they're very, very important ones. Their importance increases with their size. So the very most important one, of course, is the noun. The adjective is also important, as is the article. Do you know that some languages get by without any articles at all? It's true—some languages don't even have articles. But we do. So, we still have the article on the chart, and articles are very important to us.

Now there's something else to talk about—let's discuss why the noun's family members are shaped as they are. This might help us to understand the shape of the nouns. Nouns are a very, very, very old part of speech. That might remind you of the pyramids, because they are very old as well. Some people think that the very first word ever spoken was a noun. This certainly could be true; the first word ever said aloud might have been a name. We think it might have been "mama." A noun.

The noun family is like the pyramids. Remember that the

Hold up the chart of the nouns in the desert like pyramids, like Figure 30.

Figure 30. The Noun Family shown like the pyramids.

symbol of the noun is a black pyramid—here it is. We have already learned that it is the symbol of the noun, and that it is black, heavy, and solid. It is a pyramid with a broad, square base and it stands up strongly—the noun is solid and unmoving. The pyramid reminds us that it's old, it's ancient, and it comes from far back in time. Just like the great pyramids in Egypt that were built in the far distant past.

Because the noun is a pyramid, the adjective is a pyramid as well. The adjective is a pyramid because it serves the noun and works with the noun. The adjective helps the noun, and it's the second great pyramid of its family. The adjective has a lovely blue color.

Finally, there is the little pyramid. This is the small, light blue pyramid. It is the article; remember it's like the baby of the family. Among the pyramids, the article is the lightest and the smallest, because it is the newest part of speech. The article is much younger than the noun, and we already learned that some languages do not even need articles.

Just like the Great Pyramids at Giza in Egypt, we have the three pyramids in the noun family: the article, the adjective, and the noun. These three pyramids help us to understand how secure these pieces are—how wide and stably they stand, and how little they move. They're very solid; they like to stay in their places, especially the noun. Big, black, and immobile, it likes to stay in its place. Yes, the noun's family is very like three pyramids.

Now, let's look at this last chart. This chart shows just the

Show the chart with The Noun family represented as three triangles, like Figure 31.

Figure 31. The Noun Family in flat symbols.

symbols of the noun family, as we will use them. You can see the article, the adjective, and the noun. But, these three can't always be pyramids because we can't always work with pyramids here in school—we can't glue down a pyramid into our notebooks; we can't work with them too well unless they are flat. So, the pyramids have simply become triangles. Now we will use these three triangles as symbols of the members of the great noun family.

When naming *the huge dinosaur,* write each word on a slip of paper and set that slip in the chart right upon the appropriate symbol. If you like, you may write the word *dinosaur* in black, *huge* in dark blue, and *the* in light blue.

If you like, you can try changing the words around, like *huge dinosaur the,* or *dinosaur the huge.* If you do this, then point out that those ways are not the best way to say this phrase, because they are confusing. There is really only one correct way to say it.

The article, the adjective, and the noun. They are always in a particular order; they always stand this way next to each other. They never stand in other ways. So we could have a black noun like, oh, let's say *dinosaur.* Then if we think about that dinosaur we could use a blue adjective to describe it. Maybe we will call it *huge.* That's our blue adjective. Of course, our baby article wants to join in with the word *the.* That makes *the huge dinosaur.*

Do you see that these words really need to stand in this particular order? They do. It would mix us up to change that order around.

These three are a very, very closely-knit family who all love to be together and who all love to work together. This is a family that supports each other. So the article introduces the noun, the adjective helps the noun, and the noun is firmly in charge of its own family. It names everything. This is the family of the noun.

The Detective Triangle Game

INTRODUCTION

The *Detective Triangle Game* is a traditional activity in Montessori schools.

Presentation of this activity requires a basket or box of sixty-three different triangles, comprised of nine variations of the following seven triangle types: acute-angled isosceles, acute-angled scalene, right-angled isosceles, right-angled scalene, obtuse-angled isosceles, obtuse-angled scalene, and equilateral.

The nine variations of the seven types are comprised of each type represented in three different colors—usually red, yellow, and blue—in each of three different sizes—small, medium, and large. This means that each of the sixty-three triangles can be identified individually by its unique combination of angles, sides, size, and color. Therefore, triangles will be referred to by names like *the large yellow acute-angled scalene triangle* or *the medium*

Figure 32. The Detective Triangle Game.

blue acute-angled isosceles triangle. The children and the teacher become geometry detectives in uncovering the correct triangle.

There is a complete list of all sixty-three triangles included in the Detective Triangle Game in Appendix A (p. 335). Please consult this list. This list will be very helpful if you need to check that your set of triangles is complete or if you plan to make your own set.

This curriculum story is actually part of the language arts/grammar curriculum. In the language area, it has a goal of showing the children how powerful adjectives are. It is a great example of crossing the traditional subject lines, integrating geometry with language arts.

By using adjectives, we can identify one specific item in a large collection. It is an interesting example of how one subject, geometry, can be used to complement and enrich a second subject, which in this case is grammar.

This story was adapted and enhanced by my wife, Rose Dorer. Rose is an experienced and certified Montessori teacher with a background in both the Children's House and the elementary levels. She has specialized in the elementary school years, and is now a lower elementary guide in a Montessori public charter school.

It is not necessary to make up more details of what we are pretending may have happened. Students do not seem to question this. They are happy to be caught up in the story and game.

Source: *The Detective Triangle Game* is based upon a Montessori idea that was turned into a narrative story form by Rose Dorer.

Story

For this game, I'm going to be a detective. A detective is someone who uses clues to uncover what has happened.

Now, last night in this classroom, something unusual happened. Something occurred; it might have been an intruder. We have to find out what happened, why, and who did it. We need to find the suspect. We have only one clue, and that is a clue that I found in the dust on the windowsill. I found the markings of a triangle. I'll write the suspect's name on this wanted poster.

On a slip of paper, write the words *the triangle.*

This morning, when I got to the classroom, I put together all of the triangles that I could find, and I have them here in this box. You can see that these triangles have different colors. Some of them are red, some yellow, some blue, in all different shapes and sizes. How are we going to find out which one did it? This problem requires a detective, a geometry detective.

First, I had to get some clues. I talked to the hexagon in the Geometry Cabinet. I asked him if he could help. Maybe he was a witness. He might have seen something. He told me, "I noticed something red, just a flash of red, early this morning." Oh no! A red triangle must have done it. I'll write a new wanted poster.

On a second slip of paper, write the words *the red triangle.* Remove the first slip of paper.

All right, let's separate out all of the blue and all of the yellow triangles. They go back in the box. We have to look at the red triangles to get to the bottom of this. Oh, there's the phone. Just a minute. [*Pretend to answer a cell phone or a toy telephone.*]

"Hello? Yes, yes." [*Now pretend to hang up the phone.*]

Aha! I just learned that, last night, by good luck, one of the Constructive Triangles was awake. She discovered that not only was this triangle red, but it was also small. It was a small red triangle. All right, let's get rid of all of the triangles that are not small. Let's get rid of all the medium-sized triangles, and let's get rid of all the large triangles. Now I'm writing a new wanted poster for a *small red triangle*.

On a third slip of paper, write the words *the small red triangle*. Remove the other slip of paper.

Wait a minute! [*Look at the phone.*] I just received a text from the box of Geometry Sticks. They noticed something that is revealing.

Very good, very good. New information. It was a right-angled triangle. They could see that its corner fit right into the edge of this box. It was a right-angled triangle. That's a valuable clue. Let's write that down on a new wanted poster.

On a new slip of paper, write the words *the small red right-angled triangle*. Remove the other slip of paper.

So far, we know it was a small red right-angled triangle. Only one thing left to discover, come on! We need another informant.

Ah, the Geometric Solids were alert. [*Point to the basket or box of Geometric Solids.*] They spotted something. They noticed that the triangle moved around in a very even way, as if its two legs were well balanced. Do you know what that tells me? This was an isosceles triangle; two equal legs.

Now, we can add this piece of information, and we're going to sort the triangles again.

Now, we have only one triangle left!
Is the triangle red?
Yes.
Is it small?
Yes.
Right-angled?
Yes.
Equal legs?
Yes, it is isosceles.

This is, indeed, the triangle that is our suspect! I'm going to trace this triangle, color it in red, and put its identification onto this paper. And we're going to keep it. That is going to be the mug shot for this triangle, and it had better not do anything like this again!

And that's the end of that!

Children, when you play this game, you may choose any

triangle you like from this box, and you may ask your friends for information to try and get to the bottom of the mystery. You will be the head geometry detective, but you can also ask others to be detectives along with you.

The Adjective Picnic

INTRODUCTION

The Adjective Picnic is an interesting little language story. Its purpose is to introduce the six roles of the adjective in English: to describe, to count, to point, to distribute, to show ownership, and to question. In this first adjective story, these functions are introduced, but they are not given names. Later, after the children are familiar with the functions, the adjectives are named as descriptive, numerical, demonstrative, distributive, possessive, and interrogative.

Figure 33. The adjectives are on a picnic.

I enhance *The Adjective Picnic* with a large poster or chart that I have created. This poster illustrates the activities referred to in the story. In Montessori schools, adjectives are symbolized with blue equilateral triangles. Because of this, every person in the illustration is wearing a blue triangle.

This story is a curriculum story that can be given near the beginning of a study of adjectives. It is also an excellent culminating story to use after the children have learned the names of all the adjectives. At that time, they can identify the adjectives by name as well as by function.

Source: *The Adjective Picnic* is based upon a Montessori idea that I have turned into a narrative story form.

STORY

One day, all of the adjectives decided to go on a picnic, and the adjective children were very excited. They selected a large park, filled with beautiful green grass and large healthy trees. Luckily, the park had big picnic tables. It even had a running track for some races.

I have a picture here that shows one of the scenes from the picnic, some of the things that happened when the adjectives got together. You can see all of the adjectives here having a great time. You can tell they're all adjectives because each one has a blue triangle on his or her shirt. That blue triangle stands for adjectives.

Show the Adjective Picnic Chart (Figure 33).

Some of the children are hungry. The hungry children are in the front eating delicious sandwiches. These children are also eating whole, red apples and sliced apples. They are enjoying a beautiful day under a blue sky.

One child decided to start the races, and pretty soon more children began to race. Look, three children are racing right now! One girl got first prize. Another child received second prize. Many of the children loved racing and had a very good time.

When referring to certain children, point to that child on the Adjective Picnic Chart.

This child got a gold medal for the race. That child also received a medal. Every child had fun in the race.

Each child eventually ate lunch, which they all enjoyed. What a great picnic!

This boy in front is showing his medal to a teacher. That girl is talking about her gold medal. What a wonderful picnic. Which child do you think had the most fun? What activity would be the best one to do?

When we tell the story of the adjective picnic, we are talking about special words, the adjectives. Adjectives are very special words that do six big jobs to help the noun.

Do you remember when I told you that some children were hungry? That they ate delicious sandwiches and red apples? That there was green grass and big trees? Well, words like *hungry*, *delicious*, *red*, *green*, and *big* are adjectives that describe. So here at the picnic, some of the adjectives are describing. They are describing nouns. They're describing the sandwiches, the apples, the grass, or the trees. So adjectives can describe. Describing is the first big role of adjectives. In fact, it's the biggest job.

When we looked at this chart, we also noticed that some children raced, and one girl got first prize, another girl received second prize, many children enjoyed the race, and three children are racing right now. When I said words like *one*, *three*, *many*, and *some*, those are words that count, so some adjectives count. They can count very specifically like *one* and *two*, or *first* and *second*, or they can count generally like *some* and *many*. That's a second job that adjectives do: they count.

Now I also told you that this child has a gold medal, and that child also received a medal. We heard that these children were eating apples. Some other jobs for adjectives showed up here. *This*, *that* and *these* are adjectives that point to things, because we can point to this child or that child, or to these children or those trees. Some adjectives do that; they point things out. Pointing is another job of adjectives: it is their third role.

We know every child had fun in the race, and each child had a delicious lunch. When we say adjectives like *each* and *every*, those adjectives distribute, or share out. They are kind of like division. These adjectives take the fun of the race and pass it out to every child. The delicious lunch is also passed out to each child. We call those adjectives the adjectives that distribute. Distributing is another role of adjectives: it is their fourth job.

Then we saw a boy showing his medal to a teacher and a

girl talking about her medal. *His* and *her* are adjectives that show ownership. They tell us whose medal it is; they tell us that somebody owns it. That's a fifth job that adjectives do: they show ownership.

Finally, I asked you, which child do you think had the most fun? What activity would be the best? *Which* and *what* are adjectives that ask a question. Questioning is the sixth role of the adjective.

Our adjectives are doing many different things: describing, counting, pointing, distributing, showing ownership, and questioning. Adjectives are busy, busy words, because they have so many things that they can do.

Now, let's answer the questions. Which child do you think did have the most fun? What activities do you think would be the best?

The Noun and the Verb

Introduction

Properly speaking, the story of *The Noun and the Verb* is not a literal story, but instead is something of a drama starter. By that, I mean that the story itself ends with a challenge to the children to develop a small skit or sketch, a little play based upon the story that they've just heard. So the follow-through that happens in this particular exercise is a creative dramatics exercise. The setting is based on the idea that once upon a time, the parts of speech could speak to each other, and the noun and the verb meet and have a discussion.

While they're having this encounter, each of these two parts of speech is extolling its own virtues and qualities. The noun brags about what it does, which is to name things. The verb describes what it does, which is to show actions or states of being. At the same time, they don't look favorably upon the other part of speech. So they have a discussion in which they make these interesting comparisons.

In Montessori work, the noun and the verb each have a particular symbol. The symbol of the noun is a solid, large, black, pyramid. Alternatively, in two dimensions, to be drawn in a child's notebook or on a piece of paper, it is a large, black triangle.

The verb, on the other hand, is represented by an equally large, red sphere, or in two dimensions, a red circle. These, at some level, are meant to portray the fundamental qualities of these two parts of speech, the heavy black triangle being a thing of concrete solidity, the red ball or circle being a symbol of movement, ready to be kicked or roll away. Additionally, in Montessori work, these two parts of speech, the verb and the noun, are said to be the heads of their families.

The noun family consists of two other members, the adjective and the article. And, naturally, the family head is the noun. The verb also heads up a family, which includes the adverb and the pronoun. So those three balance against the three members of the noun family.

There are also, of course, a conjunction, a preposition, and an interjection. However, they aren't considered to be in either of these two families. They are more or less independent, and also have their own symbols.

If you like, when you present this particular story, you could expand it at some point. You could add in all six members of the two families: the noun, adjective, and article, and the verb, adverb, and pronoun. If you are particularly ambitious, you could add in the other three parts of speech, the conjunction, the preposition, and the interjection. Then a discussion could be had between all nine parts of speech. That would be particularly challenging to put together.

When the story as such is completed, I suggest a dramatic activity as a follow-up. Ask the children to think about the story, analyzing the human-like qualities of the noun and the verb. Have them look at the noun and the verb in terms of their attitudes, their looks, their colors, their sizes, their qualities—all of the things that the children can possibly think of and portray when they themselves act this out.

The children have now been presented with a situation and

they have been asked to bring it to life. In this particular iteration of the story, the children are given one day. They are then to come back the next day having planned a dramatic sketch or small play based on the story.

At the end of the assignment, tell them, "We'll see you tomorrow, and we really look forward to seeing your performance." You may give your children in your classroom more or less time as you feel is appropriate. Do you think they need more than a day or do they require less than a day? That is up to you entirely, and you will probably need to determine this over time through trial and error.

Children in the classrooms in which I have taught and in which I've worked as a consultant have really enjoyed acting out various parts. They have acted out different geometric figures, different parts of speech, different kinds of sentences, and different eras or times in history that they have been able to imagine and embody.

This leads to a holistic idea in education, which is the notion that if you can actually become the story, if you can actually come to be the thing, you are not just learning about it. Instead, you are actually learning it in an entirely different and more complete way by actually being, for example, the verb or the noun, and bringing them to life.

I included this activity to show how you and the children could structure a creative, dramatic presentation with a story at its beginning. I hope that you find this something that you could try in your classroom. It's been very rewarding for me and for the children with whom I have worked.

Source: *The Noun and the Verb* is an original story, which I wrote.

Story

A great while ago, when the world was full of wonders and even the parts of speech could talk, the noun and the verb came together one day. They began to compare themselves to each other, and they started to think about what they were, and how important they believed themselves to be.

The noun presented himself proudly to the verb. He was impressive: a large, black pyramid on a stable, square base. The appearance of the verb was very different. She was an equally large, bright-red sphere. They knew that they were each the head of an important family. And there were three important members in each of their families. The noun headed up a family that included the article and the adjective. The verb led a family including the adverb and pronoun. They knew that they each spoke for their entire families.

The noun, who was especially material in nature, launched the discussion by pointing out that he had the power to name every single thing in the language. Anything that could be named was a noun, whether it was the name of a simple thing or the name of something complicated. Even personal names—the noun named them all. Of course, that brought him a great deal of pride.

The verb, on the other hand, was happy because she had hold of every action that could possibly take place. If there was an activity or any action, that belonged to the verb. In fact, the verb knew that she was in charge of simply existing, just being. She bragged that it was impossible to make a sentence without her. No sentence could exist without the verb because she brought energy and light to the sentence. The verb brought fire, just as the Sun brings light to the Earth.

The noun thought little of the verb's accomplishments and, instead, bragged of his own huge vocabulary, which exceeded that of any other part of speech. The noun was also proud that he was levelheaded and could always be aloof. He stood above all the other parts of speech and was not moved by them. He valued his stability.

But the verb was contemptuous of that. She pointed out that she was energetic and active, that movement and involvement were the very essence of what she did. The noun thought it was essential to point out that he was a traditionalist; he had guarded words for centuries and centuries, he kept those words and passed them on. That's why his vocabulary grew so well.

But the verb, once again, was happy to state that tradition

is not everything. She reminded him that she was original and inventive, even creative because of the actions that she could perform. She was proud that she was mobile, lively, and flexible. She could move about in an exciting way. Then she pointed to the noun and brought attention to his exceptionally broad base that made him immovable.

However, it turned out the noun was proud of his base and responded that the verb must not forget that he, the noun, had all the names just as he had pointed out before. He owned all of the names, no matter what she thought of his shape.

The verb was happy to respond that she could move forward. She wasn't a stick-in-the-mud, caught in one place as she thought the noun was. She also was proud to point to her lovely color. She pointed out that she was a beautiful red, a scarlet color, glowing like the Sun.

But the noun was very proud of his coal color; he was shiny and black all over. He turned to the verb to accuse her of being flighty and impulsive, of being too changeable and not staying long enough with one thing. The verb accused the noun in return of being unadventurous, predictable, and stolid. She jeered that he remained too long in one spot.

At that, the noun pointed out that he was perfectly straight and had exact edges. He was a perfect pyramid or triangle. He was very satisfied that he had that shape; when all of his qualities were put together, they added up to an impressive black pyramid.

But the verb wasn't impressed. The verb bragged about being completely curved and rounded. The verb thought that with her round body she was like a perfect sphere. She brought to the noun's attention that being a movable sphere helped make her very active.

This argument went on and on and on. I don't know if it ever ended. As far as anyone knows, they are still arguing to this day.

What is it that *you* are going to do about the noun and verb, you may wonder. You are going to become a character. That's right. I'm going to ask you to become either the noun or the verb, and you are going to be able to tell about who you are.

Do you represent the noun? The shiny, sturdy, handsome, black pyramid? Or will you represent the red, beautiful, curved, verb, the perfect sphere? Think of what they would be like if they could be with us today. We must imagine that they could speak so that you are able to speak when you portray them.

We have to think of the expression that you could put on your face to show the feelings of the noun, if that's who you are, or the feelings of the verb, if that's who you are acting out. What actions will they take to support themselves? Or will they take any action? Will the verb be more active? Will the noun be less active, or will he be totally inactive?

Then, I want you to think about what tone of voice the verb and the noun may have. Do they have a high pitch or a low voice? Are they imperative and commanding? Is their voice kind or contemptuous? What kind of an attitude do they have toward the other parts of speech? Do they look upon the others with respect and love?

Each of them, remember, is the head of a great family. The noun is the head of a family of three; so is the verb. Each one of them has a right to be happy and proud of its family. Can you show that in your actions?

With my help, we will be choosing partners, so that each person will work with at least one partner. If you would like, we could have a narrator in the group, and that would mean a small group of three. If you want a narrator, that's fine, and we can create a wonderful, small group like that. Then the narrator will do all the talking, but the noun and the verb characters will not speak, or will speak very little.

You will have one day, so tomorrow, you will set up a small dramatic sketch, like a little play, in which you will act out the part of the noun or the verb. You will actually become a noun or a verb right here in this classroom. Then you will show us their characters, their pride, their qualities, as best you can.

Now, I want you to think about this so that you will be able come and act it out tomorrow. Each of you will put on this little sketch. I know that you will have fun with this and it may even be funny. I want you to really like this creation that you will bring to life. I look forward to seeing you perform, and I know that you will have enjoyed this, too. Okay, let's choose the groups and you can begin.

The Rebellious Pronoun
(*The King and the Prince*)

Introduction

Remember that anthropomorphism means attributing human qualities to animals, objects, or other nonhumans. In this case, parts of speech, particularly the noun and the pronoun, are given human qualities.

This curriculum story follows earlier lessons in which the children were first introduced to the idea of grammar families. They learned that there is a noun family and a verb family. The noun family consists of the noun as the head, accompanied by the article and the adjective. The verb heads its own family, joined by the adverb and the pronoun.

This leads to the question of how the pronoun ended up in what may seem to be the wrong family. In a story vaguely reminiscent of *Paradise Lost*, the pronoun is seen as jealous and angry with its rightful ruler, which is the noun.

In the imagery used in Montessori schools, the symbol of the noun is a large pyramid, colored black. The pronoun is also given a color, sometimes purple, sometimes green. This allows the story to refer to the pronoun as either purple with rage or green with envy. Like the noun, the pronoun is also a pyramid, but a tall one, taller than the noun.

Pyramids or triangles symbolize both parts of speech. However, the symbol of the pronoun is an isosceles triangle with a greater height than that of the equilateral noun. This also allows the storyteller to say that the pronoun stands up tall, reaching above the noun.

In telling this object story, the actual symbols need to be used

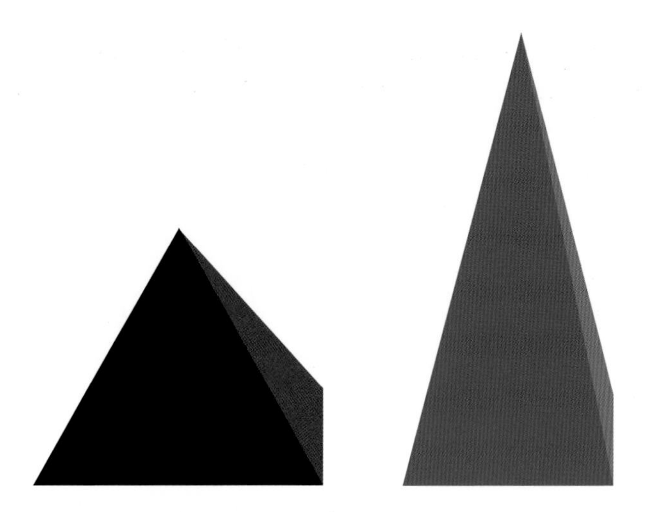

Figure 34. The noun pyramid and the pronoun pyramid.

as visual aids. The best symbols to use are three-dimensional, solid wooden pyramids that can be manipulated while the story is being told. One may also use plane triangles (two-dimensional, flat), but they should be as large as possible to make the strongest impression.

Figure 35. The flat triangular symbols of the noun and pronoun.

If you make the plane figures, the noun symbol should be a large black equilateral triangle. The pronoun symbol should be a purple isosceles triangle. The symbol of the pronoun must be noticeably taller than the noun's symbol. These could be cut from card stock or heavy construction paper.

Source: *The Rebellious Pronoun* is based upon a Montessori idea that I turned into a narrative story form.

STORY

Did you know that words have families? It's true. The noun has a family, and the verb has a family. Did you know that these families have rulers, like kings?

Well, it is told that there was once a great dispute in one of these families, and this is its story.

In the noun family, the noun himself is the ruler. The noun is completely in charge of his family. The noun is like the king, in charge of the whole family, of all naming words. The noun is also in charge of all words that describe, and he's in charge of all of the articles that introduce. Yes, the noun is the king, and very firmly in charge.

Throughout this story, point to the pyramids or pick them up as you name each one.

Now, because of that, there are more nouns, in English, than all other parts of speech put together. That is how important the noun is to us. Remember the story of the multitude. There are more nouns than anything else, in fact, more than everything else. Of course, the noun knows this and is very proud to be the king and chieftain, the head of the clan. Oh yes, the noun loves being in charge.

The noun is the king. But often, when you have a king, you may have someone jealous of the king's power—someone who wants to take over, someone who cannot understand his or her correct place in the family.

In the noun family, this is the prince. The prince wants to be the king and to have the power of being the king. The prince wants to rule. The prince wishes to take over. The prince wants to be in charge.

This rebellious prince is the pronoun. The pronoun is a special kind of a prince. He is like a prince who wants to usurp, to take over, and to kick the king out, to be in charge, to rule.

This is what happens now. When the noun king says *Ann*,

the pronoun wants to jump in quickly and say *she*. That's right, the pronoun just says *she*. He thinks that he has a better way of saying the name. Why bother saying *Ann*? The pronoun says that it is simpler to do it his way, to just say *she*.

The pronoun thinks that, with his way, there wouldn't be so many words to worry about. Doesn't it seem that the pronoun is trying to take the special place of the noun?

When the king says *Susan*, the pronoun still says *she*. And when the king says *Heidi*, again the pronoun just says *she*. The pronoun doesn't have a very big vocabulary—he hardly has any words at all, but he says, "That's okay, I'm very simple, but I want to rule. I can take the place of the noun."

So the pronoun stands up very tall, tries to get taller than his rightful ruler, the noun, and he is purple, purple with rage; green, green with envy. He wants to take over the rightful place of his ruler, the noun, and, actually, often he succeeds.

Most Montessori classrooms use both colors, since the traditional Function of Words material has a purple pronoun and the traditional Grammar Box material has a green pronoun. I like to use both colors.

But, the noun won't have it! The noun insists on having a huge vocabulary—having many, many words and speaking them all, even though the pronoun tries to make things so simple, and use only a few words, and speak just the few. Yes, the noun always insists on speaking first, before the pronoun, so that the pronoun always has to refer and defer to him.

As a result, the noun has thrown the pronoun out of his family. That's right! The pronoun was kicked out! The noun king won't allow the pronoun in his family, and the pronoun doesn't even want to be there any more. Do you know where he went?

The pronoun has gone over to serve the verb! And as we will see, the pronoun has joined the family of the verb, and serves the verb in new ways that it couldn't do as a member of the noun family.

The king and the prince. The king and the prince are at odds, and always will be. We are going to learn much more about the pronoun, the prince. But we need to remember that the noun has a huge vocabulary and always gets to speak before the pronoun. That is still true.

We also must remember that the pronoun usually may only speak after the noun. It doesn't have a very big vocabulary, it doesn't have many words, but it wants to use those words for every single noun it possibly can. It wants to take over, and it still is doing so.

That's the pronoun: purple with rage, green with envy.

The Rebellious Pronoun
(*The Angry Prince*)

INTRODUCTION

This is a second and much shorter version of *The Rebellious Pronoun*. It is a version that is used by my wife, Rose Dorer.

Source: This second version of *The Rebellious Pronoun* is based upon the first rendering of *The Rebellious Pronoun*, which is placed above. This interpretation was rewritten and simplified by Rose Dorer.

STORY

Children, you can see this solid symbol of the noun—the big, black pyramid—as well as the solid symbol that we have here for the pronoun—a tall, thin pyramid. Let me tell you a story of how these symbols came to be.

Hold up the corresponding solid wooden parts-of-speech symbols.

Long ago and far away, there was a land that was ruled by the king and the queen and the prince. They had many occasions to receive foreign visitors. When the visitors came, from far and wide, it was always the king who was first in line, followed by the royal prince. The visitors would dance for the king, bow to him, hand their presents to him, and sing his praises. The prince would then receive the gifts that people brought for the king.

Well, the prince was always a little jealous. "Why do I always have to come second in this line?" he sighed. "I never get to receive the guests first. I never get to receive the greetings and the honor." These feelings began to bother the prince a lot. Whenever the royal family had a guest, the visitor would always approach the king first. So the prince thought, "Perhaps, if I raise myself up on my tiptoes, if I am a greater presence than the king, maybe I shall receive some notice." He tried this; he made himself very tall. But he was still addressed second; the king was the first to be honored.

The prince became angrier and angrier. Finally, the prince became purple with rage. He never, ever could be the first in line, even though he tried to stand tall, even though he had a beautiful purple color, he never, ever could be first.

This is why, even today, the symbol for the pronoun is purple and the symbol for the great head of the noun family, the king, the noun, is still black.

Curriculum Stories for History

"If history were taught in the form of stories, it would never be forgotten."

—Rudyard Kipling, British author and poet

History in the Montessori tradition is a very broad and inclusive discipline. Essentially, history is considered to be anything in the past, from the beginning of the universe—as in *The Story of the Universe* (p. 65)—all the way up to the transitory nature of this day, indeed, this very moment.

Thus, history includes the creation of the universe, the beginning of this planet, the earliest evidence of life on Earth, and the evolution and development of human life. All of this is included in the *Great Lessons* (pp. 63-139). History also involves all of prehistory, ancient history, early people, wonderful migrations, great civilizations and cultures, and even modern times. In the classroom, children calculate the ages of themselves and their family members and identify months of the year, the seasons, and the days of the week—these are all history.

Another part of the study involves human needs and how they have been met over time, as well as how they are met across the globe today. In history, the children study physical needs such as food, clothing, shelter, communication, transportation, and defense. They are interested to learn how these needs are met or were met in the past by all peoples.

The young scholars also investigate what are called *Spiritual Needs*. These are needs for which fulfillment is not absolutely required for life but instead enhances the quality of life. Spiritual needs include love, religion or philosophy, the arts, and something called *vanitas*. Not to be confused with an artistic style, or with vanity, vanitas involves the human desire to be presentable, or to adorn oneself, something that varies tremendously culturally as well as historically. Again, the children are fascinated to discover how these universal spiritual needs are being met or were met in the past.

Any study of history must begin with time. Time and its passage define the past, which is historic. Additionally, young children have what is typically an undeveloped sense of time. Rightly then, the first history tale *is The Story of Time*.

The Story of Time

INTRODUCTION

This traditional Montessori tale, *The Story of Time*, is a very difficult narrative to tell and do right. The challenge is that the storyteller, for the duration of the entire story, must *never* say the word *time* until the very end of the story.

The Story of Time is a curriculum story, and it is based upon the relationships, that must have been noted by early people, between the repeating patterns of life like the seasons, human growth, aging, the rhythm of the days and nights, and more. The story tells how people had to give a name to the force that caused these recurring changes, and that the name they gave to it was *time*.

The trick of the story is to make it sound ancient and primitive, using phrases like *the great golden ball* for the Sun or *the shining silver disk* for the Moon. The goal is not to encourage the children to focus on the descriptions or to guess at names like Sun or Moon but instead to recognize the pattern of the language.

To support this goal, it is imperative that the word *time* is not to be spoken. In fact, this is so important that we cannot even call the story by its name! *Never* refer to the story as *The Story of Time.* Instead, introduce it with something like; "I want to tell you a story from long ago ..."

It is hard when thinking so intently about time to avoid saying the word while telling the story. If you do accidentally say it, just keep going smoothly on with the story, and do not try to stop to explain it. Probably no one but you will have noticed your slip; the story will still work well.

Source: *The Story of Time* is based on a traditional Montessori concept that I have significantly updated and reworked into a story form.

STORY

Long ago, when the Earth was much newer than now, early people found themselves in a place where there were very few names for almost anything.

They didn't celebrate birthdays—they had no way to honor birthdays. And they didn't celebrate anniversaries. No, they didn't celebrate or even have any record of days, or weeks, or even years. But, they did notice many important things.

They noticed that a great golden globe emerged from the Earth and brought light with it. It traveled across the sky, shedding heat and light, and then it buried itself in the Earth at the end of the period of light. This happened with a pattern, and it seemed to the early people that there might be a way to measure this pattern. This caused them to wonder about the pattern and its measurement.

The early people also noticed that there was another globe, a silver ball, which also came up out of the Earth and traveled across the sky, and at certain phases, it was wide and round and smiled. At other phases, it changed and thinned and became sharp like a knife or a sickle. This, too, happened with a pattern. It was a regular pattern, and again, it seemed to them that there might be a way to measure this pattern. This caused these early people to think deeply about this pattern and its measurement.

The early people also noted that the period of bright heat and light was always followed by a period of darkness—that there was a dark stretch, and that was when the beautiful silver ball came into the sky. After this, there always followed a bright period—and that was when the warm golden ball appeared. These regular changes of lightness and darkness happened with a pattern. It was predictable. It seemed to them that this repeating pattern might also be measured. This caused these early people to wonder about this pattern of light and dark and its measurement.

What's more, the early people observed that there was a long cycle of cold, and during that cold, there were light white things that fell and would pile up. They also noticed that a warming period followed that long, cold episode. Then the white stuff would melt away and turn into water. During this warming, plants would grow and water would fall from the sky. Soon, there would be a period of heat when the seeds of grasses could be eaten and fruits would appear on trees and vines. Now, these regular changes of coldness and warmth happened with a pattern. It was predictable. It seemed to them that there was a measurement to this pattern. This caused the early people to wonder about this pattern of coldness and warmth and its measurement.

The early people even observed themselves. They would look at themselves and think, after the very small ones came to us, they would change and they would get larger. As they got bigger, they would also grow new teeth. After that, they would seem to age, to get old, and eventually, they would die. And there was a pattern to this, too. These regular changes of growth happened with a pattern. It was predictable. It seemed to them that there was a measurement to this pattern. This, too, caused the early people to wonder about this pattern of growth and its measurement.

All of these things now have names. The golden ball was named the Sun. The silver ball was named the Moon. The white things that fell from the sky were named snowflakes. And the water that fell from the sky was called rain. The fruits of the trees and vines, and all the different kinds of grasses were named, as were their seeds. Of course, the people were all named, and so were the stages of their lives. Everything was given a name.

But the thing that was hardest of all to name was the thing

that somehow managed to measure the patterns and changes that took place. It was so hard to name because it was a very hard thing to see—the early people certainly couldn't see it at once, but they had to observe it over long periods. Yet, the early people did see changes and they did see patterns to everything. And, they saw that these changes and patterns could be measured.

Finally, a name was given to this measurement. And this name is *Time*.

And that is how it is to this day.

The Long Black Line

INTRODUCTION

The Long Black Line is a long piece of felt, ribbon, or rope that is dyed black. At the end of it, there is a small red or white section. The line represents the entire history of the Earth, and the thin red strip marks just the period of time that human beings, or *Homo sapiens*, have existed.

Maria Montessori created the line during the years of the Second World War, which she spent in India. This is explained in the story.

The Long Black Line needs to be roughly to scale. If the Earth is about 4.6 billion years old and humanity, genus *Homo,* has been around only about two and a half million years, then the red strip will be tiny indeed. In fact, it will represent only about 0.0005434 of the total length of the line. This means that if the line were made forty feet long, then the red part representing humanity would only be a tiny bit more than a quarter of an inch, actually 0.26 inch. This miniscule portion creates a tremendous impression on the children.

This story is really a commentary on the origin of the Long Black Line material—it is not the actual beginning lesson about the line and the place of humanity on Earth. I usually tell this little story to the children sometime within the presentation of the lessons associated with the line.

Source: *The Long Black Line* is based on traditional Montessori folklore that I have reworked into a narrative story-like form.

STORY

Maybe you know that long ago, from 1939 until 1946, Dr. Montessori lived in India, in Kodaikanal. The British government kept her there against her will because there was a war going on, and the British were fighting against her home country of Italy. Dr. Montessori was treated very nicely, but nevertheless, she was kept there in Kodaikanal in India during the war.

Montessori used this time to teach and work with Indian children and adults, and the story goes that she gave some of her presentations in Madras, India. During a discussion on the age of the world, it is said that the conversation got a bit heated.

One of the students told Dr. Montessori that they, the Indian people, were the oldest inhabitants of the Earth—that their civilization preceded everything else. The student suggested that the oldest civilization was in India ten thousand years ago.

To this, Dr. Montessori replied, "All of human civilization is only a very small thing compared with the whole existence of the Earth." She affirmed that no human civilization has been around since the beginning of the Earth.

To demonstrate her point, she decided to have a line made from a very long black ribbon.

When the long black strip was ready, Dr. Montessori had it brought to the school and said, "Now, I'm ready for something." Then she began to unroll it, and as she did, people saw that it unfurled for hundreds of yards. Hundreds of yards!

The funny thing is that Dr. Montessori had made this black line so very long and heavy, on such a big, sturdy, wooden spool, that it's said that a donkey was required to haul the line around. They had to put the line behind the donkey so that the donkey could undo the spool. That little donkey would unroll the long black line all the way out.

When she finally reached the end of it, there was only a very small, thin stripe, which was colored red. When Montessori showed this to the people of India, she said, "This red part is not the Indian civilization. This part is not the Italian civilization. This part is not even the Romans. It is not Babylon or Egypt. This part doesn't go back to the ancient Chinese. This red part covers all of the existence of all human kind all the way back to prehistoric time—and it's only this little part at the end of this whole line that shows the history of all of the people of the Earth."

Now, you may wonder about the donkey. Where is our donkey today?

Well, that has become a problem for many Montessori schools today, including our school here. So, our line is a little smaller because we can't afford the hay and the bedding and a barn to keep the donkey all year long for this one exercise. It's still a lot of work to unroll the spool, so our line has been reduced yet another little bit since we don't have anyone willing to do donkey work, either. So, this is the long black line, and people, instead of the donkey, will unroll it, but wouldn't it be nice to have a special place where a little donkey could come out and unroll it for us? That would be so much fun.

The Dinosaur on Your Windowsill

INTRODUCTION

Have you noticed that dinosaurs are all around us? That's true. We can see them perching on our windowsills. Or, they may be outside on a branch, on a twig of a tree, or maybe even gliding about on the surface of a pond. It just takes a moment to realize that the dinosaurs all around us are just masquerading as birds! Yes, it's definitely possible that birds are the same thing as the dinosaurs, and that's the basic idea of this story, to introduce birds as surviving dinosaurs.

The story uses anthropomorphism and features a brief

discussion with a bird and two more lengthy talks with other animals who are reached via time travel. The first discussion is with *Compsognathus*, who wants to be called Compie. Compie is a small dinosaur, which likely figures in avian ancestry. In this case, Compie may be slightly vain; I put that in to give a little character to her.

The second discussion is with *Archaeopteryx,* who likes to be called Archie. Archie is frequently thought of as the first bird, and in this story, he is very proud of that. The story also has a very short appearance by Tyrannosaurus Rex, but that is broken off because the narrator is frightened away by T-Rex's size and teeth.

This is one of my newest original stories; I wrote it for several reasons. Of course, it's aimed at supporting updated ideas about birds, and, at the same time, meant to increase interest in birds in general. More to the point, it is meant to introduce the ancestry and heritage of modern birds and to bring to the child's consciousness the idea that birds have a lineage that goes back millions of years as dinosaurs. In fact, they may even be considered dinosaurs today.

This story is also meant to relate to another story in this book, *The Gifts of the Phyla* (p. 314), because in that story, the birds receive certain gifts from the dinosaurs. It also emphasizes the concept that the past is with us still today, and that, of course, is a very powerful rationale for studying history and prehistory in elementary school. It's so important to bring up the respect for the past and to see that, even today, it is influencing who we are and who the birds are.

The story is also meant to emphasize the idea that we are enriched by events that happened in the past. Montessorians call these "the gifts of the past." Those gifts are responsible, largely, for what life is today. Certainly, the ancestry of birds is responsible, to a great extent, for what bird life is today.

Finally. the story is meant to introduce the idea that life experiences continual change. It is dynamic. It is not static.

This story introduces five important ideas in the evolution of birds. The first one of those is that birds have decreased in size from the dinosaur to the modern-day bird. Secondly, feathers are a hallmark of birds. Thirdly, today's birds have hollow bones that create efficient flight. Fourth, a wishbone is a special bone that birds actually inherited from dinosaurs, and a bone, incidentally, that may also be popular in a game, where the wishbone is pulled apart and wished upon, that children might know to play at home whenever a bird is roasted for dinner. The fifth evolutionary concept is that of beaks or bills, clear marks of a bird.

Technically, this is another tale that may not be considered a story by all, but simply a narrative. This is perfectly fine with me. The narrative is received and accepted by the children as a story, in the same way as any other story would be. There is no difference in the way that it functions in the classroom.

This story is a bit of a flight of fancy because it includes time travel. Please remember to suspend your disbelief, and also remember, to keep a lookout for dinosaurs—they're all around us.

Source: *The Dinosaur on Your Windowsill* is a completely original story that I wrote.

STORY

I'm going to tell you something that you might not believe because it may sound very strange and unreal. On the way in to school today, I saw a dinosaur, a living one. I really did; and in fact, I know that there are many of these dinosaurs living right around here. That's true. Do you know what it was besides being a dinosaur? It was a bird. This is the truth; that bird perching on your windowsill is actually a kind of a dinosaur.

I wanted to speak with that bird and find out some things about its ancestry, but I think people would have thought that I was weird for talking with a bird. Have you ever heard people say, "A little bird told me something?" Well, this little bird told me I had to forget everything I had ever heard about dinosaurs dying out millions of years ago. That's just not true. The bird was here to prove that wrong.

I did know that the time of the dominant dinosaurs ended in catastrophe and that they all, I used to think, died out because the climate changed so severely. There were gigantic volcanoes pouring out ash, gases, and lava. Even an asteroid came in and hit the earth: disaster. But what the little bird told me was that through all of this disaster, one group survived even while all of the other animals perished. Do you know what that one dinosaur group was? The birds.

After about eighty-five million years of living alongside their dinosaur relatives, when everyone else perished in that devastation, they survived and they've lived until today. Every single bird today, from loon to robin to penguin, is a dinosaur that carries on the heritage of its dinosaur ancestors.

Well, I told the bird I didn't know what to make of all this. I wasn't sure because I had always heard that the dinosaurs had vanished. The bird told me I should travel back in time and meet some of the ancestors of birds. Well, in order to do that, I had to use my imagination. I had to get into my imaginary time machine and travel to the past because I wanted to meet Tyrannosaurus Rex, the king of the dinosaurs, so off I went.

Now, I knew that every bird today is a distant relative of Tyrannosaurus Rex; that's real. Tyrannosaurus was the awesome and terrifying king of the dinosaurs who lived about sixty-five million years ago. I think you've heard of Tyrannosaurus Rex, haven't you? Everybody, almost, has heard of Tyrannosaurus Rex. Tyrannosaurus Rex is a little hard to say, so with his permission, I will call him T-Rex.

T-Rex is a kind of a dinosaur called a *Theropod.* Theropods are a big family of meat-eating, or carnivorous, dinosaurs. They stood on only two legs—just like birds still do today. Some of the theropods were the largest carnivorous dinosaurs that ever lived, like T-Rex.

But do you know what? I didn't really want to meet a Tyrannosaurus Rex. I know I'd gone back in time to meet them, but when I saw them standing there and saw how large they were and how horrifying and terrifying they were with their great teeth and their huge jaws, they were just too scary. I didn't want to have to meet one face-to-face. Even though I knew that the birds are descendants of theropods, I figured that to be safe, I had better find a smaller theropod to talk to!

The Theropod group also includes one called Velociraptor, but they're pretty scary, too. Though they're not as big as T-Rex, they are six or seven feet tall and really, really fast and very vicious. They don't sound nice at all.

But then I remembered that there's a smaller dinosaur, a theropod called Compsognathus. Maybe I could find one of them.

So, I started looking through time and space using my time travel machine and I got very lucky. I did get to meet a theropod dinosaur, face-to-face! She's a very small animal with some downy or fuzzy feathers. Her name is *Compsognathus*, which is a hard name to say and to remember. She told me her friends just call her Compie, so I do, too.

Compie was a meat eater, a carnivore who lived during the late Jurassic period, around 150 million years ago. This was a very long time ago. Compie was a very small dinosaur, which was reassuring to me. She weighs only about six and a half pounds and she's not quite two feet tall.

She did explain to me that even though she's only the size of a big chicken, some in her family are as big as a turkey. But, even though they're small like that, they're certainly not like the chickens or turkeys that we know: they are vicious hunters of small animals. Yes, they are hunters with sharp teeth and a big bite, so I was very respectful to Compie.

As I was being very polite with Compie, I noticed that she was posing and preening, turning her head first one way and then the other. She saw me looking so she explained, "My full name, Compsognathus, really means elegant or pretty jaw." Snapping her sharp teeth, she looked at me. I knew that I was supposed to admire her jaw and I did. I thought it was best to agree, to be on the safe side.

Since I had been so polite, she also told me that although I couldn't see it, her skeleton was made of hollow bones. Compie is a very sprightly little dinosaur, lively with two long slender legs that she uses to runs about. She's extremely fast, so very fast that she can easily chase down her prey, like frogs, insects, and small lizards. She's able to chase them very efficiently.

Of course, you know, even though birds evolved from theropods, they didn't change from Compie or T-Rex instantly. It took millions of years for them to get from then to today, but look at all the features that the theropods like Compie already had. They had feathers. They walked on two legs like birds do, and lots of them even had a wishbone inside. Some had hollow bones, like Compie.

Compie suggested that I should go talk to a real ancient bird, an actual bird from very old times. Once again, I got into my machine and decided to time travel to visit somebody named *Archaeopteryx*. I knew that birds evolved from the theropod dinosaurs, but I wasn't really clear—I'm still not—on how Archaeopteryx fits into that progression. Maybe Archaeopteryx is closely related to the ancestors of living birds, or maybe other theropods like Compie are more closely related.

To find out, I went about 145 million years back to the late Jurassic Period and there, I finally got to meet Archaeopteryx. The animal that I saw certainly seemed to be a bird or, well, maybe it was just sort of like a bird. But he was happy to meet me, and he told me that he was named Archaeopteryx but he said I could call him Archie for short.

Archie was beautiful with lovely light and dark colored plumage and many black feathers. The feathers were all over him, especially along his arms, legs, and tail. And those on the arms made them look, well, sort of like wings. Inside his body, Archie told me he even had a wishbone, like birds still do today.

While we talked, Archie kept very busy munching on some insects, small reptiles, amphibians, and even a few small little mammals kind of like mice. Huh, what a lunch! Archie was different from any birds that we see around us nowadays. He showed me, for example, that he had a long, bony tail. Archie also had teeth, and I know that no bird today has teeth.

Archie didn't really look entirely like a bird, and he probably was a little more like the other small dinosaurs than birds. But Archie told me that he was actually the first known bird even though he didn't look like one. He was quite proud to say that, so I didn't want to dispute it. He said that scientists consider him the first bird, or at least they did—even though he might not be a true bird.

His name, his actual name, Archaeopteryx, comes from the ancient Greek words *Archaeos,* meaning ancient, and *teryx,* meaning wing. So: *ancient wing.* That was a great name for him because of his wings, which, of course, he showed off by flapping them for me. He was showy, but Archie wasn't very big for a dinosaur.

The largest Archie and his relatives could grow was about a foot and half long and they weighed about two pounds. They were smaller than Compie, but bigger than a lot of today's birds. So, it seems that Archaeopteryx had some features of dinosaurs and some features of birds. The thing was, like Archie told me, he was something like our birds, but probably not their direct ancestor. But both Archie and Compie had a lot that birds have inherited and use even today.

Well, I had heard one interesting idea and I wanted to see what they thought of this. It might just be true. Maybe birds evolved from dinosaurs by somehow blocking their own development early on in life. Birds do look a lot like baby dinosaurs that are still in their eggs. It's possible that birds developed by making themselves into small, miniature, baby-like dinosaurs. It could be true, but I couldn't get a sure answer about its truth from either Compie or Archie.

But, we were able to decide on five big things, critical things that happened in the evolution of dinosaurs into birds. Of these five, number one is their size. These gigantic dinosaurs like T-Rex, these huge, hungry, carnivorous dinosaurs, constantly shrank to smaller sizes for more than fifty-million years. They just got smaller and smaller. That's right.

For example, the theropods had an average weight of 360 pounds, with some gigantic ones in there like Tyrannosaurus Rex, and then they started to scale down and get smaller until they reached a new average weight of about one and three quarter pounds before becoming modern birds. Think of that, losing over 350 pounds on the average.

There is something else that's really interesting about their getting smaller. Compie was careful to point it out to me because she was so pleased by it. Did you know that the theropods were the only dinosaurs to get continually smaller? Yes, at that time, most of the other dinosaurs were actually growing bigger and getting gigantic.

Moreover, these theropods sped up their shrinkage a lot more once some of them grew wings and began trying to fly. It seems like it must have been a great advantage to be smaller. It must have been very useful, because so many of them did it. Maybe it was helpful that their wings could help them fly up into and perch in trees—can you imagine why? Either way, they did get a lot smaller.

Now the second big feature we figured out is feathers. Birds have feathers, but they weren't the first fuzzy ones. Even the king of the dinosaurs, the terrifying, awesome, terrible Tyrannosaurus Rex, may have been a little bit fluffy. Some people call that dinofuzz and T-Rex likes that name, but, of course, everybody we met today had feathers of some kind.

Maybe those first downy-like feathers kept the animals warm. Maybe they helped in brooding eggs, so that the eggs could stay warm. Possibly, they were for some kind of attractive display that they could show off, as peacocks do even today. Maybe feathers were useful as camouflage or possibly identifying different species. We really don't know what the first purpose of feathers was, except that they were successful enough that they stuck around for generation after generation. But it was only later that they were used for flying, that's for sure. Flying wasn't one of the early purposes of feathers. Of course, now feathers are essential for birds that fly.

Let's look at the third thing: hollow bones. Remember that Compie told us that she had hollow bones? Mm-hmm. So do modern birds; their bones are also hollow. After Archie, that's Archaeopteryx, many of the birds' bones were reduced and fused together, which may make them better flyers. At the same time that that was happening, the walls of their bones became thinner and thinner. That means that birds now have lighter, hollow bones, and that leads to flying that is more efficient. But they got the hollow bone idea all the way back from the dinosaurs.

A fourth thing is a wishbone. Maybe if you have ever eaten a whole turkey or a whole chicken or been at a dinner where people did that, you might have seen a wishbone. The real name of the wishbone is the *furcula,* or little fork. The wishbone is actually made up of the collarbones of the bird fused together in the center. It really helps them in flying because it can be springy.

Archie explained that birds from his time on have had wishbones. However, Compie was quick to say, "Way before birds, the wishbone was widespread among the theropods." The birds just kept that great idea. You know what? If you ever happen to eat a Tyrannosaurus Rex or another theropod for Thanksgiving and you carved it up, you might be surprised to find a wishbone right there in the dinosaur's breast, just like a turkey or a chicken.

Of course, I don't think you'll probably have one of those for dinner, but maybe.

Now let's look at the fifth thing: beaks. Birds have beaks. Some people call them bills. Beaks are remarkable arrangements that are used for many things by birds. A beak is the mouthpart for the bird, isn't it?

Birds use beaks for finding food, for making nests, for cleaning themselves, and even for caring for their young. It's possible that one reason that birds are so successful is because they have beaks. In other words, maybe beaks have led to their success. But birds have had beaks for a long time. The first known bird to have a modern beak is an eighty-five-million-year-old bird called the *Hesperornis* bird.

In modern birds, there are two bones in the beak, called the *premaxillary bones*. These bones fuse together to form the beak, an idea that the birds have had for more than eight-five million years. Even before that, dinosaurs had those premaxillary bones; they just hadn't fused together in the way they do with modern birds.

All of those five things that I've talked about connect today's birds with Archie and Compie and all of the other theropod dinosaurs of prehistoric times. But, I need to wave goodbye to my friends Archie and Compie now. And even to T-Rex, who's not really a friend. I need to come back from my trip to the prehistoric time.

Now that I'm back here, in modern times, I know that I'll see dinosaurs today. Yes, I will—real ones, right outside. They're here, many of them. I know that it may not be quite as exciting to see a robin on your windowsill as it would be to see a Tyrannosaurus Rex sitting there. But you have still seen a dinosaur. After talking to that bird, I think that I'll always remember what a bird is: a modern dinosaur.

And that is how it is, even to this very day.

The Chicken or the Egg

"Story is the best vehicle for passing on factual information."

—National Council of Teachers of English, 1992

INTRODUCTION

When we study the early development of life, at a certain point, the egg becomes very important. If life began in the water, as science teaches, then the migration of animal life to the harsh dryness of land must have been an extreme challenge. One particular challenge was reproduction. Eggs require wetness—perfect for fish. However, if animals are to live far from water, then the egg must contain its own wetness, or *amnion*. So, animals that live away from water developed what is called the *amniotic egg*.

A chicken egg, such as can be bought in a grocery store, is an example of an amniotic egg. This egg's design has solved the problem of keeping its developing life wet. The shell protects the egg and blocks evaporation—two great evolutionary achievements that allowed reptiles and birds to cover the Earth.

This story uses the familiar question, "Which came first, the chicken or the egg?" to introduce the notion of the amniotic egg. Although the question is usually rhetorical, in this story, we do answer it. The story of *The Chicken or the Egg* is an excellent introduction to the idea of the egg and its importance to life.

When presenting this story, I use two props. One is a large egg. I like to use a jumbo duck egg or even a goose or turkey egg if I can get one, but a regular chicken egg works just fine.

I also use a model chicken. Of course, I am careful to use a hen rather than a rooster, since the hens are the ones that lay eggs.[3]

Source: *The Chicken or the Egg* is a completely original story that I wrote.

Note: For technical reasons, some people may not consider this a story, but a narrative. However, if it is orally told like a story, called a story, and treated like a story, the children will perceive it as a story. They will receive all of the benefits of storytelling from this sort of narrative.

STORY

Have you ever heard the question, "Which came first, the chicken or the egg?"

"I wonder," people will say, "Which came first, the chicken or the egg?" When they say that, you know what they are really saying is that there is no way to figure it out.

I have a chicken here, and I also have an egg. This is so that we can be thinking, "Which came first? Which one, the chicken or the egg? The egg or the chicken?" We are going to answer that question—we're going to solve that problem, right here and right now.

Point to the model chicken and to the egg.

The egg came first!

We know that the egg had to come first, because long before there were chickens, long before there were birds even, there were other animals that laid eggs.

You may remember that egg-laying animals are called *oviparous*.

Who were the first animals to lay eggs? They were not

[3] Although any hen may do, I use a model ceramic hen from Happy Hens in Dunedin, New Zealand. I went to Dunedin for a Montessori conference and was charmed by the beautiful hens. They can also be purchased online from www.HappyHens.co.nz. One of their larger hens is perfect for this story. Just be sure that it's not a rooster!

chickens, nor any other birds. There was something else, before the birds.

Were they reptiles? Reptiles do lay eggs, and they were on Earth before the birds. But no, the first eggs came even before the reptiles. There was something else, even before the reptiles.

Were they amphibians, then? Amphibians lay eggs. They were on Earth before birds or reptiles. But no, the first eggs came even before the amphibians.

Even before the amphibians, there were fish already laying eggs. Even insects and other invertebrates laid eggs. Eggs were a great invention!

An egg is nothing more than the fertile seed of a new life. That beginning of life is often laid in a specially prepared place, like a nest.

Many kinds of fish are good examples of egg-layers, who make a kind of nest for their eggs, but some fish just swim away from their eggs, and others die as they're laying their eggs. And just like this egg, which some people might want to eat for breakfast, some of those eggs laid by the fish might be eaten by some other fish or sea creature that swims up and finds them. In that case, of course, if the eggs are eaten, those fish never hatch. There are also many people who enjoy eating the eggs of fish, which are called *caviar*. You may have heard of it. How delicious!

Hold up the egg and show it to the children.

So it is important to remember that fish actually do lay eggs, but their eggs are laid entirely in water, and during one of the earliest times on our Timeline of Life, the Age of Fishes, all eggs were laid in water.

A little bit later, something very important happened; maybe you remember it. A little bit later, some fish emerged from the water. Over many millennia, these fish evolved into amphibians.

So, what did they do about their eggs? Amphibians lay eggs just as fish do. But where do they lay them? In the water, that's right. Most amphibians, like fish, have to go to the water to reproduce. Their jelly-covered eggs are in the water, their young hatch in the water, and swim around like little fish. They are, at first, kind of little fish-like things. Even though they may be baby frogs, baby salamanders, or baby toads, they swim about like fishlets, and they are called tadpoles, or larva.

The amphibian really lives two lives: a watery life in which it grows as a little tadpole or larva, and then, all of a sudden, a new life beginning when legs sprout out of its end. At this point, it must think, "I can come up out of the water." Once it does come up on land, it usually still lives near the water—the amphibian is always tied to where it can lay its eggs. Amphibians can't leave the water too far behind. They always need to be in a moist spot.

Now, let's look at our Timeline of Life around the Permian Period. Somewhere right around the Permian Period, there was a great ice age, and during this ice age, lots and lots of water froze into ice. When it became ice, the water was no longer out there in the ocean. As it says right here in the timeline, "trapped seas dry up." So there was a lot of drying up of watery places, and this caused great extinctions for many animals.

This was a particularly hard time for amphibians because amphibians are so closely linked to moist and wet places. This is when the greatest innovation of all time, as far as eggs are concerned, happened. That is right, the best thing of all—for eggs—the most important development, more important than the chicken, more important than the fried egg—this is the most important thing of all time for eggs! A truly great idea came along. First, I'll tell you what the idea was, and then I'll tell you who thought of it.

The idea was to put the moisture inside the egg instead of putting the egg into the water. It's that simple! Brilliant!

What a great notion. Now some animals won't have to lay the eggs in water because the water would be inside the egg—and the shell would be waterproof so the water wouldn't leak out.

That might seem simple to you and to me, but actually, it isn't. It's a phenomenal idea. There's a special name for this new kind of egg with the water inside. It's called an *amniotic egg*. The amniotic egg is an egg that contains fluids—just like a little ocean—right inside of it. Those fish and amphibians had to be in or go find the pond or the ocean to keep their eggs wet enough, but this new egg has a lake inside of it. It contains an ocean. It is a sea. It has its own little ocean inside so that the young can swim in the water even if the egg is laid in dry places. What a great idea!

Who was it that thought of that? Was it some great modern inventor? No, it was the reptiles. Reptiles. That's right; reptiles came up with this idea. This, in fact, is what made them reptiles.

They came up with another great idea, too, which was having dry skin protected by scales, but their first great idea was an egg that didn't have to be in the water. The egg with a marvelous shell that doesn't let the inside dry out but it can still let air pass through so the young inside can breathe. Isn't that an amazing egg?

That egg came way before there were chickens, but that reptile egg started a whole revolution of animals, especially vertebrates, that were able to live completely on land. They didn't have to be in or next to the water anymore. Now they could finally go somewhere else and lay their eggs in almost any place.

Nowadays, reptiles live in forests. Reptiles live in the desert. Reptiles live in mountains. Reptiles spread all over the Earth for one reason: the egg. The wonderful amniotic egg that freed them from the water.

Now, many people think that birds, like my chicken right here, are just transformed reptiles, as you know. And birds are free from the water, too, because they also have this astonishing egg. They are able to lay an egg, and they don't have to lay it in water, because it contains the water inside it. So smart, so simple, so elegant. Such a great idea.

By the time the first ancestral chickens came around, there had been eggs for over a hundred million years. It is a good idea to have an egg, but this isn't the end of the egg story; there's more about eggs. Because mammals even took the whole thing a step further. You might not know that mammals have eggs, too, but most of them keep the eggs completely inside their bodies, and their eggs don't even require a shell at all! But that's another story. This is the story of the chicken and the egg, and we now know that first came the egg—and then, much later, came the chicken.

And so it was, and so it is.

The First Farmers

Introduction

One of the greatest of all human inventions has to be agriculture. With agriculture, humanity was able to settle in one place and establish villages and cities. The development of agriculture can be dated to at least seven thousand years ago, and possibly as many as ten thousand years ago. Many people believe that it happened in the area of the Middle East known as the Fertile Crescent.

The thing that marks an agricultural society is their planned planting and care of plants; this contrasts with societies that gather wild seeds or plant parts. The earliest cereal grains to have been domesticated probably include emmer and einkorn, both of which are related to modern wheat. Barley is another early grain. All of these developed from ancestral grasses in the Middle East.

This story imagines the inception of agriculture as an accidental event, one that may have been replicated in many locations, and the key discovery is that seeds are both the beginning and the end of the growing cycle. The story imagines a time in which food was extremely scarce because people believed that the gods had prohibited spilling seed upon the ground. As a result, intentional planting was not yet practiced.

Stories like this are imaginative. They do not purport to tell with historical accuracy the exact sequence of events that may have happened. Their intent is to stimulate the imagination, motivate, initiate speculation, begin discussion, and lead to writing and research.

In this story, as in many stories I have written, I let the discovery lie in the hands of a young child. We really have no idea who the very first farmer may have been, so the character of that individual is open to speculation. I like to imagine that it might have been a child—in this way, I aim to empower the children in my class, to encourage them to consider that they, too, might discover something great.

The First Farmers is a curriculum story, to be given when the children are studying the origins of civilization. In Montessori schools, this is usually undertaken in the fifth grade, or the second year of the upper elementary class.

Source: *The First Farmers* is a completely original story that I wrote.

Story

There was once a girl who lived in a very warm climate, in a place that may have been close to a river. This was long, long ago, almost ten thousand years ago. At that time, people really did not have established villages, and they had to go from spot to spot to follow whatever food they could get. If they did settle in one spot, they did not really stay very long.

When the girl was very small, her name day came and the wise woman of the tribe observed her, for this was how naming took place. The wise woman saw how curious the little girl was, and once she saw this characteristic of being curious, the wise woman said, "She is a curious one, and so she shall be known." Thus, the girl's name became Curious One.

And so she was—very curious about all sorts of things. Sometimes, she even got in trouble because she was so curious. In fact, this story is about one time when she was very curious and she got in trouble for it. But, it's also a story about how her trouble turned out. We will find out about Curious One and her trouble.

Curious One lived in a group of people that liked to live by great fields of tall grass. In the late summer, after the grasses dried up and turned golden, they would go out to the field and they would cut the stalks of the tall grass, which bore seed. Then they would carry the grasses back to where they lived, and all of the stalks of grass, with their grainy seeds, would be piled in a dry place.

Then the men would play on drums and pound on other objects. Some of the men and women would get on top of the grasses and dance and stomp up and down. This would separate the grass stalks from the seeds, and then the men and women would throw the seed up in the air and let the wind carry away the light things that they had stomped off. After carrying away the stems, the people would get down on their knees and pick up every single grain, every seed, for they had been told that the gods did not allow seed to be spilled on the ground, so every seed had to be recovered and saved. This was important not only to please the gods, but because these grains were the food that they ate.

Then, during the fall and winter, they would pound that grain into powder, mix it with water, and spread it out on stones made hot from the sun to make a kind of bread. Or they might put the grain in a pot, which they had made from clay, along with water and let it boil until it could be eaten, like a porridge. They were probably also able to take small handfuls of the grain and just chew it up. But there was only so much seed until the next grass grew and not one single seed could be wasted; if it were, someone might go hungry. No seed could be spilled; no seed was wasted.

Now, when all of the seed had been gathered from a field, these people would leave their old dwelling place behind—they would find a new field full of the same sort of tall grass that bore nice seeds of grain. They repeated this over and over, moving from place to place, for they did not farm, they simply went from field to field, always looking for spots where they could get seed.

Curious One was curious, of course, and when she lay in her bed at night, she often thought of how hungry she was. Because she was so curious, she thought "Wouldn't it be good to have some more of that seed? Wouldn't it be good to have just a handful, just a small handful, right now? I would like to have some of it."

But she couldn't have more, because the seed for the whole tribe was kept in special containers, and only the wise woman was allowed to go there to fetch the grain. No one else in the tribe would try to get it, because the gods had warned them that no one should take the seed.

But one night—and this is where she got in trouble—Curious One decided she wanted to go see if the seed was all right. It was just curiosity—was the grain all right? So, she got up very quietly, as not to wake up anyone else, and slipped off to the hut where the grain was stored. When she looked in the great pottery jars where the seed was stored, she could see that, in fact, it was all right.

The next night, she was once again curious. Again, she got up in the deepest darkness of the middle of the night and slipped out very quietly so that no one would hear her. Once again, she checked and saw that the grain was all right.

On the third night, she checked again, but this time, just before leaving, she thought, "Well, maybe as long as I'm here checking on it, I should try a small bit of the seed, just a taste, just a pinch to see if it's really still good. That would probably be all right." And she did take just a tiny pinch, but she didn't put it in her mouth for fear that she was stealing the seed from the whole village. Would something happen to her? After thinking it over, she decided to put it in her mouth. She chewed and chewed and went back to bed. There was no problem.

Well, this got a little bit worse and eventually you will hear what happened. Curious One went back night after night, and finally one night she thought, "Why not just take a whole handful? I could go back and I could lie in my bed and munch it there, and no one would notice." So, she took a handful of the seed, covered everything up, and started back to her place where she slept.

Now, this was a very dark night and, of course, you have to understand that nobody had lights on at night, nobody had flashlights, no one had candles, no one had lamps. It was very dark.

All of the people except Curious One were asleep. It was very, very dark. And as she crept carefully along, she tripped and spilled all of the seed on the ground. The very thing that the gods had warned them not to do—she'd spilled the seed on the ground.

Now listen to what happened. Curious One got down on her hands and knees and felt around for the seed. But in the darkness, she couldn't find it all. It was just too dark. She started to smooth around, and covered it all up with soil to try to hide it from everybody. "Maybe," she thought, "the gods wouldn't see it. Maybe there would be no trouble." So, she went around and smoothed the ground, hoping to bury any of the grains. Then, the first thing in the very earliest morning, she came out and looked around and covered up the few seeds that were still there to be sure that no one would find out. She walked on the spot where she covered the seeds with dirt so that no one would know that she had committed the terrible crime of spilling the seed on the ground.

The next day, Curious One was still okay. Nothing had happened to her, even though she still felt worried and guilty. She went over to the spot where she had spilled the seed, and there was no problem. "I guess the gods may not have noticed." Every day for the next several days she checked and everything seemed to be okay.

But one day when Curious One came to check on things, she saw that in that very spot where she had spilled the seed, little plants were sprouting. When she looked closely at the little sprouts, she could see that they were the very same kind of grass that made the seed that the people ate. It was the very same thing! Curious One thought, "Well, I'll just wait and see," and she came back the next day to see them growing even more. As the days passed, the grasses kept growing, more and more. Then Curious One was worried and she thought, "I have to go to the wise woman and tell her what happened. I have to tell everyone so that they can see what happened."

So, she went to the wise woman of the tribe and she confessed. The wise woman seemed very upset and said, "Curious One, what you have done is a terrible thing. You don't have the right to go into our food and take food from us. But show me the place where the spilling took place."

So, they walked to the spot together, and they looked at it. Then the wise woman said, "I think that the gods have smiled upon us. Growing here is the very same plant. We may have discovered something."

"What?" thought Curious One, "What?"

The wise woman said, "Let's watch it for the next few days." So they studied the plants. Indeed, it grew up into the very kind of plant that produced the grass seed that they liked to eat. Then the wise woman discovered that the seed is both at the end and at the beginning of life. She helped Curious One to see that, too. They saw that the seed produced life at the end, which gives life to us by eating it. But when carefully put in the ground, the seed begets new life, which can grow. If people put seeds in the ground, maybe they wouldn't always have to move to new fields where the plants grew.

So they tried it. They put a few seeds intentionally in the ground. Many people were frightened for fear the gods would punish them for it. They still also kept gathering as they had always done. But, indeed, the seeds sprouted and grew. They grew not only into the plant that they ate, but also into some of the best and fattest seeds they'd ever seen. Those were the ones they saved and planted again for next year.

Year after year, they again saved the fattest, nicest seeds and sacrificed them by planting them in the ground. Year after year, they grew the finest grain they'd ever eaten. Indeed, the village never moved again. It stayed where it was, and many years later, it became a great city. As it grew, the people kept harvesting the grain and planting new grasses to grow all around them.

And Curious One? Well, when she grew up, she became the wise woman of the tribe. She became the wise woman herself, for what she had done had given life to her entire tribe. Furthermore, she gave us the idea of growing and planting, of planting seeds and of agriculture, a great discovery for all human kind.

And this is a true story. And if it isn't, it should be.

Curriculum Stories for Mathematics
(Arithmetic and Geometry)

"Tell me the facts and I'll learn. Tell me the truth and I'll believe. But tell me a story and it will live in my heart forever."

—Native American proverb

The mathematics work in Montessori schools is tremendously rich and varied. Like any quality mathematics program, it includes the basics of numeral recognition; the idea of place value; the four operations of addition, multiplication, subtraction, and division; fractions; decimals; and ideas from pre-algebra and algebra.

Much more than this, however, the Montessori program takes a unique holistic view of mathematics. The Fifth Great Lesson (p. 125), along with the other Great Lessons, serves to place mathematics in a cosmic context. This means that its connections to other areas are emphasized along with its origins. The central idea of holism is to consistently give the whole before the parts whenever possible. This means that the idea of our number system, the decimal system, is offered right at the beginning of the program, with all of the component parts under the umbrella that it provides.

Additionally, geometry has immense importance in this program. It is given an emphasis at least equal to arithmetic. This sets up an almost binary mathematical program, until, by the upper grades, these two subjects increasingly cross-fertilize and inform each other.

Stories are exceptionally useful in mathematics. There is an idea in our culture that mathematics is all about right and wrong, black and white. This hard-edged perspective is one of the causes of the problems so many children have with mathematics. Infusing the narrative element of story into the math curriculum enriches and deepens it while simultaneously increasing its accessibility to all learners.

These mathematical stories address both arithmetic and geometry through narrative. Many times, older children and even adults have come to me to tell me that they still remember these stories. Frequently, these stories have engendered a love of mathematics in these people. That, indeed, is a Gift of the Memorable (p. 13).

Enjoy these stories and witness the enjoyment, pleasure, and understanding that these can bring to children learning mathematics.

The Four Strange Brothers

INTRODUCTION

This fun, fanciful arithmetic tale is a curriculum story about an unusual family of four brothers. These four strange brothers represent, in order, addition, multiplication, subtraction, and division.

The four brothers dress in four special colors that, in Montessori schools, are associated with the four arithmetic operations. Red stands for addition, gold or yellow for multiplication, green for subtraction, and blue for division.

Along with the oral component of the story, I make signs using four regular 8½ x 11-inch sheets of paper. There is a large red "plus" sign, a large golden "times" sign, a large green "minus" sign, and a large blue "division" sign. I hold these up when I speak about "the strange symbol" that they had mounted on their shirts.

The red is usually a primary red. You may also use cherry, rose, or crimson. The green is usually a pure green. You may also use forest green or medium green. The blue is usually a primary blue. You may also use a Persian blue or royal blue. For all of these colors, use what you have available. Almost any tint, shade, or tone will work.

One note about the multiplication. The times sign is meant to be golden in color. This could be a metallic gold, old gold, honey, or other gold. This has posed a problem for some people who were unable to locate gold in a craft shop. If a gold tone or shade is difficult for you to acquire, use a golden yellow, amber yellow, or another shade or tone of yellow. In the story, I will simply refer to the color of multiplication as gold.

I first envisioned this story while on an airplane, traveling to a math workshop I was to present. I did end up presenting a rudimentary form of the story there, and since then, I have worked on it quite a bit and it has become very successful.

This is also a wonderful story for creative dramatics. After telling the story, the children can act it out. Children may play each of the brothers (or sisters), and someone could be the narrator. Others may be the villagers. One group I worked with inserted a new character, the mother. She was at first frustrated by her sons' behaviors, but she ultimately grew proud. I thought that was a creative addition.

Enjoy this story. I know that the children do.

Source: *The Four Strange Brothers* is a completely original story that I wrote.

Story

Long ago, in a far away place, there were four very, very strange brothers. When you hear about these four brothers, I think you will agree they were very strange. Everybody in the village knew that they were strange. And they certainly were.

Display the red "plus" sign.

Figure 36.
The red plus sign.

The eldest of the four brothers always dressed in red. He wore nothing but red; all of his clothes, even his shoes, were red. On the front of his shirt or jacket, he always had this strange emblem sewn on. Whatever clothing he was wearing, if he had a jacket, he had this sign sewn on his jacket. No matter what red clothes he wore, you would see this symbol sewn on.

This first brother, in red, with this sign, always wanted to put things together to make more. Whatever he saw, he would put them together. "Oh there are some spoons. I'll take one and one and make two spoons." Or he might say, "There are some papers, I'll take three and two and four, and I'll make nine." Another time when he spotted something, he would think, "I'll go and get one and seven and make eight."

He just wanted to put things together to make more. He went around the house. If anybody left something around—plates, candy, dog kibbles, ties—he would bring them all together and count how many he had made. If somebody had left out silverware, he'd get all of it together and count how many he'd made in the pile. You see, he was strange. When people went to the garden to harvest vegetables, other folks might be interested in bringing in the carrots, but he only wanted to put them all together in one big pile and find out many there were. That was his only interest. So, he was a little bit unusual.

Display the gold "times" sign.

X

Figure 37. The gold times sign.

Now, the second brother dressed all in gold. He was completely dressed in gold, and on his chest, he had this emblem, this X-like shape. Like his older brother, he only wore one color, even on his hat and shoes, except in his case, it was always gold.

He was a lot like his older red brother in many ways. He was really pretty much the same. He liked to put things together and make more, too, but he only liked to put groups of the same size together. So he would say, "Well here are three and three and three and three—four threes, that's twelve." The elder red brother might take one and two and five oranges, to make eight oranges, but not this one, he wanted the same thing many times. That meant that he would want to group the oranges and then take two and two and two and two. "There," he would say, "four twos make eight."

The gold brother told his older red brother, "You and I do practically the same thing. But I am faster. I just do what you do repeatedly. I do the same thing, but I repeat."

Between those two brothers, you could imagine the piles of things that they gathered. They would have had nothing but huge piles around their house and everywhere else—except for their third brother, who dressed completely in green and was also strange.

Display the green "minus" sign.

This third brother would dress all in beautiful green from his hat to his deep-green shoes. Like his two older brothers, he also had a symbol sewn onto his front. It looked like this.

Figure 38. The green minus sign.

The green brother just liked to take things away. He wanted to come over and take away. Whatever they'd put together, he would try to take away. If he saw some apples, he might say, "Well now there's seven over here, I'll take five away and leave two." Another time he might say, "I see you've got those four coffee cups. I'm taking one away and leaving three."

He would take things away all the time. You could imagine what their house was like with the other two brothers putting things together and him doing nothing but taking things away. No wonder the people thought that these brothers were strange. Not only did they dress strangely, with those odd symbols sewn on them, but they worked against each other all the time, and somehow it all worked out to balance.

Finally, there was a fourth brother. The fourth brother thought that the most important thing was to be fair. He wanted to be fair to everyone. He dressed completely in blue, even up to his bright-blue hat and down to his beautiful blue shoes. Like his brothers, he had a strange emblem sewn on his chest. It looked like this.

Display the blue "division" sign.

Figure 39. The blue division sign.

This youngest brother wanted everything to be fair, completely so. So he might go around and say, "Look there's a pile of oranges, why don't I give one to you and one to you and one to you and one to you ..." and he would pass them out so everybody got the same amount of everything.

He always said, "I believe in fairness." If it didn't work out just evenly that everybody got the exact same amount, he would leave some to the side as a little remainder left over. He'd never let one person get more than the other. Fairness—that was the most important thing.

At this time, show a handful of golden beads. These can be any kind of beads. If you cannot find golden beads, use red or green beads and simply change the color of the apples in the story.

When each brother speaks, hold up the card with the corresponding symbol.

Can you imagine this family's house? It was very different, with these four brothers and their peculiar activities!

Well, it so happened that one night, there was a great windstorm in the village. In that village was a large apple orchard, and in that orchard, there were many luscious golden apples growing. Now these beads might give us the idea of some of those apples that were all around. Beautiful golden apples.

Because of the windstorm, all of the apples—so many of them—were knocked off the trees and had fallen on the ground. They lay all about under the trees.

When the first brother got there, dressed all in red, he became very excited. "Oh," he said, "I know what I need to do. I need to put them together and I'll end up with more in my big pile than in any small pile." So, he went to work. "Here are six apples, here are twelve apples. I'll get thirteen more apples and bring them over." And he started building big piles with all the apples.

The next brother, the one in gold, thought that the first brother was making such a waste of time. "I'll just get four and four and four and four and four—which makes twenty—and that way I will have so many because I'm just repeating the same number over and over. I can go so much more quickly and work so much faster." The two of them kept busily cleaning up all the apples.

Now what do you think that their third brother, the one in green, did? He began to take the apples away. "What a lot of apples there are. I will take away as many as I can, and there will be fewer in each pile." He moved those apples into other, far-away piles.

But because the older two brothers were working as sort of two-against-one, eventually they got all of the apples into several big piles. Then, all three brothers rested because they were tired from their work.

Then their youngest brother, dressed in blue, started to work, saying, "Now comes the time when I am going to make sure that every villager gets their fair share of apples." Then he went to the piles of apples and started giving them to each person, and he went around just as we could with these beads, and gave one to you, and one to you, and one to you, and one to you, and one to you, and so on until everyone in the whole village had gotten an apple. But there were still more apples, so he did it again, and he did it again, one to you, and one to you, and one to you, and one to you, and one to you, and so on. He did it again, and again until everyone had their fair share of apples and all of the apples in the piles had been shared out.

Show the twelve golden beads to the children and pass them out equally to three or four adults or children.

The four strange brothers looked over their work and were happy.

Then the eldest red brother said, "I helped with this by getting everything together and making more. I shall call that *addition*. When we bring things together and we make more, it is addition. I did addition."

Then the second brother, the one dressed in gold, said, "I helped too, because I did just what you did. I did something like addition, but I repeated the same quantity so many times that I was faster. I shall call that *multiplication*. When we bring the same quantity of things together many times, we are repeating addition, and that is multiplication. I did multiplication."

The third brother, dressed in green, the one that liked to take things away all the time, said, "Well I guess I really didn't help much at all, but I had fun doing it. I kept taking things away. I call that *subtraction*. When we take things away and leave less, we are subtracting. Subtracting just means taking away. I did subtraction."

Finally, the fourth brother, the one dressed in blue, spoke up. He announced, "I solved the problems for everyone by doing *division*. Division means sharing out equally." He smiled, and went on, "Division is the fairest process of all because everybody gets a fair share. I did division."

He was right. Everybody did get a fair share. And then, the villagers were happy that those four brothers lived nearby, even though they were very strange.

And that is how it is, even to this day.

The Three Shapes

INTRODUCTION

The Three Shapes is a story designed to accompany the introduction of the triangle, the square, and the circle. In the Montessori classroom, these are kept in a special place called the Presentation Tray, which usually sits on top of the Geometry Cabinet, an assemblage of shapes used for plane geometry. It is as if these three very special shapes open the entire study of geometry—and they do.

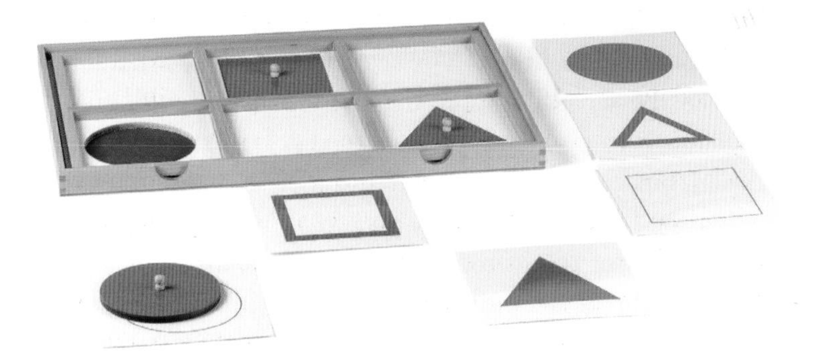

Figure 40. This is the Presentation Tray.

If you do not have a Presentation Tray, you can easily make these three figures. Using heavy card stock, cut out an equilateral triangle with ten-centimeter sides, a square with ten-centimeter sides and a circle with a ten-centimeter diameter. The traditional Montessori color is red or blue, but you may certainly use any color, so long as all three are the same.

Montessori teachers tell the children that the triangle is the constructor, the square is the measurer and, the circle is the calculator, and they do, indeed, serve these functions.

I wrote this curriculum story, my newest in this volume, to add an imaginative dimension to concepts in the Presentation Tray. I am pleased to report that the children have received it very well.

Source: *The Three Shapes* is a completely original story, which I wrote.

Story

Once upon a time, in a far-away land, there lived three men. These three men accomplished wonderful and great things—things we still think about today. So, let's talk about what they did and listen to a story about these three very interesting men.

The first one was a constructor. He could build anything—oh yes, just about anything! He built things so strongly that all people admired him for his beautiful building. Now, as he got older, there was great worry as to who would build and where his skills would go when he was no longer alive. He was such a great builder; certainly, no one else would ever have his powers.

His work was so noble that even the gods high on Mount Olympus took notice of the remarkable things he had done and wondered what might happen when he was gone. Finally, even the great god Zeus took interest, and gave thought to what would become of this distinguished constructor.

This builder, however, didn't accomplish everything on his own. For there was a second person that measured everything, making sure every measurement was just perfect. Because building and measuring are very closely related, these two had to work together: the constructor and the measurer. Now, this measurer was able to measure more accurately and more perfectly than any other person—his measurements were precise and absolutely perfect. Because of this, the constructor and the measurer were partners and worked together on many things.

The measurer could determine the exact size of things so accurately that all people admired him for his magnificent thought. Now, as he got older, there was great worry as to who would measure and where his skills would go when he was no longer alive. His appraising was so ideal; certainly, no one else would ever have his powers.

His work was so noble that even the gods high on Mount Olympus took notice of the remarkable things he had done and wondered what might happen when he was gone. Finally, even the great god Zeus took interest, and gave thought to what would become of this distinguished measurer.

There was also a third partner involved. This person was a calculator. I don't mean a little handheld calculator, but someone who could do many calculations in wonderful ways, all inside his head, all mental. Of course, construction requires calculation—these are very closely related—so the constructor and the calculator had to work together and be partners. Measuring and calculation are also very closely related, so the measurer and the calculator had to work together and be partners, too.

The calculator could compute the exact value of things so accurately that all people admired him for his magnificent thinking. Now, as he got older, there was great worry as to who would calculate and where his skills would go when he was no longer alive. His evaluations were so ideal; certainly, no one else would ever have his powers.

His work was so noble that even the gods high on Mount Olympus took notice of the remarkable things he had done and wondered what might happen when he was gone. Finally, even the great god Zeus took interest, and gave thought to what would become of this distinguished master of calculation.

And so these three humans—the constructor, the measurer, and the calculator—continued through life as three closely-knit partners. They shared so many projects that even the gods high on Mount Olympus took notice of the great things they'd done and wondered what might happen to their alliance when they were gone. Finally, even the great god Zeus took interest, and gave thought to what would become of these three and their grand partnership.

At last, the great god Zeus made a decision. He decided that the world could not lose these three: the constructor, the measurer, and the calculator. He thought, "We have to preserve them forever; there has to be a way that we can care for these three remarkable people forever. But, of course, only the gods are immortal—not human beings." Then Zeus hit upon a wonderful idea. As these three got older, he gave them a special kind of eternal life.

First, he turned the constructor into a triangle. Yes, a perfect equilateral triangle. Now, we are granted the power to view and use that triangle, which is the constructor of all figures. It's true—every figure we have can be built out of triangles! We can even imagine very tiny triangles building up into circles. The triangle, the great constructor, constructs it all and gives strength to so many figures. Triangles are still with us. Even here today—immortal!

Display the equilateral triangle from the Presentation tray.

Next, Zeus considered the great measurer. Carefully, but with a single stroke, Zeus transformed the human measurer into a square. Now, with the square, we humans are granted the power to precisely measure any surface; we can find out the size of everything. The square measures all things—the measurer lives on as a square even today. The square, the great measurer, is also now immortal. It's true, squares are still with us. Even here today—immortal!

Display the square from the Presentation Tray.

Finally, the great god Zeus looked down upon the human who was the great and wonderful calculator. With one more single stroke, the calculator was instantly and permanently transformed into a perfect circle. For it is true that the circle can calculate the hidden angles and measurements of all things. The magnificent circle became the third and ultimate everlasting figure.

Display the circle from the Presentation Tray.

The circle, the great calculator, is also now immortal. It's true, circles in all their perfection, are still with us. Even here today—immortal! The circle is also a universal symbol of wholeness, perfection, eternity, and the infinite. With this circle, we are also pointed towards infinity, pointed towards eternity.

So, the calculator completes our triad of the three great and immortal figures: the constructor, the triangle; the measurer, the square; and the calculator, the circle. Now these three live forever and we can imagine that they once were changed from three very interesting people into these three shapes: the triangle, the square, and the circle.

You see, that was just the beginning. These three figures still live on and, as far as we know, they will live forever.

Figure 41. The three shapes.

The Point, Line, Surface, and Solid

Introduction

Several years ago, I had the wonderful opportunity to attend a day of African storytelling. I listened to magnificent, moving, and sometimes very funny tales from peoples like the Igbo, Zulu, and Yoruba, among others. I was struck by the way that some of the tellers used clicks, hums, buzzes, and other sounds to punctuate their stories.

That very night, this curriculum story came to me in its earliest form. The curricular context is that there are four fundamental concepts or ideas in classical geometry. Dating back to the ancient Greek geometer Euclid, these concepts are the *point*, the *line*, the *surface*, and the *solid*.

These four concepts are usually offered to six- or seven-year-old children in a Montessori early elementary lesson that had previously struck me as both too dry and too abstract. Not seeming to inspire or draw the young students to the study of geometry, this lesson really had not worked well for me.

After the African storytelling experience, I knew that a story was needed, so I began to formulate one that gave voice to each of the four concepts, anthropomorphizing them and associating each with a distinctive sound.

As I told the story the first time, I noticed the children instantly caught on and began to use the sounds themselves. When I would get to a certain point in the tale, they added the sound. To me, this meant that the story was working.

Since that time, I have told this story many times. It is a wonderful, good-humored tale that really engages both children and adult listeners. It is also a lot of fun to tell as I go through my sound repertoire. Most importantly, it works; through it, children get interested in the four fundamental concepts and acquire a basic understanding of each one.

This story associates each of the four geometric concepts with its own corresponding unique sound that aims to be onomatopoetic. I do not know exactly how to write these sounds, so I will try to describe them. Of course, you could invent corresponding sounds of your own.

Whenever I mention the point, I make a sound by pursing my lips and blowing out with a kind of /p/ sound. For the lack of a better way of writing it, I have spelled this *pchew*.

Whenever I mention the second fundamental concept, the line, I partially close my mouth and make a sound that seems to combine a whistle and the beginning of the word zoom. I have spelled this *zyoo*.

The third fundamental idea is the surface. This is the easiest sound to describe. I close my mouth and hum loudly, which I spell *humm*.

The final fundamental concept is that of the solid. To demonstrate the solid, I extend my hands in front of me, palms down, and make a motion toward the floor. At the same time, I make a sound like a grunting version of "huh." I spell this sound *huunh*.

Source: *The Point, Line, Surface, and Solid* is a completely original story, which I wrote.

Story

It is told that long ago, when geometric shapes made sounds and talked like people, there came a time when the points were all around. All there were, in every place, were points. Pchew. Pchew. Pchew, pchew, pchew. Points: pchew, pchew. They were everywhere. Pchew, pchew. They were so small you couldn't see them. Pchew, pchew. They were all around, and that's all there was. Point, pchew. Point, pchew.

Now, for some reason, sometimes, some of the points bumped into each other, Pchew-pchew. Pchew-pchew. Probably because points—pchew—are invisible. And then two or three points—pchew—might stick to each other, and maybe even more: pchew-pchew, pchew-pchew. They'd stick, and then maybe another point would stick on.

I really don't know why this happened. Maybe they liked

each other and were friendly. Maybe they were in love. But they would stick to each other, pchew, pchew.

Now, when they were stuck together—pchew, pchew—some of them looked around and said, "Zyoo. I'm a line. Zyoo." Many points make a line. "Zyoo, I'm a line." Then another group of points did it. "Zyoo, I'm a line, too." Before long, there were many lines—zyoo, zyoo, zyoo.

And the other points—pchew—were like, "We're just being points here, and all of a sudden you think, what, you're a line?" "Zyoo," answered the line. And the lines—zyoo—were long. The points looked around and they were still points—pchew—everywhere, but there were also more and more lines—zyoo. They were everywhere—zyoo—lines.

Now, for some reason, some of the lines—zyoo—sometimes bumped into each other—zyoo, zyoo. Zyoo, zyoo. Probably because lines—zyoo—are invisible. And when they'd bump into each other, sometimes they'd stick—zyoo, zyoo, zyoo. Maybe two or three or even more lines would stick together—zyoo, zyoo. And when they did that, they looked at each other and said "Humm. We're a surface. Humm. Many lines make a surface. Humm."

I really don't know why this happened. Maybe they liked each other and were friendly. Maybe they were in love. So, they would stick to each other—humm, humm.

The points were looking at this and thinking, "We were just points—pchew—here a little while ago." And the lines thought, "We're just being lines—zyoo—here, and all of a sudden you think, what, you're a surface?"

"Humm, we're a surface. Humm." Now many of the surfaces were flat, though some were curved and some were twisted, but they were all surfaces.

So now, there were points—pchew; lines—zyoo; and surfaces—humm.

Then some of the surfaces began to bump into each other, probably because surfaces—humm—are invisible, and sometimes they'd stick—humm, humm. Maybe two or three or even more surfaces would stick together—humm, humm, humm.

Then many of them stuck, and many more, and suddenly, they looked around and they went "Huunh! Solid. We're solids." And everyone could see them suddenly, because they were solid. They were visible. Many surfaces made a solid. "Huunh! Solid."

I really don't know why this happened. Maybe they liked each other and were friendly. Maybe they were in love. They certainly would stick to each other—huunh! Solid!

And do you know what? Even to this day, they are still here, even now, all around us. There are points—pchew, pchew, pchew—in the corners. There are lines—zyoo, zyoo, zyoo. There are surfaces that are on the sides of things—humm, humm, humm. And anything that you can touch or hold or pick up or feel—huunh—is a solid.

How about that for a real story!

The Discovery of the Degree

Introduction

This mathematical story focuses upon the idea of the degree as a measurement for angles. It takes children back over 2,500 years, to ancient Babylon.

Babylon was the capital of a great empire in the fertile land between the rivers, called Mesopotamia. Its location was on the Euphrates River, in what is now Iraq. It was famous for its power, and for its learning, including astronomy, and for its famous hanging gardens, which are considered one of the Seven Wonders of the Ancient World.

It is known that astronomy in Babylon has a history that goes back at least 3,800 years. According to David Darling (n.d.), the early work of the ancient astronomers of Babylon "centers mainly on the problem of establishing an accurate calendar" (para. 1). In the story of *The Discovery of the Degree*, it is suggested that the work of defining that calendar led to the use of astronomic measurements to measure angles.

The Discovery of the Degree tells how, when, and where the division of the circle into 360 parts may have originated. Photogrammetrist David Wallis verifies the Babylonian origin. In 1936, a clay tablet was excavated … some 350km from the ancient city of Babylon, The text provided confirmation that the Babylonians measured angles using the figure of 360 to form a circle (2005).

Lendering (2015) offers the thought that "The astronomers of Assyria and Babylonia, usually called Chaldeans, are the fathers of science—or at least of the scientific method…" (para. 3).

This story is interesting and appealing to the children. It is amazing to them that these ancient people accomplished so very much. It is usually offered to them in the second year of lower elementary while studying angles, at the beginning of angle measurement. It is a curriculum story as well as an origin story.

Source: *The Discovery of the Degree* is an original story based on concepts in Montessori geometry and on many outside sources.

Story

Very many years ago, there lived an ancient people called the *Babylonians*.

I want to take you to their wonderful city that is so very, very far from here. It is a great distance from here in two ways: it's far away in space and far away in time. It's a long way that we have to go, in distance, but we also have to go back about 2,500 years in time to get back to this beautiful, incredible city. Let's see where it is.

Show the Persian Gulf region on a globe.

If we take our globe and we look to this area right here, there is a great body of water called the Persian Gulf. Right above this body of water, here are two great and wonderful rivers. One of those rivers is called the Tigris and the other, the Euphrates. There on the Euphrates River, lay a city the like of which had never been seen before. Two thousand five hundred years ago, this city, under its ruler Nebuchadnezzar, was at its great peak.

Show a picture of the Ishtar Gate.

Babylon is the name of this city, and it's called Babylon—from *Babel*, which meant the gate, because it had a great and wonderful gate, which I'll show you a picture of. This is its gate, and there were several gates, but this is the famed Ishtar Gate that gave its name to the city. *Babylon* means "The City of the Gate," and this gate that you see was covered with glazed tiles so beautiful that it's said that from a distance, the outside of the city gleamed in the sun and people could see it from miles away as the sun reflected off the glazed tiles.

Here's a map of the Babylonian Empire from a very long time ago, about 2,500 to 2,600 years ago. It will let you see where it is. There is Babylon.

Show a map of the ancient Babylonian Empire.

Now Babylon was known for many things, and it had one of the most wonderful things of the ancient world. One wondrous thing that Babylon had was nowhere else. It is called The Hanging Gardens. Babylon was famous for gardens that hung on its walls and hung down from all over. Nebuchadnezzar is usually given credit for building these fabulous gardens that hung down, and they were one of the Seven Wonders of the Ancient World. Can you imagine coming along the river and seeing these gardens hanging, with the glazed tiles behind them? You would see the beauty of the blooming garden and you would smell its lovely scents. It was one of the most beautiful and amazing places to go.

In this city, this great city of Babylon, there was a class of people that were priests, and the priests were exclusively men, only men. In fact, only men of the wealthier classes were allowed to be priests. They were the only ones who were allowed to learn to read or write. It was limited just to them. So, not many people in Babylon could write, and not many people could read, but those few that did could achieve great things.

Now the priests held sessions of worship and astronomy high in a building like this, which was called a *ziggurat*. It looks a like a temple, or perhaps it may look to you like a pyramid. This is a ziggurat, and the ziggurat has a stairway that leads up to it. On the very top, there's a building; a house or a small hut where the priests went at night to observe the stars. From there, they could watch the heavens. The special priests who studied the heavens were called *temple astronomers*. They went to the very peak and looked through the top of that building to observe the stars.

Show a picture of an ancient Babylonian ziggurat.

Now, why did they do that? Because they were the great

scientists of their age. They were great astronomers. They studied the stars. These ziggurats stood high above the city. You must understand that in ancient times when it became dark at night, the city was dark—there were no streetlights. There were no competing lights, so they could go high up above the city, above anybody's oil lamps, and they could see the stars in all their splendor.

Now, the temple astronomers went high up into the ziggurat and there, they would look up at the stars, and they noticed over the course of years that the stars seemed to move around in the sky every night. But, over the course of time, they seemed to follow a pattern. It was as if the stars circled the Earth—as if the Earth stood still. Now, we know that's not what happened. To the temple astronomers, it was as if the Earth stood still and the stars seemed to go around in a great circle, around a single star that's relatively unmoving at the very center. This polar star was at the center of their observation.

Now, the way they wrote in those days was into wet clay. So, they decided to keep a record, and we know that they kept these records because they've been found. Today, they are called the *Astronomical Diaries*.

These priests decided to keep a record in the clay of what happened with the movement of the stars, and that meant that they had to keep a damp cloth on the clay for an entire year so that they could continue to mark it. They marked the clay with a wedge-shape tool. This kind of writing is called *cuneiform*, which goes back to a word that means "a wedge." And that's what they used to make their marks in the clay.

By writing down their observations, they found out that over the course of a year, the stars appear to move in a great circle all around. They seemed to move about the same amount every day. They studied this and studied this.

Now, the Babylonians had a number system that was based on sixty. There were special sacred numbers to the Babylonians: six, sixty, and 360, because that's sixty taken six times. So, as they watched the movement of the stars, it seemed quite logical that it would take exactly 360 days for the stars to make their traverse around the Earth, which is what they thought was happening. Now we know that it was close, but the stars took a few more days than 360. Because that didn't quite fit with their sacred number, they defined a year as 360 days—and they gave five extra days over to celebration and religious holidays; they didn't count those five as part of the year. Otherwise, they thought, there had to be a miscalculation. Since six sixties had been given by the gods, it had to be the right measurement, and that's what they used. In fact, they were extremely accurate!

The passage that they marked on their chart each day was one of the 360 markings that they had for the day—1/360th as it went around and around. Do you know what gift the Babylonians gave us by doing that? They gave us a way that we still use today to measure angles.

We measure angles by the method that the Babylonians used to measure the stars. The gift of the Babylon priests who looked through the hole at the top of the ziggurat was the way we measure our angles.

Today, I have with me something that we call a protractor, which is a measuring tool for angles. When I look right at the very center of it, I imagine the spot where the priests sat. Now, I can't see through this metal, but I imagine that I can. I imagine that I am priest, and I can look right up and see through the metal and see a whole circle of movement above me. That measurement of the circle, as it goes around and around, has numbers that could represent days, but instead of days, we call each mark a degree. It actually goes back in etymology to mean a step.

Display a metal protractor.

When we write with the protractor, we will make a little circle, which we're going to make in red to start with to bring everyone's attention to it. That little red circle reminds us of the path that the Babylonians saw in the stars. That little circle is a reminder of the gift from the past that we've received from the Babylonians. The gift of the degree. And when we say *degrees*, I hope we'll remember the Babylonians and their priests high above that Ishtar Gate, high on top of the ziggurat, way up above the gardens hanging down but looking up at the stars far above them. They probably were not thinking of us 2,500 years later,

Draw a small red circle to indicate a degree.

but they gave a gift that lasted all that time, long after they were no longer here.

That's the story of *The Discovery of the Degree*, and that is how it is to this day.

The Love Story of the Lines

INTRODUCTION

I learned a rudimentary form of this story while I was a student in Montessori teacher training. At the time, I was amazed that such a truly corny story could be offered to us as a lesson that could be given to children! I was convinced that the story was boring and useless.

After graduating, and teaching in the classroom with children, I eventually came to the place in the geometry curriculum in which convergent, parallel, and divergent lines are introduced. That is the lesson with which this story is offered. With no other idea as to what to do, I simply went ahead and gave a cursory telling of the story.

Amazingly, the children loved it! The next time I did the lesson, I buffed up the story a bit, gave it a stronger performance, and they loved it even more.

I must admit that my initial reaction to this story was wrong. It really does work, and the children adore it.

The Love Story of the Lines is a curriculum story as well as an object story. It uses two interesting Montessori materials as essential elements. The first material is the set of Geometry Sticks with the corresponding Geometric Plane. These special sticks are available from a number of manufacturers. If, for some reason, you do not have this particular material, any set of sticks of equal length, such as smooth dowels about eight-to-ten inches long, would suffice. This story requires six of these sticks.

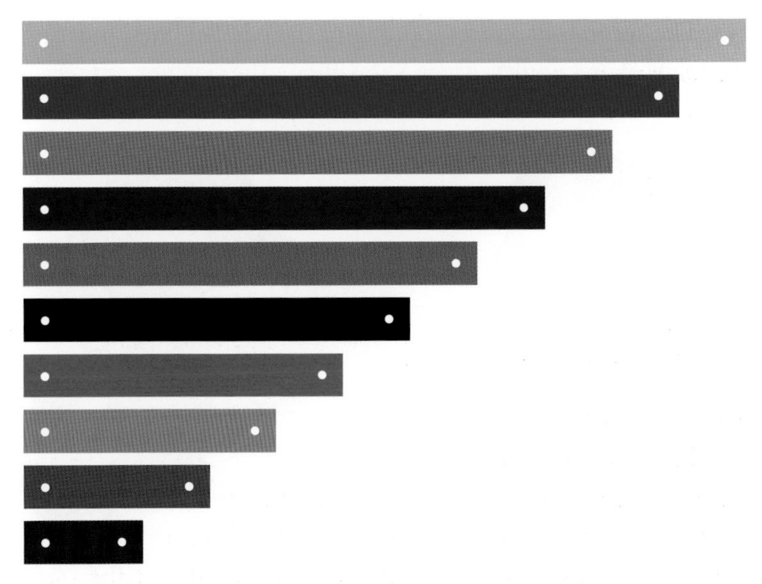

Figure 42. These are the Geometry Sticks.

The second requirement for this story is a set of six small dolls. These may be paper dolls or actual dolls. The dolls are arranged in three sets, each containing a boy and a girl, selected for the following attributes:

- The first set, to accompany the divergent lines, have sad faces.

Figure 43. The sad, divergent children.

- The second set, corresponding to the parallel lines, must have expressionless faces, showing neither joy nor sadness.

Figure 44. The neutral, parallel children.

- The final set, to pair with the convergent lines, should have joyful, happy faces.

Figure 45. The happy, convergent children.

In all other respects, the dolls should be alike.

This is to be a love story, so I keep the dolls in a special red, heart-shaped box, which is brought forth with a great show of reverence and rapturous expression. I tell the children that this will be a very sad story, at which time, I parody a sniffle and show a downhearted face. Perking up a bit, I tell them that there will then be a bit better part, though it will not be really happy. Lastly, I allow an expression of sugary-sweet joy to transform my face as I announce that the story will end with a romantic tale of true love.

This ostentatious and campy presentation of the story thoroughly captivates the children.

Source: *The Love Story of the Lines* is an original narrative presentation, based on a traditional Montessori model.

STORY

I want to tell you three stories today. A love story in three parts, really. It's a love story about the lines. The first part of the love story will probably make you sad, and maybe it will even make you cry. The second part of the love story will probably make you say "So what?" And, the third part of the love story will probably make you laugh with joy.

The first part is a story of moving apart. Then, there's a story of indifference. Finally, there's a story of true love. It's a beautiful set of stories that we keep in this red, heart-shaped box that reminds us that it's a story of love.

Bring out the two dolls wearing sad expressions.

It is told that long ago, there were two children. Here's one of them right here, and here's the other one. There were two children, and these two children were good friends.

Place two sticks down on the work surface, side by side and touching. As you complete this small section of the story, move the sticks into a "v" shape so that they remain touching at one end but move apart at the other end.

They lived by each other, and they played with each other. They held hands. They were such good friends. I'm going to put out these sticks to show a line along which these children could walk. It shows the direction of their pathway. Though their pathway started very close when the two were very close friends, as they walked along the path of their lives, it turned out that they moved apart from each other. Then they saw each other less.

And then it happened that they hardly saw each other at all. The sad news is that they never, ever met again. I'm sorry, but this makes me so sad, I may sniffle a bit. It's a story of moving apart. It's when you need the tissues. It's a very sad story because the children never see each other again.

Parody a sniffle and show a downhearted face.

Well, this is a very hard story to take, with all the sadness, but there will then be a bit better part. Perk up a bit with a small smile. Still, even this second part will not be really happy. Let's go ahead and look at that next story.

The next story also tells of two children—two different children. The story tells us that these two children also lived very close to one another. I will set out two sticks to show the path that they walked along, as well.

Place another two sticks in the work area. These two are to be parallel to each other, a few inches apart.

These two live close to one another, maybe only about a block away. They could be such good friends, except they don't know each other. Such good playmates they could be, except they never get to meet. They always live very close as they go down the path of their lives, but they go to two different schools. They live very close as they get older, but they get two different jobs. They live very close as they become adults, but they live in two different houses and never, ever know that each other even exists. They never meet. They never hear of each other. So this is a story of indifference. It's not quite so sad because they never get to meet, but still it's not happy.

But wait! There's a third pair of children that I want to tell you about, and this third pair, we'll put over here. Now, these two children do not live near each other at all. In fact, they live quite far apart, at a great distance. One child lives in the heart of a great city, and the other child lives in a small community many, many miles away.

Place two more sticks in the work area, this time in an upside-down "v" pattern.

But as time goes on, they move a little bit closer. Each family moved and they were a bit closer. The families move again, and then the two meet. They become friends, and they become even better friends. They hold hands. And then, they fall in love. Life is good because they get married in the end and everything is beautiful. These children have a happy life. A happy ending. And that is how it is to this day.

The first two children I talked about started very close together and the paths got wide apart. We say that their paths are *divergent*. These lines are divergent. That means they move apart. When the two children moved apart from each other, their lines *diverge*. That's the sad one, when we cried. When the lines diverged.

Now, the next two children, their paths were perfectly the same all the way through, and we can even measure that to be sure that the pathway is the same all the way, the same distance. They never meet, and they never will meet. Their paths, we say, are *parallel*. Parallel lines never meet. It's not that sad, but it's indifferent. It's as if they don't really care.

But the last two come together in the end, and our hearts overflow with joy when we hear about them. We're so happy for them. Their lines are said to be *convergent*. That means that they come together. As you can see, they do come together. Divergent lines move apart. Parallel lines never meet. Convergent lines come together.

These are three love stories. The love stories of the lines. The first story tells of leaving, when the children left each other. It was sad that they diverged.

The second part is a story of indifference, when the children never even knew each other and never met. Their lives were parallel.

The third part told the story of true love. In this happy story, children came together. They met and converged.

Now, how about that for a real story!

The Family Gallery

Introduction

The Family Gallery is a curriculum story and, at the same time, an object story. The story is about the quadrilaterals. In geometry, quadrilaterals are four-sided figures. This story is told and presented toward the end of the children's study of the quadrilaterals. Before the children are ready for this story, they should already know the names of all of the quadrilaterals as well as their parts.

What this story will introduce is the relationships between the quadrilaterals.

There are seven possible quadrilaterals: the common quadrilateral, the trapezoid, the kite, the parallelogram, the rhombus, the rectangle, and the square. One of the points of the story is to make it clear that these are the only possible quadrilaterals.

The common quadrilateral is sometimes called a trapezium

All of the quadrilaterals are related in special ways. This story makes use of the image of a family gallery to make this point. The family gallery is a collection of photographs or paintings of family members, often going back many generations. In this story, the common quadrilateral is portrayed as the ancestor of all of the quadrilaterals, the founder of the family. At the end of the story, we meet the square, the most modern quadrilateral, which we will introduce as the most perfect quadrilateral.

In presenting this story, you will need a set of all seven quadrilaterals. These can be made from wooden sticks. In the Montessori elementary classroom, the Geometry Sticks material (as shown in Figure 42, (p. 215) is ideal for this purpose. The figures may also be cut out of blue card stock.

You will also need seven labels with the names of the seven quadrilaterals written on them. Remember that these are:

- the common quadrilateral [*The common quadrilateral is a quadrilateral with no parallel sides, and which lacks adjacent equal sides.*]
- the trapezoid [*The trapezoid is a quadrilateral with a pair of opposite equal sides.*]
- the kite [*The kite is a quadrilateral with two sets of equal adjacent sides.*]
- the parallelogram [*The parallelogram is a quadrilateral with two pairs of opposite parallel sides.*]
- the rhombus [*The rhombus is an equilateral quadrilateral.*]

- the rectangle [*The rectangle is a quadrilateral with four right angles and opposite parallel sides.*]
- the square [*The square is an equilateral quadrilateral with four right angles and opposite parallel sides. It is presented here as the most perfect quadrilateral.*]

Finally, you will need eight cards with arrows drawn on them. These are placed to show relationships.

Speaking very strictly, this may not really be a story. Perhaps it is a narrative including actions and objects. However, the presentation is offered in a story-like manner and the children perceive it as a story, so I have included it here. I do hope that you enjoy it and that you use it. The children really do like it.

Source: *The Family Gallery* is based on a traditional Montessori presentation, which I have enlarged to include more narrative elements.

STORY

Many people like to go to art galleries. I like to go to art galleries, and I'm going to talk today about a special kind of gallery. Not just a regular art gallery, but a family gallery where you can go and see pictures of many, many people who are all with one family.

Sometimes, I see these in people's homes. You go to their house and there on the wall is a picture of grandma and grandpa, or cousins, and sometimes there is a great-grandparent. In some families, there might even be paintings of people from so long ago, before cameras were even invented!

Sometimes, I visit people's homes and they have their family pictures along a stairway so as you go up the stairs, you can go back in time. As you're climbing the stairs, you can look at all of the people who are their relatives.

Occasionally, friends have these pictures in a scrapbook so that as you go through the book, you're traveling through time. They might tell you, "Here's a picture of my grandfather, and oh! This is my grandmother by her old car, which was new in those days." Then they might find an even older picture and tell you that it is their great-grandmother. Maybe their book goes even farther back that that. That is a family gallery.

I have some exciting news for you. This is something that you probably do not know. The quadrilaterals have a family, too. Today, we're going to build their family gallery so that they can have a portrait gallery of their family just like you might have a portrait gallery of your family. Now, the quadrilaterals will have the same thing.

It is always good to start your family gallery with your earliest known ancestor, who would be the oldest person you can find in your family. This is the person who was your grandparent's great-great-great grandmother. Something like that.

It might be the first one to settle in this area, the oldest one. Well, the oldest and simplest of all the quadrilaterals is the *common quadrilateral*, so let's start the gallery with the common quadrilateral.

Set the common quadrilateral, and its label, out in the work area.

There he is, in all his simplicity. The common quadrilateral is so simple, there's nothing special about him at all. He has nothing but four sides going for him. He has four sides and that's it. There is nothing else worth mentioning.

He is the ancestor of all the other quadrilaterals, so that is very special. The common quadrilateral is the most primitive of the whole quadrilateral family and the ancestor of them all.

Set out two arrows, both pointing down and away from the common quadrilateral, and diverging from each other, as in Figure 46.

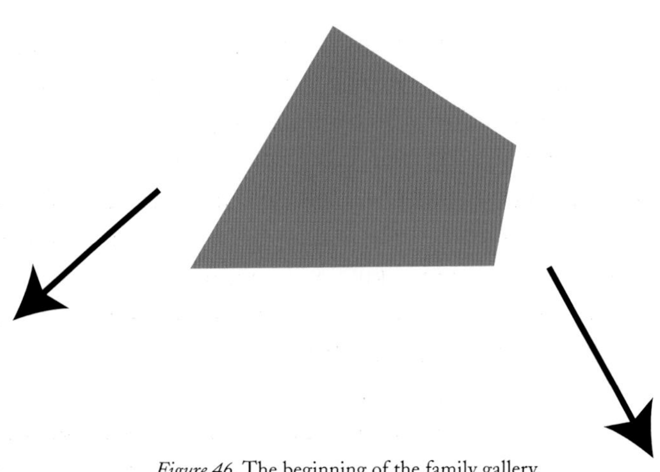

Figure 46. The beginning of the family gallery.

The common quadrilateral founded two branches of the quadrilateral family; we will show these two branches with some more arrows, so that we can set out one branch and then the other. This side of the family on the left is the *trapezoid* branch, so let's put out a trapezoid over here. This trapezoid shape stands for all possible trapezoids.

Show the trapezoid shape, and then place it, with its label, beneath and to the left of the common quadrilateral.

The trapezoid does have something special going for it—it is a quadrilateral like the common quadrilateral so, of course, it has four sides. We can see that the trapezoid has something extra: it has opposite parallel sides, two of them. Two parallel sides—isn't that great? That makes it special! It has improved from the common quadrilateral in this one special way.

The common quadrilateral has another member of its family. It starts another branch over there, on the right, that we call the *kite* branch.

Place a kite shape, with its label, beneath and to the right of the common quadrilateral.

This kite shape stands for all possible kites. Kites are members of the quadrilateral family, so they are quadrilaterals with four sides. But, there is something special about the kite. The kite is special because it has adjacent equal sides, but nothing is parallel. Yet, there are pairs of sides next to each other that are equal in length.

Look at the difference between the two branches of the family. They are like two brothers or sisters. The kites have equal sides; and over there on their branch, we see that the trapezoids have parallel sides. This is turning into an interesting family.

Place an arrow pointing down from the trapezoid

Let's come back to the trapezoid side, because the trapezoid has a descendant as well. There is a specialized, more perfect descendant, and that is the *parallelogram*. This parallelogram stands for all possible parallelograms. Oh, how special!

Set a parallelogram, and its label, at the end of the arrow pointing down from the trapezoid.

Parallelograms are still members of the quadrilateral family, so they are also quadrilaterals, with four sides. The special part is that the parallelogram is a kind of a trapezoid that has not just one pair of parallel sides, but two pairs of parallel sides. It is like the trapezoid has been raised to a higher level and it has. It's a perfected, improved trapezoid.

Not all our families show improvement every generation, but this one does. So, the parallelogram is an improved trapezoid. It has two pairs of parallel sides, instead of only one.

Now let's go back here to the kite side. We can see that there is an improved version of the kite as well. The kite has one descendant: the *rhombus*. Naturally, the rhombus is a quadrilateral, but also the rhombus is a kind of a kite. A kite with four equal sides. Remember that the kite has two pair of equal adjacent sides, but what an improvement the rhombus has made!

Set down an arrow pointing down from the kite, and at its end, place a rhombus with its label.

Look at that rhombus; it has all four sides equal. It is equilateral. So, the rhombus is a specialized kind of an equilateral kite. This rhombus stands for all possible rhombi.

Look at the family tree that we have built so far. It's as if the parallelogram and the rhombus are cousins.

We're going to learn something else about the rhombus in just a minute, though, some sort of internal family story. It's going to be interesting that we're going to find out something about that family. First, let's look at the parallelogram here and find out what its descendant or descendants are.

The parallelogram has a descendant that is a specialized trapezoid and a specialized parallelogram. It is called the rectangle. So let's put out the rectangle right here. The rectangle belongs to the quadrilateral family, and to the trapezoids, and to the parallelograms, but it also has right angles. So not only does the rectangle have opposite parallel sides, but it also adds that one more important feature: it has right angles, four of them.

Set out an arrow pointing down from the parallelogram, and place a rectangle with its label at its end.

In this large family, and this happens in many families, something interesting happened. To show that, I'm going to draw a line right here between the parallelogram and the rhombus. That is because the rhombus also has the parallelogram for a parent. We know that one parent is the kite. Now we can see that the other one is the parallelogram. That means that the rhombus is not only a specialized kite, but it crossed over from the parallelogram, from its cousin, from the other side of the family. That is a good thing in many ways. We just have to remember that the rhombus belongs a little to the parallelogram side of the family, so it's a kind of parallelogram, and it also belongs a little to the kite side of the family, so it's a kind of kite. Don't forget!

Draw an imaginary line with your finger.

Still, the quadrilateral family gallery is not complete yet, because at the end of the entire family lies true perfection. The genuine purity that lies at the end of the entire family is the square. This square stands for all possible squares.

Set down two final arrows, pointing down from the entire family tree. One is from the rectangle and one from the rhombus. Arrange them so that they converge. At the end of the arrows, place the square with its label, so that the entire array looks like Figure 47.

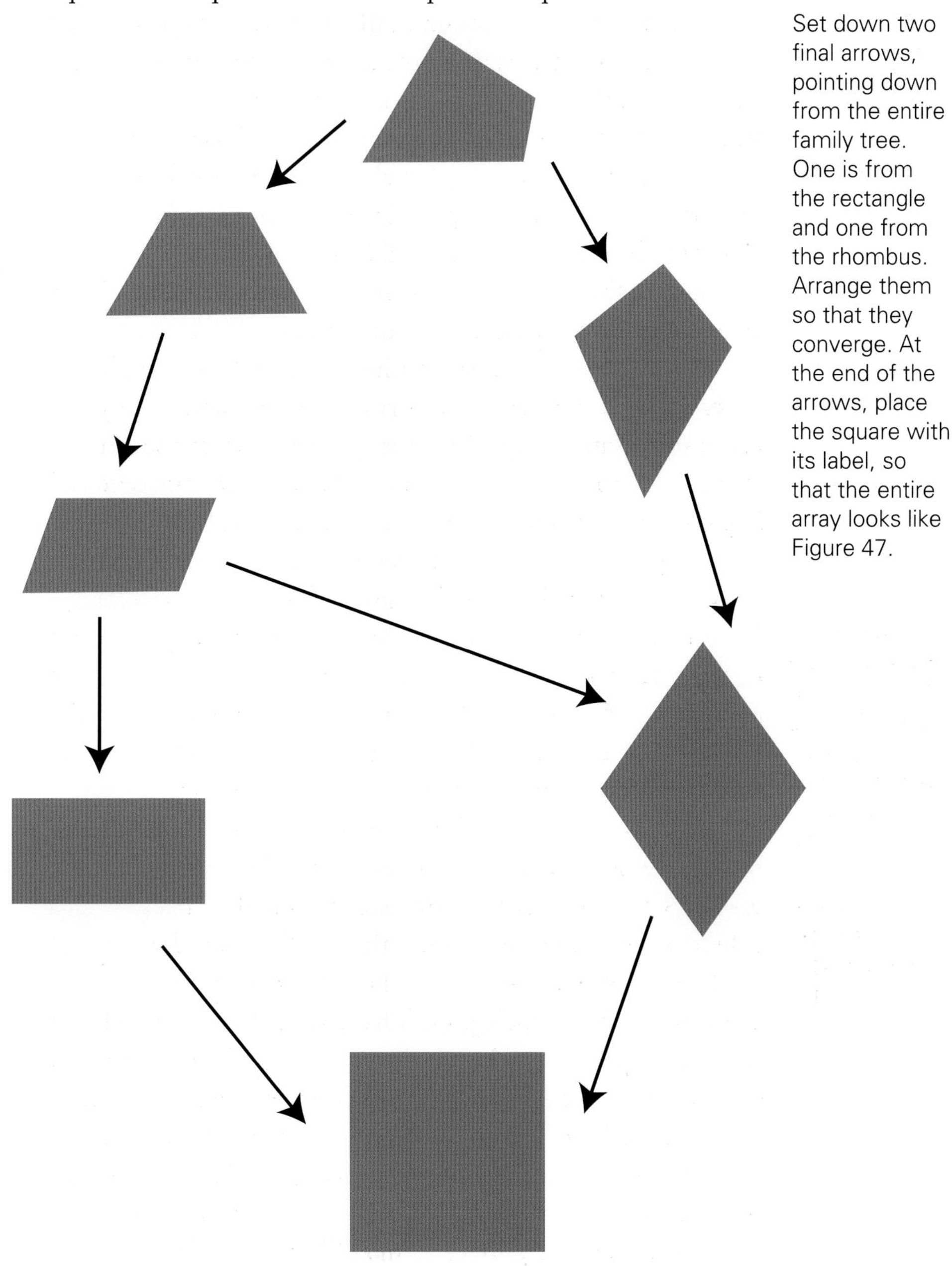

Figure 47. The complete family gallery.

What makes the square so perfect? The square is a rectangle that is perfected by having all four sides equal. It is the equilateral rectangle.

But wait! The square is also a rhombus that is perfected by having four right angles. It is an equiangular rhombus.

It is both equilateral and equiangular. It is the only quadrilateral that can say that about itself. All so equal!

The square brings both branches of the family together. The square is the ultimate end of the family gallery. It is the most perfect of all of the quadrilateral figures.

Now, we see that there are exactly seven quadrilaterals. In truth, there are only seven possible quadrilaterals that can possibly exist. All quadrilaterals must find a place in this family tree somewhere. This is the family gallery of the quadrilaterals. It's a beautiful family, starting with the common quadrilateral and ending with the square.

The Story of Tan

Figure 48. The complete Tangrams.

Introduction

The Tangrams represent a traditional mathematical puzzle that is said to have its origins in ancient China. It is believed that they may have originated in the Song Dynasty somewhere around the year 1000 CE.

The puzzle set consists of seven precise geometric pieces that can be made of metal, wood, heavy card stock, or other material. In the Montessori classroom, they are related to a special metal material, which shows the square divided by successive diagonals. This metal material is colored red and is based upon a ten-centimeter square. As a result, in Montessori classes, the Tangram pieces are also colored red, and when assembled, make a perfect ten-centimeter square.

Mathematically, it makes no difference what color is used—red or any color. The Tangrams may also be of any size. It is not necessary that they make an exact ten-centimeter square. These are simply matters of tradition.

There are many available books and puzzles for the Tangrams. They are fascinating and can be used for much more than making a square. Try making a standing crane, an elderly woman carrying a sack on her back, or a child crawling across the floor.

Source: *The Story of Tan* is an original story based on folktales.

STORY

Far, far away and long, long ago in ancient China, there once lived a poor man whose name was Tan. Now, Tan was a potter—he worked with clay. It so happens that next to his small hut, there was a flowing stream with fresh water. On the bank of the stream was a rich source of clay so that Tan could go in and dig and dig and bring out clay.

Now, that clay was not ready to be made into anything. First, he had to spread it out and let it dry, because when he dug it up, it would be wet and sticky. Next, he would have to let it dry, and then he would have to grind it very fine and pound it. When he did that, he'd find every little pebble, or any part of a root, or any sort of an insect, or anything that might be in the clay. Then he'd sift it with a big bamboo sifter so that a powder came out that was pure white. Finally, he would take that clay and mix it again with clear, filtered water, and then his clay was ready to work with.

Only after all of that work was Tan ready to work with his clay, but he was usually exhausted by that time. Very, very tired from having done all this work, he would require quite a bit of rest before he could go to the next thing, which was to make something from his clay.

Now, Tan didn't make just anything from his clay. Most potters made pots for different things, but Tan made beautiful, exquisite flat tiles, like plates. Then he would take these flat tiles to his kiln.

Now a kiln is a place like a furnace that gets very, very, very hot, an oven where people bake clay so it becomes hard. But in order to have a kiln, you need to have something to burn to make it hot. So, Tan would have to go into the forest and cut wood. It would take him many days to cut the wood. Then, Tan would come back to his hut with the wood and bury it underground, where he would burn it without the presence of air. Burning it without air turned it into charcoal. That's how charcoal was made. Then, Tan would open up the fire pit and take out all the charcoal that he had made. Finally, he put the charcoal into the kiln so that he could burn it, because that makes a very hot heat, hot enough to properly fire his clay.

But, still he wasn't done! Tan did one more thing. He made a special glaze, something that he could paint onto the surface of his plates to make them beautiful. Before he painted them, he would fire the clay once by putting his beautiful tiles into the kiln, adding the charcoal, and starting the fire. Once it started burning, Tan would cover everything up, and then he'd go and make his glaze. To do that, he would have to grind some stones that produced a red color very, very fine. These special stones had a red color in them, and when he ground them, they would become a vibrant red powder. When the first firing was done, Tan would mix that red powder with certain liquids and spread it on top of his tiles before firing them one more time. The glaze would melt into a glistening, deep, beautiful red color for which Tan was famous.

This was absolutely backbreaking work for poor Tan. Think of all he had to do. He had to dig the clay out from the side of the stream. He had to clean it and dry it and do all that work. He had to build the kiln. He had to make the clay plates. Then he had to go find the trees and make the charcoal. Then he had to fire the kiln with the charcoal in it while he found the special stones that made the glaze that he wanted to use. He had to grind the stones and mix his glaze, and then finally he would glaze the pot and fire it one more time. So much work for his beautiful red tiles.

Tan was always tired. He was always very tired. Then, when he sold his pieces, his beautiful tiles, he often got almost no money at all. Sometimes, people would just give him a handful of rice, which he liked. Or, they might give him a piece of fish or meat, which he liked. Or maybe some vegetables, which he also liked. Or even beans. And he needed all those things too. And they were good.

One day, in the emperor's palace, the emperor of all China made a proclamation. He said, "I will give a reward to he who comes forth with the greatest piece of pottery in the whole kingdom. Send this word to all potters throughout all of China that that piece which is most beautiful will receive a wonderful reward."

When the word reached the village where Tan lived, you can imagine how excited he was. He went to the mine and began to dig clay. He got the finest, purest, whitest, most perfect clay that he could find. He ground it to the smallest powder so that it was smooth. He screened it so that it was as clean as possible. He was more careful than he had ever been in his life. He got the finest charcoal, free of any impurity. For the glaze, he was extremely careful that it was perfectly smooth, beautiful, and deeply red. Then, Tan proceeded to make the finest square plate he had ever made. His work was simple. But it was said that one could look deep inside the glaze and it was like looking all the way to the center of the Earth, it was so beautiful. He knew he had something of great beauty. It was done. He showed it to his neighbors and all were in awe, all were amazed at the perfection by the square piece that Tan had created, its beauty combined with its simplicity.

Tan took his piece of pottery, his beautiful red square tile, and he began to walk, carrying his square in his hand. He started to walk all the way to the capital, to the palace of the emperor. It was a long walk, and as he walked, over the course of time, he began to think, "Wouldn't it be wonderful if I could win the reward? Wouldn't it be amazing? It would make me so happy to win this reward. Perhaps, the emperor would be kind enough to give me a pig. What a reward that would be! I could eat for a month. It would be wonderful." And he thought about the wonder of having a pig of his own.

As he walked a few more miles, Tan thought, "What if I were to receive a copper piece? With a copper piece, I could buy a pig and I could even buy vegetables, I could have so many things; a copper piece would be a wonderful gift from the emperor to me." And Tan dreamed about life.

As he walked further and further, Tan began to think, "What if he would give me a silver piece? With a piece of silver, I could hire a boy to help me and I would not have to dig that heavy clay every time I make anything. I would have a boy to work with me. And I could buy a pig. And I could have vegetables. Oh, this would be wonderful. This would be so wonderful."

Tan still walked along. As he walked another few miles, suddenly, a new idea hit him, "What if the emperor were to give me a piece of gold? What if I were to get a gold piece from the emperor? I could have a boy to help me, I could have a pig, and I could have vegetables. I could even build a new house!" Without thinking, he threw his hands up in joy. When he did, his plate flew up, then fell down, and hit the ground—SMASH—shattering into seven pieces. Tan looked at the ground and he saw his broken plate, and he fell to his knees and wept. His beautiful plate had been shattered into seven pieces.

Figure 49. These are the Tangram pieces.

He began to try to put it together. And as he brought the pieces together, he saw a crane standing tall, and he moved the pieces in another way and he saw an elderly woman carrying a sack on her back. He moved the pieces in still another way, and he saw a child crawling across the floor.

Tan saw many other pictures as he moved the pieces back and forth. As he looked at them, he saw these seven pieces had become items of wonder. They were no longer just a beautiful plate. Now, Tan couldn't fit them all back together into a perfect square again, but he didn't mind this because what he'd seen was so beautiful.

Tan gathered up his seven pieces, and continued on his way. When he reached the emperor's palace, he told the guard, "I'm here to enter the contest for the greatest piece of pottery in the kingdom." The guard stared at him and said, "Peasant, where is your pottery?"

Tan said, "Right there," and showed him the seven broken pieces in his hand. Then the guard became angry and shouted, "Be gone. You cannot come into the presence of the emperor carrying broken pieces of pottery." But Tan dropped to his knees and spread the seven pieces out, and when he did that, he began to move them and the guard looked at them, and he saw a crane standing tall. He saw an elderly woman carrying a sack on her back. He saw a child crawling across the floor. He saw many other pictures as he moved the pieces back and forth.

And the guard was amazed and entranced, for he saw these seven pieces had become items of wonder and he said, "Surely, this is a gift that all must see. Please bring it in to the emperor."

As he entered the throne room, Tan dropped to his knees, for that's how one approached the emperor. He crawled in, holding his broken pieces in front of him. When he reached the emperor, he said, "Oh Mighty Emperor, I have brought an entry into the contest for the greatest piece of pottery in the kingdom." Then the emperor said, "Where is the pottery then, for what you hold is nothing but broken shards."

Tan replied, "Oh Great One, this is my entry. Please look at what it can do." And he spread the pieces out on the floor and began to move them around.

As he did, the emperor saw a crane standing tall. He saw an elderly woman carrying a sack on her back. Then he saw a child crawling across the floor. He saw many other pictures as Tan moved the pieces back and forth. The emperor was amazed and entranced, for he saw these seven pieces had become items of wonder. Then, the emperor noticed that the Sun had risen and fallen, and an entire day had passed in his great fascination.

The emperor let Tan rise to his feet and he said, "Tan, surely you have brought the greatest piece of pottery in my kingdom. You have brought the most wondrous thing I have ever seen, for in these seven pieces, I see hundreds of pictures. I see wonderful things. Can we put it back together in a square again?" And Tan replied, "Oh Great One, I have yet to solve that problem, but I shall work on it." And he did.

The emperor let Tan go home, saying, "You may now go home, Tan, and return to your village and take this pig as a gift." Tan was so grateful. Then the emperor said, "And take this coin of copper as a gift." Tan couldn't believe his great fortune. Then the emperor said, "Tan, you may also take this silver coin as a gift." Tan was amazed at the magnificence of his great fortune. Finally, the emperor brought out a small sack with golden coins within it and said, "And please take this sack with many golden coins." Tan was able to live happily from that time on, and left for us this wonderful gift from the past, which we call the Tangrams, in his honor.

We shall now see if anyone here can put the seven pieces of the Tangrams together and do what Tan tried to do and make them into one square. That shall be our challenge.

And that's the end of that!

The Clubs for the Shapes

INTRODUCTION

At some point in elementary school, children will study the three forms of geometric equality: congruence, similarity, and equivalence. Although these three notions are essential, they are often presented in such a way as to be bone-dry and very hard to assimilate. Too many adults with whom I have spoken have unpleasant memories of stiflingly boring geometry lessons, often including these three concepts. The good news is that the imagination involved in stories can bring interest and enthusiasm to almost anything, including basic geometric concepts like these.

I wrote this curriculum story to add excitement and fun to an area that really needed it. The story humanizes the triangles and other figures using anthropomorphism. They speak among themselves and form three special clubs.

I have used this story, like many others, before the technical lesson. Thus, it is important that while the tale is fanciful, it also contains geometrical truths. The children love this yarn because of the way that it imbues geometric forms with human qualities.

Source: *The Clubs for the Shapes* is an entirely original story, which I wrote.

STORY

It is told that long ago, the triangles were all gathered together in a big room. They were sitting around, thinking of things, and talking, when one of them—I think it was probably an equilateral triangle—looked around and said, "You know, we need a special club here. We need a special group. There are too many different kinds of triangles that are allowed in here, all in the same room. I think we need to have a more exclusive group, where we could have folks just like us—only triangles that look exactly like I do."

The other equilateral triangles, the ones that were exactly the same, thought that was a good idea. "Maybe that's what we need. A club for the other triangles that are just exactly like us." And the first triangle—now I'm sure it was an equilateral triangle—said, "And I mean exactly the same. Not just the same shape, but the exact same size. That's what I want. Just like me!"

So, that is precisely what they did. They formed a club, and they called it *The Congruent Club.* Congruent means "exactly the same." The triangles had to be exactly the same size and exactly the same shape to get into this Congruent Club. Then they would be together. Just with others that were exactly the same. These triangles loved it.

Eventually, the word got out among all the other shapes—the circles, hexagons, squares, and all the rest. All of the other shapes eventually heard that the equilateral triangles had started a Congruent Club, and before long, the circles formed their own Congruent Club. You had to be a circle, of course, and exactly the same-sized circle. Other shapes were not congruent, so they could not join.

Then the hexagons got in on it. They wanted a Congruent Club of their own. Of course, none of the triangles could join, because you had to be exactly the same, which meant a hexagon with the same exact size and shape. No triangles were welcome.

I think some of the others, like the squares, were doing it, and the pentagons, too. It was all over the place. Many other shapes made their own Congruent Clubs. It was all about being congruent. Exactly the same size and exactly the same shape. They were the only ones that could call themselves congruent. If they weren't exactly the same size and exactly the same shape, then they couldn't call themselves congruent. That left a lot of other shapes and sizes out.

So some of the other triangles were standing around outside the Congruent Club, thinking about being left out and complaining, and another one—I think that it was an isosceles triangle—looked around and said, "Maybe we need a club for those of us who are the same shape. Who cares if we are the same size or not? All the isosceles triangles can join this club if they're the same shape as I am. But, they can be bigger or smaller. Let's call this the Similar Club. That's right, we'll make a club just for those that are the same shape, but they can be bigger or they can be smaller. Who cares? Size doesn't matter."

So, that club got started, too. All sorts of triangles could belong to the Similar Club as long as they were the exact same shape, and they could be many different sizes. Similar.

Word got out about this, too. This always happens! Before long, all of the other shapes formed their own Similar Clubs. There was even one for some special scalene triangles that all had the same shape. I heard that even some trapezoids formed a Similar Club, but that might be wrong. Of course, the rule was always same shape, but any size; then you were similar. Exactly the same shape, but any size.

Well, you probably know that circles tend to be very clever. Before long, some of them noticed something. They were all similar. Every single circle in the whole world was similar. They thought "This is great; we can have a club of every single circle in the world. They all can join this one. It's open to all." Because they were all the same shape. Different sizes, but they were all circles.

Now, squares aren't quite as quick at thinking as circles, but they finally figured it out, too. Every single square in the world could join the Similar Club of squares. What a great club!

Some of the others had a little more trouble, like the ellipses, because they were different, so they had to have different similar clubs for different ellipses. That was tough for them because they were always feeling like something left out.

Then, the other polygons got in on it, but, oh—it got all over the place, and there were still some that were left out. They weren't able to join the Congruent Club because they all weren't exactly, *exactly* the same size and exactly, *exactly* the same shape. They also couldn't join the Similar Club because they weren't all exactly the same shape.

Finally, somebody else—and I know for sure that this was a scalene triangle, one with obtuse angles who was particularly artistic—came up with a new idea: "Let's get a club for anybody that's the same size. We'll make it open to circles, squares, and triangles. I don't care what their shape is—if they're the same size they can join. They could be any shape. Even the ellipses can join, if they're the same size"

One of the trapezoids who was lounging around spoke up, "Even the common quadrilaterals? Would we let them in, too?"

"Yes, they can join, too, as long as they're the same size," said the scalene triangle. "We'll call it equivalent, because that comes from a word that means equal value and we think that we all have equal value." So, that got started up, too, and they called it the Equivalent Club.

Now, that was a wide-open club, open to everybody, so long as they were the same size. The Equivalent Club. Same size—who cares what your shape is? You are welcome in here; this is open to anybody. You have to be the same size, but you can be any shape you like.

Even the ones that are a little bit snooty, like the square and the equilateral triangle, and especially the circle, can join, too. Even though they sometimes get up on their high horses because they think they're so perfect. But they can join, too. It is open to everyone, so long as they have the same size.

Now, those clubs are still here with us today. Those three groups are still around, believe it or not.

Congruent shapes are exactly the same size and exactly the same shape. They are exactly alike. They have to be perfectly identical. Then, they are congruent.

Similar shapes have exactly the same shape, but they can have different sizes. Their shapes have to be perfectly identical, but size doesn't matter. Then, they are similar.

And equivalents are still around, too. They can have any shape at all, so long as they're the same size. Don't forget, their sizes have to be just the same, but shape doesn't matter. Then, they can be equivalent.

And ever since then, that is the way it has been. Now, wasn't that a good idea to form those three clubs?

The Very Thirsty Man

INTRODUCTION

The Very Thirsty Man embeds a strange mathematical problem within the framework of a curriculum story. Because it uses real things to support the story, it is also an object story. This story deals with fractions, using them repeatedly to solve a complex mathematical puzzle.

The story itself tells of a man who is so tremendously thirsty that he must drink and drink and drink. In doing so, he continues to dilute his drink (wine) with water. Eventually, a question is put to the children: what part of his drink is water, and what part is wine?

I first heard a version of this story at the International Center for Montessori Studies in Bergamo, Italy, posed simply as a math problem. True to its Italian roots, the story as told in that setting included the man drinking a delicious red wine, probably an Italian varietal! Some American educators have objected to this, believing that another liquid, such as juice, should be substituted. That certainly may be done, and, in fact, I would definitely suggest that juice rather than wine be used as a prop in a school setting. The actual story, as I tell it and as I write it here, remains true to its source—I allow him to drink wine, although he dilutes it with water. When you tell the story, feel free to substitute juice for wine.

To make this story fun and more of an enjoyable display, I act it out as it is being told. To do this, I prepare a clear glass carafe of faux wine, actually cranberry or cherry juice, and a clear glass pitcher of plain fresh water. Be sure that your juice is something with a deep-red color—it is easier to see the color dilution as the "wine" is watered down. Use a clear wine glass to see the liquid as it is being drunk.

As you tell the story, you must actually drink the liquid. Be sure to offer evidence of enjoyment and pleasure as you sip your diluted beverage. Be especially careful to follow the story in drinking the correct amount each time.

I find this story to be interestingly different. It is a story, but it is also a mathematical story problem. The children really like it and enjoy acting it out, making it a creative dramatics piece as well.

I won't give you the answer to the problem here. Accept my challenge and figure it out for yourself!

Source: *The Very Thirsty Man* is based on a traditional Montessori arithmetic word problem. I have expanded and reworked it to place it within a narrative, storytelling framework.

Story

Did you ever hear the story of the very thirsty man?

It is told that so long ago that no one can quite say when, there was a very, very thirsty man. I can't tell you why he was so thirsty, because I don't know. Maybe he'd been outside. Maybe he'd been exercising. Maybe he'd been for a long walk. I do know that his throat was dry and he was very thirsty.

When the man got to his house, he thought, "What can I do about my thirst?" So, he went to his cupboard where he got a small glass pitcher of wine, and he got a beautiful wineglass. He filled the glass completely with wine, which exactly used up all of his wine. With the glass now completely filled with wine, he looked at it and thought, "Aaah, now I shall quench my thirst!"

From the carafe of red juice, pour one glass full. Be sure that you measured the juice first, so that it completely empties the carafe.

At last, he began to drink. He drank exactly one third of the glass of wine, and then he thought "Uh-oh. If I keep drinking all of that wine, it may soon be gone, and I'll still be thirsty. I can't drink it all right now, because there's no wine left in my pitcher."

You also drink exactly one third of your glass of juice.

"I have no wine left. Since it's all gone, I'll still be thirsty," the man thought. Then he had an idea. He got a pitcher of water and filled that same glass up with water, all the way to the top. He poured it right into the wine, so that the wine and water mixed together. That exactly filled his glass.

You fill your glass all the way up with water, diluting the juice.

"Aaah," he thought, "I now have a full glass again, and I can drink as much as I want, so he began to drink. He drank exactly half of the mixture of water and wine, so the glass was half full—or half empty. He then stopped and thought, "Wait a minute, if I drink all of this, it will be all gone and there'll be no taste of

You also drink exactly one half of your glass of the juice and water mixture.

the wine left in my glass. I don't want that. I had better fill it up again."

Fill your glass all the way up with water, diluting the juice even more.

So, he went back to his pitcher of water and he filled the glass all the way to the top so that the wine and water mixed. "Aaah, now I can drink and maybe I won't be thirsty anymore." And he began to drink, and drink. He drank exactly two thirds of the mixture of water and wine. Then he stopped, and he thought, "Hmm, I'm still thirsty. What would happen if I drank it all? It would be all gone. I had better fill it all the way back up."

Now you drink exactly two thirds of your glass of the diluted juice and water mixture.

So once again, he took his pitcher of water, and he began to fill the glass all the way to the top one more time, until the glass was completely full, all the way to the top. He picked the glass up one more time, but he looked at the glass, and he thought, "Now, what part of that glass is wine, and what part is water? How much wine is left in this mixture, and how much water?"

Fill your glass all the way up with water again.

And that's the problem for you to solve. You can figure out how much wine and how much water is left in that glass.

Think hard, think long. And perhaps you will find the answer to this riddle.

And now the story is yours.

The Very Strange Continent

INTRODUCTION

In the Montessori classroom, there is an interesting piece of equipment called the Bead Cabinet. Please see Figure 50 (p. 241). This cabinet is a beautiful display of materials that find many uses in mathematics: counting, skip counting (counting by fours, counting by fives, etc.), multiples, squaring, cubing, and polynomials, as well as work with other base systems.

The Bead Cabinet is essentially a large wooden board, especially made to hold two sets of bead chains: long and short. The long chains equal the cubes of the numbers and the short chains represent the squares of the numbers. There is also a set of prepared squares and cubes, also made of beads. Presenting this story will also require a set of ten short bead bars, each of which simply represents a number from one to ten. One additional single red bead will be required to use as the unit bead.

The Cubes of the Numbers (sometimes called the *Bead Cubes* or *Cubes of the Beads*) are actual geometric cubes of the numbers one through ten, composed of beads, either fused or wired together. These are stored along the top shelf of the Bead Cabinet; there is one for each number, one through ten.

Figure 50. The Bead Cabinet.

Each number is color-coded with a distinct hue, usually using the following system:

One	Red
Two	Green
Three	Pink
Four	Yellow
Five	Light Blue
Six	Lavender
Seven	White
Eight	Brown
Nine	Dark Blue
Ten	Gold

The Squares of the Numbers (sometimes called the *Bead Squares* or *Squares of the Beads*) are accurate representations of the numerical squares of all the numbers one through ten and are constructed of beads fused or wired together. There are as many squares of each color as the number of that color; thus, there are four squares of four, seven squares of seven, and so on. There are fifty-five squares in total. The squares are kept on shelves in the Bead Cabinet.

The Long Chains hang on the Bead Cabinet. There are ten of them, one for each number, one through ten. They are constructed of the same matching beads as the preceding material. Each chain corresponds to the cube of the number; thus, it contains precisely the same number of beads as the Bead Cubes, except that the chains are arranged in linear fashion. The chains are made of bead bars of the appropriate color linked together. A large ring is placed at the spot on each chain where the square of the number is reached.

The Short Chains are kept in specially designed "troughs" on the Bead Cabinet, although sometimes, they may be kept hanging on a separate wall hanger. There are ten short chains, each made of colored beads matching the corresponding Long Chain. The Short Chains are exactly equal to the Squares of the Numbers (the Bead Squares), but in linear form.

These colorful materials are especially attractive to children. Usually, children begin using them in the preschool years and continue with them through upper elementary, doing different mathematical exercises along the way.

By the time that the children reach the middle or upper grades, they have seen this material many times. This story, *The Very Strange Continent*, refreshes interest in the material and renews the students' motivation at the launch of a new unit on the multiples of numbers.

The story leads the children to imagine the Bead Cabinet as another continent made up of ten countries. Each country is related to one of the numbers, one through ten. Because the cabinet is too large and heavy to easily move around, to tell this story, we walk over to the cabinet and sit in front of it. Then the story can be told with the entire cabinet serving as a prop. I also use a globe as a prop at the beginning of the story, to reintroduce the word *continent*.

Because this story ties directly into the mathematics curriculum plan, it is a curriculum story. At the same time, its use of the specialized Montessori materials makes it an object story.

This is a popular story because it is so fanciful. Telling it always attracts older children from around the room who aren't part of this particular lesson now, but who want to hear it again.

Source: *The Very Strange Continent* is based on a traditional Montessori presentation, which I have substantially enlarged to include narrative storytelling elements.

STORY

I love to travel, and I am planning a long trip today. I know that some kind of map just might help. I think that the best help might be a globe.

Display a small globe on which the continents can be pointed out.

Here is a globe. Does anybody know how many continents there are on the globe? Seven. That's right. There are seven continents: Antarctica, North and South America, Africa, Europe, Asia, and Australia. Seven continents on the globe.

Some people prefer the term Oceania, rather than Australia.

Today, we're going to take a trip to a continent. We're going to go to a continent, but it's not going to be North America, where we are right now. I can also tell you that it's not going to be any one of the seven continents that you just heard about, either. There's actually another continent, a very strange continent.

This is not a continent that you have ever seen on the globe. And we will never see it on any globe. It's not a continent that you'd see on a map, either. We'll never see it on any map. That is because this is a very strange continent. It's a continent made up of ten countries, and each country is a very strange country. Some are stranger than others. Did you know that this continent is right here in our room, right now? It is. So, let's go take a trip over to this continent.

Now, walk with the children over to the Bead Cabinet and have them sit in front of it.

Here it is! This continent has been in our room all this time. You may think of it as the Bead Cabinet, but it has really become a very strange continent. We are now on our trip to the very strange continent. Let's take a look at it.

This is a continent made up of ten strange and different countries. They are countries of numbers. There is the Country of the Tens, there is the Country of the Sevens, there's the Nation of the Fives, there's the country where the Threes live—there are all these different countries.

Now the Country of the Tens is the biggest, and they take up the most space on this continent, whereas the Nation of the Ones is very small and it doesn't take up very much space at all. The countries of the Sevens and Sixes are about in the middle; they take up some space, but not as much as the Tens. The Tens know that they are in charge, and that is why they are colored golden—they are very, very important, and the shining gold color shows that they are really important.

Every single country on this continent has its own special color. You know now why the Tens are colored golden; it's to show that they are very important. Every other country has a color, too. So, the Country of the Fives is colored light blue—that's one of the laws in this country. Everybody in the Country of Fives has to be colored light blue. It's one of their rules. In the Country of the Sevens, the rule is to be pure white. The Land of the Fours must all be bright yellow. They are all red in the Country of the Ones. Each country is like that; they have their special color.

So, each nation has its own laws. There is a law that's kind of the same in every country, but it's a little bit different, and that's what makes the countries different. For instance, if we go to the light blue land of the Fives, the Fives have a law and it's called the Law of Five, and that law is that everything has to be in fives. That's their whole law.

The golden Tens also have a law. Their law is called the Law of Ten. That Law of Ten says everything in their country has to be ten. Ten is the law.

It is different among the Eights. In the Country of the Eights, a brown country, the law of eight is simply that everything has to be eight. That is their rule, that's their law. If you don't follow their law, you can't be an Eight.

If you were to say, "Well, I want to have seven," then you will have to join the Country of the Sevens, which is white. You can't be in the lavender Country of the Sixes unless you're a Six. There, everything has to be sixes—that's their rule. They're very exclusive. Each country, except for one of them, is very exclusive and wants only certain numbers to be there.

Now, each country has a government. The government rules the country. Each country also has a ruler, someone who is in charge of the whole country.

Let's look at the Fives, for instance. This is the ruler of the Fives. The ruler is always a cube. So, this light blue cube is the ruler of the Fives, which we call the king. The king of the Fives is a cube. So let's put the king of the Fives over on the table so we can see it. That is the king of the Fives, and it follows the Law of Five, as we'll see. It's the most important of all of the fives. The king is the Five that has the greatest power. You will see that another important thing about this board and this very strange continent is that everything is judged according to power. The king, who is a cube, is the one with the most power in the Fives.

Display the light-blue cube.

Now among the Fives, which we're looking at now, there are also some light-blue squares. These squares are the princes and the princesses. They have some power. They don't have as much power as the king, but there are five of them, and all five of them put together would have just as much power as the king.

Show the children the five squares of five.

Likewise, in the Land of Sixes, there are six princesses. The Land of Eight has, of course, eight of them, because that's the law, remember? Everything has to be that way. Here, in the Fives, because there are five of them, it takes all five together to have as much power as the king. Each prince has some power, but not as much as the king does.

Now let's look at the next piece. This is a lord or lady—a light-blue five bar. The lord or lady of five has a little power. They don't have much power, at all really, but it does have some. However, five of these lords or ladies can have as much power as one prince. Of course, in the Tens, it takes ten of the golden lords to have as much power as a prince. In the Twos, it only takes two green bars to have as much power as the square green prince. Because that's the law. The law always has to do with a number. Yes, these ladies and lords have very little power, but they do have some.

Finally, at the bottom of all of the power is the common citizen. This is the everyday citizen, who is the same in every single country. This citizen is the same in every country; it's the red unit. Here is our common citizen, a single red bead.

Display the single red bead.

This is because every country is made up of units. So the citizens, just like the world we live in, are really the same from country to country. Their rulers may be different, and their laws may seem to be different, but the people are pretty much the same, except that on this continent, these citizens have no power. They have zero power. That's right—absolutely zero! The citizen is powerless, completely without any power, in all of these countries—with one exception. The Nation of the Ones seems to be made up of just common citizens, but it is actually the only country on the very strange continent that is a democracy. Here, the king, the prince, the lady, and the citizen are all the same. They are more democratic.

If the citizen has no power at all—has zero power—then we could say that the lord or lady has one level of power. They are one power step above the common citizen. In the Country of the Fives, it takes five of the common citizens to equal the power of just one lord. So, the bar-shaped lord has one level of power. A first power, that is one up from zero.

When we get to squares, which are the princes and the princesses, we can say that they have two levels of power because they are two up from the citizen. Zero, one, two. A second power These square princes and princesses have two levels of power, a little more power, but it takes five of the ladies or lords, remember, to make one prince or princess.

Then, could we say that the cubic king has three levels of power? That's right. Zero, one, two, three—three levels of power. A third power. It takes five of the princes or princesses to equal the power that's held by one king in the Land of the Fives.

It's truly a strange continent. A continent populated by common citizens. A continent filled with princes and lords. A continent filled with ten kings who are cubes. There are princes and princesses who are colorful squares. There are many lords who are colored bars. And there are the common citizens who are little units, and are all red.

There is more population in the Tens than in any other country, but they have the same power structure: the king, who is a golden cube, the prince, who is square, the lord or lady, who is a bar, and the same common citizen. This is truly an unusual continent, isn't it? A very strange continent with ten very, very different but strangely similar countries.

We're going to learn a lot more about these countries, and we're especially going to learn about the powers that the different levels have. We are going to learn about what it means that some have more power and some have less. We're going to understand how the power is different for the Ones, the Twos, and the Threes, all the way up to the Tens.

That's all there is! So now, let's leave the very strange continent and let's travel all the long way back to North America, to our school, back to our classroom. Now, we'll begin to learn everything about the powers of all of the pieces that live on this very strange continent.

Measuring the Farm

INTRODUCTION

This is a story that is particularly dear to my heart. It was the first original curriculum story that I ever wrote. I was teaching the upper elementary level at a school in Minneapolis, Minnesota, and I wanted to develop a kickoff story to the geometrical concept of area that had a bit more pizzazz than what I had received in my own teacher education.

One day, as I was thinking about it, my (then) small, blonde daughter came into the room with her two much older brothers and made several insightful comments that had all of us scratching our heads. It occurred to me how often we can be wrongly dismissive of comments from the youngest children.

With this rumbling around in my head, I proceeded to write *Measuring the Farm*. This is a story that introduces area, but it also introduces a basic notion of social justice that is addressed in many folktales: the sudden and surprising ascendency to greatness of the one who was once considered the most insignificant.

When telling this story, I have three cautionary notes. First, be somewhat dismissive of Marigold at first. She seems not to be one of the main characters. This is hard for many people, because they do not want to be dismissive of this charming small girl. Still, that is essential to the notion mentioned above that the insignificant ascend.

Secondly, do *not* mention the word *area* at all in naming the story, nor anywhere within the story until the very ending. Finally, do not call this *The Story of Marigold* or *The Story of Area*. Call it *Measuring the Farm*. Using either the words *Marigold* or *Area* in the title gives away too much.

In presenting and telling this story, you will need a special set of materials. If you are in a Montessori classroom, these will be the four rectangles from the Montessori yellow-area material. These are rectangles of wood twenty centimeters long by ten centimeters wide, and painted yellow. The first rectangle should be entirely blank. The second rectangle is ruled lengthwise into five long strips, each two centimeters wide. The third rectangle is ruled in the other direction into ten strips, each also two centimeters wide. The final rectangle is crosshatched into fifty squares, each two centimeters on a side.

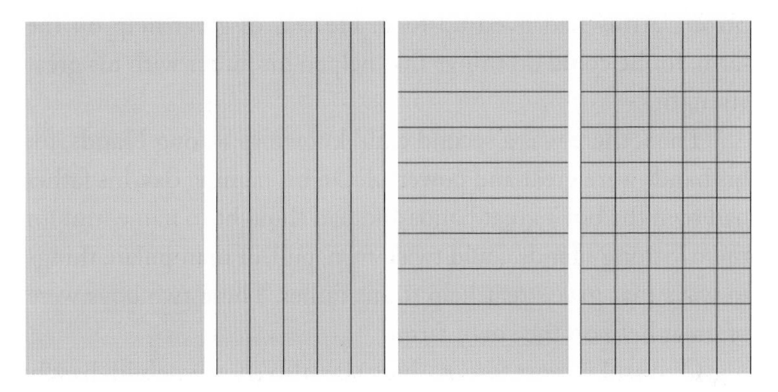

Figure 51. These are all four rectangles from the yellow-area material.

When presenting the story, hide the rectangles until the time comes to bring them out. Do not display all of them at the beginning.

Because this story ties directly into the curriculum of geometry, it is a curriculum story. At the same time, its use of certain specialized materials or objects makes it an object story.

Source: *Measuring the Farm* is a completely original story, which I wrote.

STORY

Long, long ago in a faraway land that lay in a well-watered plain somewhere between two great rivers, there was a beautiful and fertile place. In this rich and favored spot, there lived a farmer. Now, this farmer had a very, very small farm. It was so small that he could work all of it by hand and with his family, for in these days, there were no such things as horses to work the land. Oh, there were horses, but no one had harnessed them to work the land. No one had even thought of using oxen to work the land. People thought of using their own muscle and brawn to work the land. Luckily for him, he was strong and worked very hard, and he also had two strong sons.

His eldest son was a strong, strapping young man known as Strong Arms, for his arms were every strong, with powerful muscle. On the boy's naming day, his father had seen the youth's strong arms and had thought, "That shall be his name," and Strong Arms had lived up to it. He was of great help on the farm, for he could do things that helped his father with his great strength.

Then, there was a second child known as Strong Hands, for his hands were great and powerful. On his naming day, his father had seen the boy's great hands and had thought to name him for them. Strong Hands could twist, turn, pull, or manipulate things in ways that gave great help to his father. These two boys were of great help on the small farm.

Oh yes, I almost forgot, there was also another child, hardly worthy of mention, a small, blonde daughter named Marigold.

Now, this small family lived and worked on their little farm. Here is a rough map of the farm. But this map is blank. It just

Pick up and show the children the first rectangle.

Figure 52. The first rectangle.

shows that the farm was shaped like a rectangle and it lay somewhere in the rich land watered by the two rivers.

The farm was so small that every year the farmer himself had to go out and plant row after row of vegetables, fruits, or grains, patch after patch of other things. Well, he was getting quite old, and he thought that the time had come for him to think of who would receive the farm when he could no longer farm it himself.

So, he called his two sons to him, and Marigold came along as well, as she tended to do. He called his two children together and he said, "My sons, the time has come for me to think of who shall get the farm when I am no longer able to farm here." And both boys said, "I should have the farm, I should have the farm." However, the farmer said, "Well, I've come up with a plan for you to be able to earn the farm from me. This is the plan. I shall ask you to measure the size of the farm, and the one who gets the measurement right shall inherit the farm." The boys looked at each other with confusion. What does he mean? What does this thing *measure* mean? What is *size*? But the farmer wouldn't say.

As it turns out, it was soon time to till the soil and to plant, and they planted their farm in five great long beds, great beds of vegetables, great plots of fruit. Great patches of grains and root crops. And the farmer said to his elder son, "This year you, Strong Arms, shall have the chance to win. You will have the first chance because you are older. You will go first."

So, as they planted, Strong Arms looked and tried to figure it out. As the plants began to sprout and grow, he walked around the farm and examined things to see what he could see. As the plants grew and matured, Strong Arms looked at the farm and he looked at these five great rectangular plots or beds of plants. Finally, at the time of harvest, it dawned on him. "I have the answer; I can measure the farm. I know what he wants to know. Why didn't I see this before?"

Well, his strength was mostly in his arms and not in his head. Strong Arms came back to his father and in great joy he said, "Father, I have solved the problem and I shall inherit the farm." His father was overjoyed, saying, "Strong Arms has inherited the farm, Strong Arms has inherited the farm." He invited friends and he invited neighbors, and they had a great dinner.

Finally, his father said, "And now, Strong Arms, you shall tell us all what is the measurement of the farm?" So Strong Arms said, "Why Father, it's five. One, two, three, four, five." He got down in the dust on his knees and he drew this very picture in the dust at their feet and he showed the five long strips representing the beds of plants.

Show the children the second rectangle (on next page) and count the five horizontal strips, using your finger.

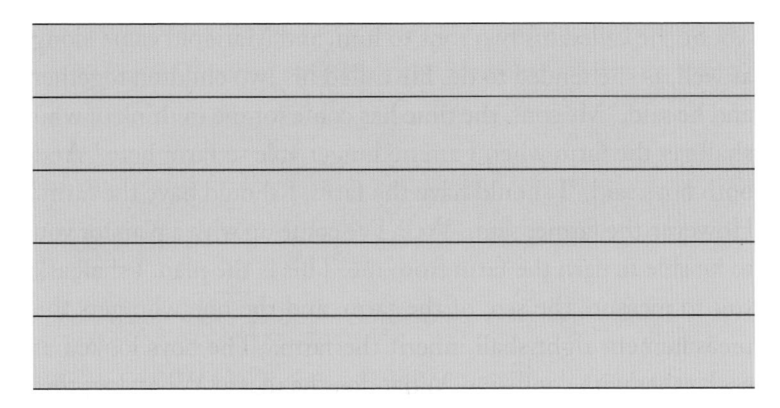

Figure 53. The second rectangle.

But then, they all heard a small voice, a small piping voice. It was Marigold! She said, "That is not quite right," in her high and piping voice. How dare she speak at a time like this?

They looked at her and she was shaking her small, blonde head in disappointment. Now, her father had learned that sometimes Marigold spoke in wisdom beyond her years, so he said, "Marigold, what can it be?"

Again, show the children the second rectangle.

Marigold got down on her knees and she drew the same picture in the dust. Then she said, "My brother, Strong Arms, says the measurement is five and of course he is right that there are five beds." But, she showed them that if we simply keep drawing the picture longer and longer and longer and longer so that it's very long, it would still be five—and that is what Strong Arms would call the measurement. But we can see that it's much longer. Five cannot measure the whole size of this farm.

When they looked up from the drawing, all the guests had left. They all had heard the wisdom in her young voice and knew that she was right.

Well, the next year, the next summer, they were to plant again, and once again, the farmer brought his children to him, and Marigold joined them, as usual. And he said, "Once again, I am going to try to give my farm to one of you. And this time, it is your turn, Strong Hands." Strong Hands smiled because he knew he would probably be able to do this better than his brother would. He knew that he must measure the size of the farm. First, he had to figure out how to do it.

Now, every year, they changed the direction of the planting of the beds. So, this year, they planted their beds in another direction. They did that every year.

As they planted, Strong Hands, like his brother, looked around and tried to figure it out. As the plants began to sprout and grow, he walked around the farm and examined things to see what he could see. As the plants grew and matured, Strong Hands looked at the farm and he looked at the ten great plots. Finally, at the time of harvest, it dawned on him, and suddenly he said, "I've got it, I see it. My stupid brother can't count. One, two, three, four, five, six, seven, eight, nine, ten—the measurement of the farm is ten. It's ten."

Show the children the third rectangle and count the ten strips, using your finger.

Figure 54. The third rectangle.

In great joy and happiness, Strong Hands raced back to the farmhouse to tell his father that he had measured the farm. When he arrived he said, "Father, I shall inherit the farm, for I have measured the farm." His father clapped his hands and cried, "Let's let everyone hear this," so even Marigold came over to listen. Then Strong Hands said, "The measurement of the farm is ten."

Then they all looked at Marigold to see if she would do something, and as you probably have guessed, she did. She shook her head in disappointment. In her high and piping voice, she said, "Oh, my brother is wrong again."

"How, Marigold," her father asked, "is this wrong? If five was wrong, why is this also wrong?" Marigold got down on her knees in the dust and she drew this very picture with the ten beds of vegetables and fruits and grains. And Marigold showed how if you just kept drawing the lines longer and longer or shorter and shorter, you would still count ten, even though the size would change

Again, show the children the third rectangle.

Both boys hung their heads, and their father said, "Marigold, you have spoken with great wisdom. Next year, you shall have a chance and you shall be able to measure the farm." But Marigold said, "No Father, I can tell you the measurement of the farm right now. I already know the measurement of the farm from the work that my two brothers did." And they looked at her in wonder as she said, "You see, both of the boys were correct." Then she once again drew a picture, this very picture.

Show the children the fourth rectangle.

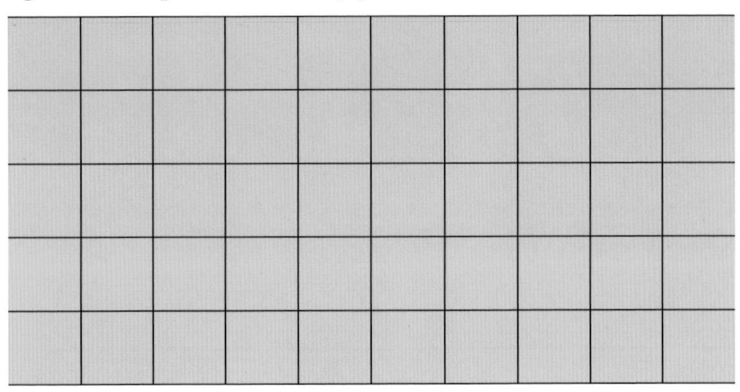

Figure 55. The fourth rectangle.

"When Strong Arms said the measurement was five, that was part of the answer. And when Strong Hands said the measurement was ten, that, too, was part of the answer. But what we have to do," she said, "is that we must put both pictures together—like this." And she crossed them all.

Refer to the fourth rectangle.

Marigold said, "You must make squares, Father. For each square is the same, and the measurement of this farm is fifty squares, each with the exact same number of paces on the side."

Those fifty squares would be exactly the size of the farm. It cannot be lengthened, it cannot be widened, it cannot be changed in any way, or the number of squares will change.

While discussing this, again point to the fourth rectangle.

They all knew that she was right. They could hear the wisdom in her young voice. In amazement her father said, "Marigold, you have solved the problem. You, Marigold, shall inherit the farm." But one more time, she shook her small head back and forth, and she said, "No Father, no. Let the boys have the farm and they may share it. For I shall go to the great city to seek my fortune. And there, I shall found a new science. I shall call it *area*. Area shall be the name of the science that measures the surface of all things. And when I do that, I shall measure everything." And indeed, she did.

And that's the story of Marigold. She and her brothers grew to be very old, and lived happily all the days of their life.

A Root Is Like a Radish

INTRODUCTION

In Montessori schools, square root and cube root work are offered in the upper elementary years. This work involves the special sign for extracting a root, called a *radical.* This curriculum story uses an actual radish, the vegetable, as a prop or visual aid to enter into the discussion of roots. This is based on the idea that a radish is, after all, a root.

Along with this are certain illustrations of the some of the great innovators in the history of the radical sign. These pictures are available widely, in books and on the Internet.

When you finish the story, it is up to you whether you choose to eat the radish!

Source: *A Root Is Like a Radish* is an original story, which I wrote.

STORY

Show the children a real red radish, ideally with green leaves attached.

Let's take a look at what I have right here. Does anybody know what I'm holding in my hand? What is this thing?

This is a radish. Now, a radish gets its name from an Italian word which comes to us from Latin, *radice*, and that means "root." A radish is really like a root. In fact, it is a root. The old Italians and the Romans must have used the word *root* to describe this thing. It's a root: *radice*. When you think *radice*, you see how that word can become, in our language, *radish*. The etymology of the word is just root. Isn't that an interesting thing?

Now, around the 1100s, some people were thinking, just as people had thought before, as long as 2500 years ago in Babylon, that some numbers have roots, too. Can you imagine that a number could grow a root and be like a radish? Well, in fact, a number can grow a root, or even better yet, many numbers grow from roots. We are going to be talking about roots, especially number roots, a lot more. There was one special root, the square root of a number, which was interesting to many, many, many people.

Hold up a picture of the letter r.

Now, I want you to remember one thing as we talk about roots, that the word *radice* and the word *root* both start with an *r*. I'm holding up this picture of an *r*, because it will help you to understand something about how a radish and a root are like each other.

Figure 56. An ancient lower-case letter *r*, the earliest radical sign.

There was a man who lived in the late 1100s in Italy named Leonardo. You may have heard of Leonardo da Vinci, but this is a completely different man, also named Leonardo. He was called Leonardo Pisano. *Pisano* in Italian indicated that he was from Pisa, Leonardo of Pisa. That meant that he was from the city with the famous Leaning Tower.

Leonardo has been called, as sort of a nickname, *Fibonacci*. That really wasn't his name, and he never called himself that in his entire life. He always called himself Leonardo. Still, he has been called Fibonacci for the last few hundred years.

Leonardo's father's name was Bonaccio, so some people think that the nickname Fibonacci is a short version of the Latin words *filius Bonacci*, which means "the son of Bonaccio."

Leonardo was a great mathematician, and he did many things that were very interesting. We think Leonardo was responsible for introducing the Arabic numbers—the ones we heard about in the Fifth Great Lesson—to Europe. Leonardo was also responsible for a great sequence, or theorem, of numbers that are called Fibonacci's Sequence, or Fibonacci's Numbers, even though he didn't use that name for himself.

Well, one of the things that he did like to do was to explore roots. He especially wanted to find the roots of numbers. What would be the root? And once he started to look at roots, like all mathematicians, he wanted to use a symbol. He wanted some kind of a symbol to show the root, the square root of a number. Now, knowing that *root*, or *radice*, starts with the sound *rrrrr*, an *r*, Leonardo used this symbol. It's looks like an "R" with a little "X" down at the bottom, and he would write this letter, this symbol, followed by a number, and that means "find the square root of this number." You may have also seen this symbol somewhere else. It is also used when people get a prescription for drugs at the pharmacist. But it was used by Fibonacci to indicate the root of a number. The "R" is because of *radice*, because a root is really sort of like a radish after all.

Display a picture of Fibonacci's radical sign.

Figure 57. Fibonacci's radical sign.

Now, Leonardo's symbol caught on because other people started to get interested in roots, too, but that symbol was pretty complicated. It's a capital "R" with what looks like an "X" drawn across its leg, and that's a lot to write for a mathematician because they're always looking for shortcuts. They're great "shortcuttists," and they always want to find shorter ways to do things. So, many people still used that the little lowercase "r" that I showed you before, but they started to write it in a different, quicker way.

Here's a picture of a mathematician named Christoff Rudolff, and in the 1400s and 1500s, he started to use a sign like this, called a radical sign. Do you hear *rrrrr* in "radical radice?" It's like a radish sign; it means find a root. Do you see that it looks sort of like a rapidly drawn "R"? Somebody started by drawing an R and it became, instead of a root, well, a thing called a radical. We know that it's still our old friend *radice*.

Display a picture of Christoff Rudolff.

Display Rudolff's radical symbol.

√

Figure 58. Rudolff's radical sign.

That almost was the end of the development

of this special sign until another fellow came along known as René Descartes, who was born in France in 1596. Descartes is famous for his work in geometry. He was also a philosopher—and, of course, he was French. In the 1600s, René Descartes was still very interested in roots. It is so interesting that 500 years after Fibonacci, people were still playing with the symbol. Descartes liked the symbol that Rudolff used and he kept it, but he made one little change. Descartes drew a line across the very top of the symbol, and to this day this is the root, or radish, or radical sign that we use where we're finding roots. It took five hundred years for the development of this sign to take place, all the way from the radish to the radical. Now we all call it the radical sign, but we know that it started as a simple radish.

Display a picture of Descartes.

Display Descartes' radical symbol.

And that is a story of how it all happened.

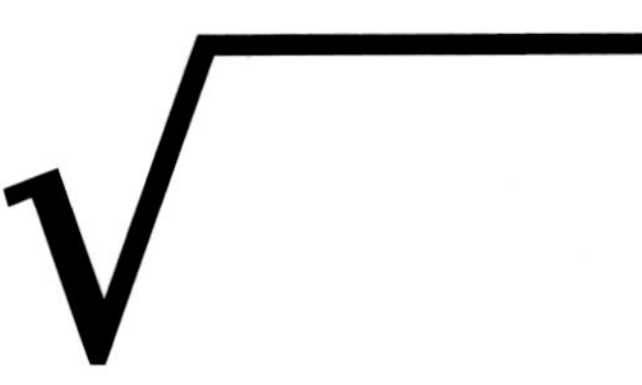

Figure 59. Descartes' radical sign.

The March of the Three Kings

INTRODUCTION

This tale is a special mathematics curriculum story that is linked to two very specific Montessori materials. These are two wooden cubes, each divided into twenty-seven parts. Called the *Trinomial Cubes*, these are a quite complex mathematical material, unlikely to be found anywhere but in Montessori classes. Their hands-on nature makes them user-friendly, even to preschoolers, but this story is usually aimed at children in the upper grades of the Montessori elementary level. The first cube, the *Algebraic Trinomial Cube*, is in use by children starting in preschool, and it is generally used as a three-dimensional puzzle. In the Children's House, they simply call it *The Trinomial Cube*.

The second cube, the *Arithmetic Trinomial Cube* (sometimes called the *Hierarchical Trinomial Cube*), has twenty-seven pieces of the same shape, but the pieces are colored differently; this is because these two cubes have related, but different purposes.

Figure 60.
The Algebraic Trinomial Cube,
in its box, and open.

Figure 61.
The Arithmetic Trinomial Cube,
in its box and open.

They both are material that expresses the trinomial expansion, which is:

$$(a+b+c)^3 = a^3 + 3a^2b + 3a^2c + 3ab^2 + 6abc + 3ac^2 + b^3 + 3b^2c + 3bc^2 + c^3$$

You will note that in both of these puzzle cubes, there are three small pieces actually in the shape of cubes themselves, representing a^3, b^3, and c^3. The remaining twenty-four pieces in each set are various rectangular prisms, all colored uniquely. This cube material is used both for cubing and for cube root.

Obviously, these are complex ideas, so a delightful story is ideal as an introduction. This story imagines that the three small, cube-shaped pieces are kings. They each lead their retinue out for a stroll. While on the walk, they are all transformed, their colors change, and in some cases, their allegiances change. This leads the children to move from the algebraic cube to the arithmetic cube, and eventually back again.

The procedure is to begin with the Algebraic Trinomial Cube.

For your reference, the arrangement of the twenty-seven pieces in the Algebraic Trinomial Cube is listed in Appendix B (p. 339). The twenty-seven pieces of the Arithmetic Trinomial Cube are listed in Appendix C (p. 341).

Figure 62. The contents of the Algebraic Trinomial Cube.

This illustration shows the all of the pieces of the disassembled Algebraic Trinomial Cube. Its three cubes, representing the three kings, will lead their retinues of the remaining twenty-four prisms to an imaginary bridge leading to the *Land of Numbers*. They will stop there, contemplating, then one king at a time, they will lead their followers across the bridge. This will be interesting and shocking to the kings.

Meanwhile, the teacher (or storyteller) has taken all twenty-seven cubes from the Arithmetic Trinomial Cube and carefully concealed them in a basket or tray out of sight of the children. Its empty box is also hidden.

As the kings lead their followers across the bridge, the teacher switches the blocks from the Algebraic set for the corresponding ones from the Arithmetic set. As this is done, the Algebraic set is put into the secret place where the Arithmetic set had been hidden.

Coordinating the various movements in this story with the narrative is very challenging. It does require a great deal of practice. Practice repeatedly, one section at a time, until you can get it down. Do not despair—it will involve many rehearsals. Be sure to practice with the actual materials; don't just try to imagine the movements. Be patient; it will pay off. If this is told and done deftly, it is especially appealing to the children.

Source: *The March of the Three Kings* is an original presentation and story that I wrote based on ideas originally proposed and developed among several elementary Montessori teachers.

Remember to have concealed the disassembled Arithmetic Trinomial Cube and its box. I usually put a cloth over it as well to discourage curious eyes.

STORY

Many hundreds of years ago, there was a distant kingdom far across the sea. Now, it so happened that in very middle of that very large kingdom, there was a forest, and in the very middle of that forest, there was a town, and in the very middle of that town, there was a great palace, and in that splendid palace, there lived three kings.

Display the entire assembled Algebraic cube in its box.

Their palace where they lived was unusual, for it was a perfect cube. It is told that each of the three kings was also a cube, and that these three cubical kings were allies and friends. They worked together and they helped each other but, still, they were separate and each had his own personality.

Point to each "king" as you name his size and color.

The first of these kings was a large, handsome red cube. The second king was a beautiful medium-blue cube. And the third king was a fine-looking small, yellow cube. These three kings together ruled their cubical territory. They were in charge of a great domain, including all sorts of territory.

From the disassembled cube, take out the three cubes.

Figure 63. The three kings from the Algebraic cube.

The importance of each of the three kings was different, and it was determined by their size. The largest king, the red king, was the most important. And the red king was the most adventurous as well; he was always the leader, always going first.

Point to the red king.

Point to the blue king.

After the red king, the blue king always comes next. The blue king is second—second in importance. The blue king likes safety and security. The blue king enjoys being surrounded by others, so he is happy to be right in the middle where others are on either side. The blue king enjoys being centered with the others all around him.

Point to the yellow king.

Finally, there is the yellow king. The yellow king is kind of shy. He is a little bit nervous and does not like to put himself forth too much. He likes to be at the end of everything, coming last because he's somewhat bashful.

It so happened that every once in a while, the three kings would leave their palace and go on a walk. They would march from place to place. Maybe they would go to a ball. Maybe they would go to war. They might go out to explore new territory, or perhaps, they might simply take a hike.

One day, the red king said to the other two kings, "Today, we shall explore new lands. We shall go to other places and find new territory." Because he was the chief of the three kings, they did as he wished. One of the rules of the three kings is that all three must march in a certain way, a certain pattern. They always follow this special pattern.

And this is it:

First comes the red king, then the blue king, and then the yellow king. And each one of them has six attendants who wear jackets that match the king, and these attendants surround them. Each one also has two bodyguards, and the bodyguards follow them as well.

So, let's find the six attendants that follow and march with the red king. Here they are.

As you begin to discuss the three kings and their attendants and bodyguards, you will be carefully and neatly arranging the pieces of the Algebraic cube in a very particular pattern as shown in Figures 64 through 90.

Set out the red king and his attendants with the two bodyguards, following the pattern in Figure 64. First place the red king (cube), then arrange the attendants behind him.

Figure 64. The red king and his retinue.

The red king starts the march with six of these attendants behind him, and they're all wearing red jackets that match the color of the red king. Finally, bringing up the rear, are two of the black-suited bodyguards for the red king. The red king is able to start the entire march lined up, always in the front, followed by all six of his attendants and the two bodyguards.

Then, as always, the next king is the blue king. I'm sure you remember that I said that the blue king likes to be surrounded by people. So, his attendants start to come out first, ahead of him. You can see that they are wearing blue jackets. First, three of the attendants line up, followed by the blue king, and then come the other three of his attendants behind him. They all line up so that they are all arranged around the blue king, and then in the center next to him come his two bodyguards in their black suits. The blue king does not like to lead the way, but likes to be in the middle. I told you he likes security; he likes to be surrounded completely.

Set out the blue king (the blue cube), his attendants, and his bodyguards as they are shown in Figure 65.

Figure 65. The blue king and his retinue.

I hope that you remember that I said that the yellow king is a bit bashful and likes to come at the end of everything, so the yellow king always orders his attendants to go first. First come three tall attendants wearing yellow jackets, and they all line themselves up. Then come three shorter attendants wearing yellow jackets. Next come the two bodyguards, all in black, who

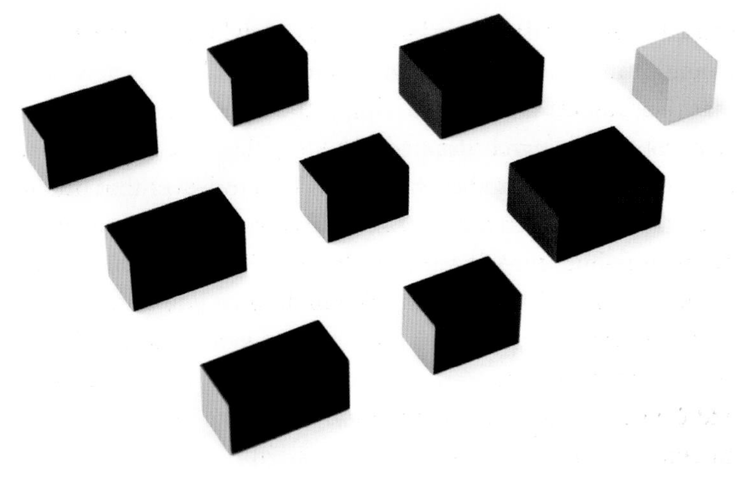

Set out the yellow king (the yellow cube), his attendants, and his bodyguards as they are described and shown in Figure 66.

Figure 66. The yellow king and his retinue.

place themselves behind the whole group of the yellow-jacketed attendants. Finally, at the very end comes the yellow king himself. Now they are finally all ready for their great march.

The red king looked back at everyone to make sure that the march was prepared. "We are ready to go forward. We are ready to go. Is everyone ready?" The blue king said that his group was ready. The yellow king said that his group was also ready, so they began to march.

Pause to admire the complete layout of all 27 pieces representing all three kings and their retinues as shown in Figure 67.

Figure 67. They all begin the march.

They marched up hills and down. They marched over and around. Finally, they arrived at a new land. This is a new land that they'd never seen before. And just before entering the new land, the whole march stopped.

There appeared to be a bridge, and to cross over that bridge, the red king would have to go first. It seemed that the land that they were going into was a land of numbers, a land marked by numbers of some variety or type which were unusual to these three kings, for they knew nothing about numbers. So they looked at the bridge and wondered whether they could go there and cross it. Of course, as we know, the red king was very bold and very strong and heroic, and he insisted right away that they must go into this new land.

Have a line of tape or some other mark that indicates the stream to be crossed and the bridge. Point to this line.

So they started off, led by the red king himself. Yes, he marched right across the bridge, but instantaneously, as soon as he got across it, something marvelous and miraculous happened. At the very moment when he crossed the bridge, he changed color and became blue.

As you say this, switch the red king (4x4x4 centimeters) from the Algebraic cube for the exactly congruent blue cube from the pieces of the Arithmetic cube from the concealed tray. This is called the new blue king. You will need to practice this so that you can do these switches smoothly.

Nobody knew what to think. Why was the king blue? What had happened to turn him blue? Was he all right? No one knew. They could all see that he had turned blue. His three attendants

Figure 68. The new blue king has crossed.

came across to try to help him and to try to do something to save him if he needed saving. But no sooner had they crossed the bridge than they turned green. Oh my goodness. They were green. They didn't even have jackets to match their king anymore now that they had changed to green!

The king's next attendants had started to cross and they were very nervous, thinking, "What's going to happen right now? What will we do?" Guess what happened? As they crossed over the bridge one at a time, they became brown!

As you say this, smoothly switch the first set of three attendants from the Algebraic cube for the exactly congruent 4x4x3 centimeter solid green prisms from the parts of the Arithmetic cube that are in the concealed tray, as in Figure 68.

Switch the second set of attendants for the three brown prisms that each measure 4x4x2 centimeters and bring them across the bridge, as in Figure 69.

Figure 69. The first seven have crossed.

They didn't match their king and they didn't even match the first three attendants. The two bodyguards were so frightened by this that they decided to back off and not go forward. Even though they were supposed to be bodyguards, they did not cross the bridge. They just stood back and watched to see what would happen next.

As in Figure 70, keep back the two black prisms. They measure 4x3x2 centimeters.

So the first blue king, not knowing what was happening, sent his first set of three attendants on ahead, and as they crossed over the bridge, they all suddenly became brown, and then they stood up tall. When they did this, they realized that their allegiance was not to their old blue king any longer. They would join the

These three are the attendants that each measure 3x3x4 centimeters.

These three are the attendants that each measure 3x3x2 centimeters.

As you tell this part of the story, smoothly switch the three blue-jacketed 3x3x4 prisms and the three blue-jacketed 3x3x2 prisms for the exactly congruent brown prisms from the concealed tray. Turn them so that they stand vertically to be equal in height to the new big blue king. Finally, group them behind the new big blue king, as seen in Figure 71. Leave the two black bodyguards behind; they will still be waiting to cross the bridge. They are not shown in Figure71.

Figure 70. The bodyguards are fearful and hold back.

new blue king, the new big blue king—the king that used to be red. They then became followers of the new king.

Then, the second set of three attendants went on ahead, and as they crossed over the bridge, they also all became brown, and then they stood up tall. Finally, all of the greens and all of

Figure 71. The new blue king and his nine followers have all crossed over.

the browns joined the new blue king, so that he now had nine followers.

At this point, the first blue king had no one in front of him, so he felt that he could go ahead and cross the bridge since the way was clear. So, he began to cross the bridge, and as soon as he did, he changed color as well. He became a red king. He changed completely to red.

At this point, switch the medium-sized blue king (the 3-centimeter cube) from the Algebraic cube for the exactly congruent red cube from the concealed tray, as in Figure 72. The black bodyguards will still be waiting to cross.

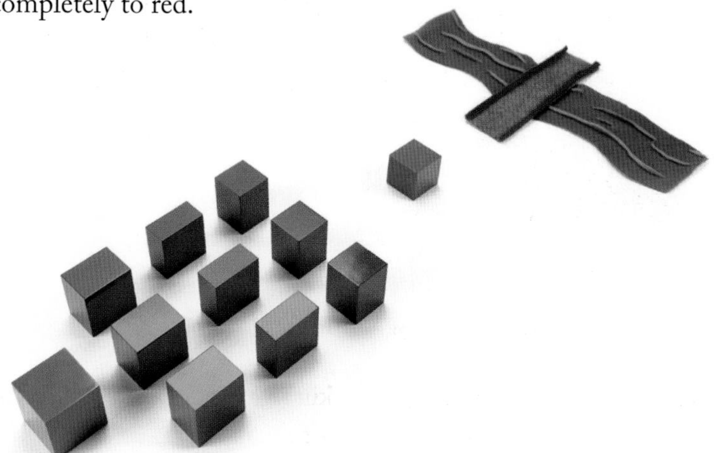

Figure 72. The new red king has crossed, there are now 11 pieces across the bridge.

Finally, both of his bodyguards decided that they'd better see what was up, and they both came forward and rushed across to see if they could help. It was about time, too, that they came across. But as they did, all of the other bodyguards joined them. Suddenly, they all changed—every single one of the six of them changed to red. So, there were then six red bodyguards. And knowing that the old blue king (the new red king) liked safety and security, they arranged themselves around him so they completely encircled him, as in Figure 73. There will now be a total of seventeen pieces that have crossed the bridge, as in Figure 74.

This made the new red king so happy, because although the new blue king did not have attendants who matched, at least *his* attendants matched his coat of beautiful red.

Of course, the yellow king had yet to cross, because he liked to be the last one. I'm sure that you remember that he's a little bit shy. He was nervous about coming too soon, anyway. He knew

Smoothly switch the black prisms (4x3x2 centimeters) for the exactly congruent red prisms from the concealed tray. Arrange them surrounding the new red king as in Figure 73.

Figure 73. This is how the red pieces are arranged.

Figure 74. Their are now seventeen pieces that have crossed the bridge.

that he had to cross, but instead of going first, he told everyone else to go across ahead of him.

Well—look at this. This first group isn't even his followers—the old blue king left three attendants behind. They didn't

Point to the three attendants left behind, as in Figure 75.

Figure 75. The old blue king left three attendants behind.

know what to do, but the yellow king said, "You have to cross, I command it! I want to bring my people across and I can't go until you go across." So, across they went.

They went marching all the way across the bridge into the new territory, where they immediately changed into orange. I don't know why they were orange, but they didn't mind too much because they were kind of like the red, but a little bit different, and kind of like the yellow, but in between. That made them feel a little more comfortable.

Switch the blue-jacketed prisms (3x3x2 centimeters) for the exactly congruent orange prisms from the concealed tray.

Then, the yellow king said, "All right now, my loyal followers can move forward," and he sent his attendants ahead to cross

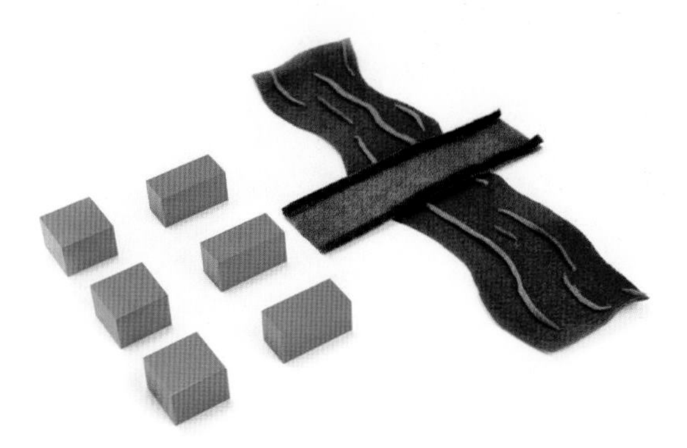

Figure 76. All the orange prisms have crossed.

Smoothly switch the first set of yellow-jacketed prisms (2x2x4 centimeters) for the exactly congruent orange prisms from the concealed tray. Arrange them behind the red prisms.

the bridge. His first three attendants went ahead, the tall ones—and much to their surprise, they, too, became orange. So, now there were six prisms that had become orange standing between the red and the remaining prisms with yellow jackets, and these

They should be arrayed as in Figure 77.

Figure 77. Now twenty-three prisms have crossed the bridge.

last three yellow ones were very frightened. Would they have to cross the bridge? What color would they turn? What would they become? They were used to being yellow, and they didn't know what would happen.

With a great deal of fear, they began to cross the bridge to see what would happen. As they crossed the bridge, they changed to solid yellow. They were still yellow, what joy! But now, instead of

Switch the second set of yellow-jacketed prisms (2x2x3 centimeters) for the exactly congruent yellow prisms from the concealed tray, like Figure 78.

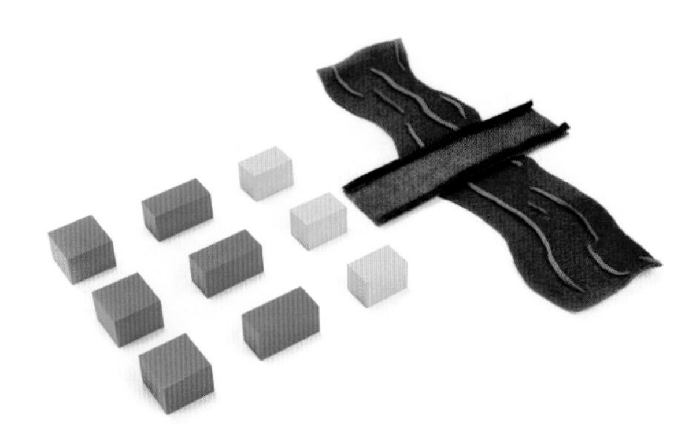

Figure 78. The three yellow prisms have lined up behind the orange prisms.

only having yellow jackets, they were a beautiful yellow all over. How gorgeous they were.

This made the last one left, the small yellow king, very happy. He saw that he could continue being yellow and that when he crossed over, he would match with the ones he had—there would be no problem. So, he decided he would cross the bridge and join his attendants.

But, guess what? When he finally crossed, he lost his yellow hue and he turned white! He wasn't yellow anymore after all—he

As you say this, switch the yellow king (2-centimeter cube) from the Algebraic cube for the exactly congruent white cube from the concealed tray. It should be the last piece on the concealed tray.

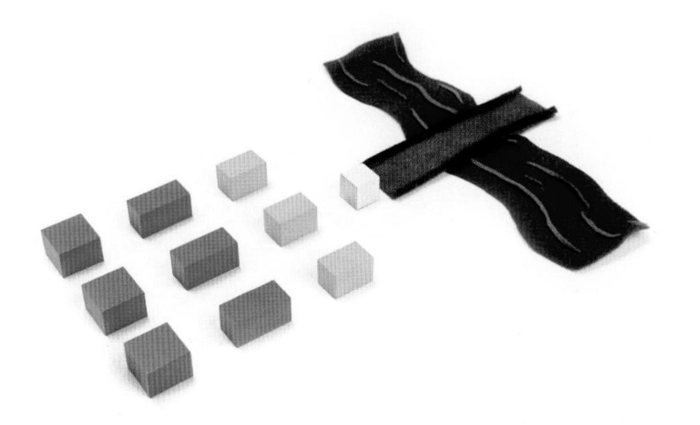

Figure 79. The white king is behind the yellow prisms.

had become white. All twenty-seven pieces have now crossed over, as in Figure 80.

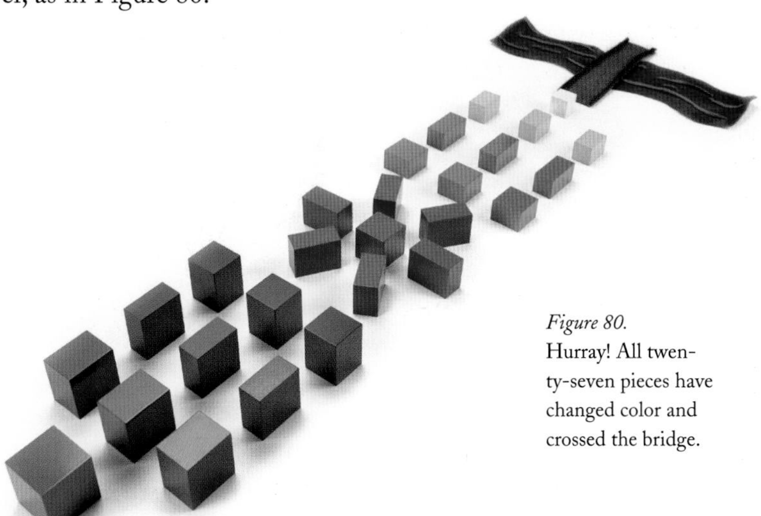

Figure 80. Hurray! All twenty-seven pieces have changed color and crossed the bridge.

The three kings looked around themselves and saw that now there was a blue king, a red king, and a white king. The three kings were so tired, so exhausted by their long march into a new land, that they decided to go home. But, when they got up to go home, they found they couldn't change their colors back; their colors stayed the way they had been changed. So, they marched back to their cubical palace, where they decided to enter their homes. What a surprise. Even the palace had changed color!

Set out the open Arithmetic cube.

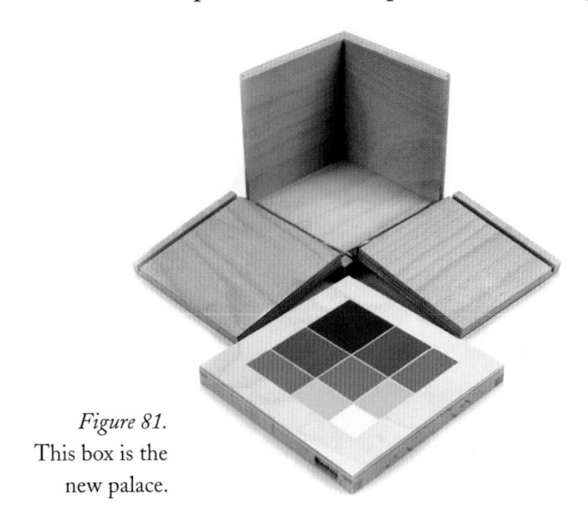

Figure 81. This box is the new palace.

The first king, as always, the first one to enter, was the new blue king. He became the first king to enter their new palace when they got home, and he was very happy to be home and he went in like this. But now, his three green attendants came rushing after to cover him and protect him. They covered him completely, protecting him from anyone else. Now, he couldn't even be seen anymore. When this happened, the brown attendants decided to make sure that this was the safest place. The brown attendants came

Place the blue cube in the box.

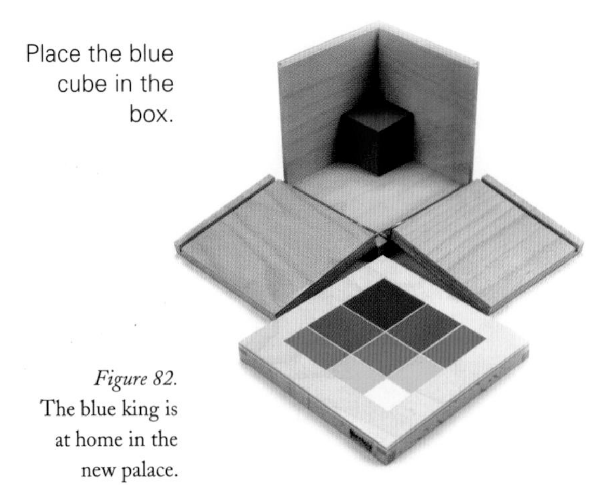

Figure 82. The blue king is at home in the new palace.

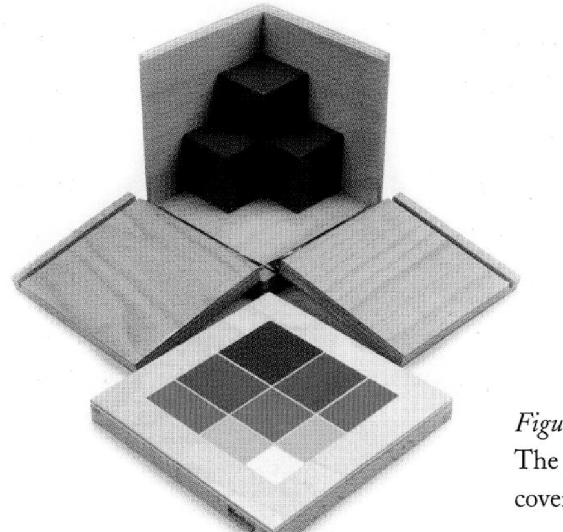

Place the green prisms in the box, covering all three exposed faces of the blue cube.

Figure 83.
The green prisms are covering the blue king.

in at the same time and began to cover all of the green ones so that they were completely covered up and there was nothing to be seen but brown.

Place all of the brown prisms in the box, filling all spaces made by the green prisms.

Figure 84.
The brown prisms are in the new palace.

The new red king had rather hoped that there would be a special place for him, so he watched closely. When all of the brown attendants had finally found their places, he noticed that a high throne had been prepared for him, a special place where he could sit. Hurray! So, he immediately went and sat on that throne, which was just for him. His bodyguards, all six red ones, immediately came to protect him and surrounded him in every area, covering up as much of the brown as they possibly could, making

Put the red king in place.

Figure 85.
The red king found a seat in the high throne.

Place all six red bodyguards in the box.

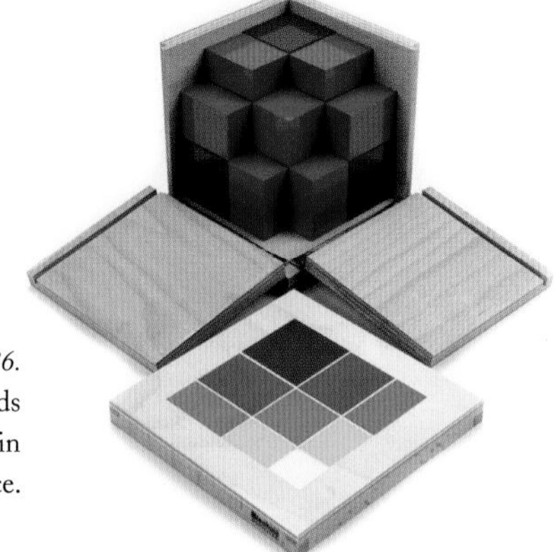

Figure 86.
The six red bodyguards joined the red king in the new palace.

it nothing but red. He felt exalted and impressive because he was in the very middle, just as he liked to be, right in the center.

Then, the orange guards and the white king peeked in. The white king had also really hoped for a throne of his own, but he was disappointed to see that there was none. Apparently, being the one who always had to be last, he was not powerful enough to deserve a throne. So, unhappily, he told his orange attendants to go ahead and find places for themselves.

The first orange attendants went into the palace and immediately found a place where they could be at home. When they were done, the rest of the orange attendants joined in. Then, the white king told his yellow attendants, the last three, to also find a

Place all of the orange prisms in the box.

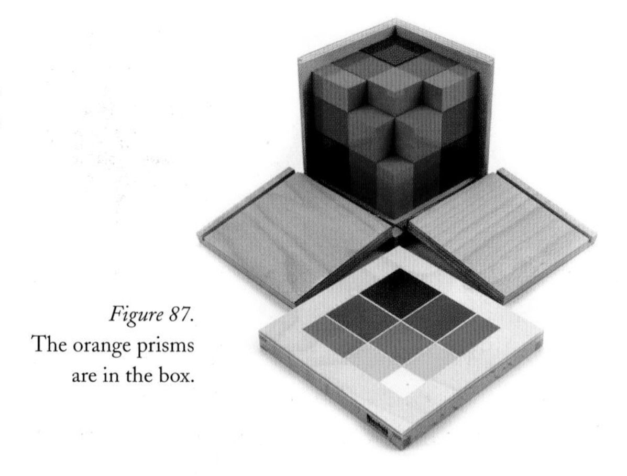

Figure 87.
The orange prisms are in the box.

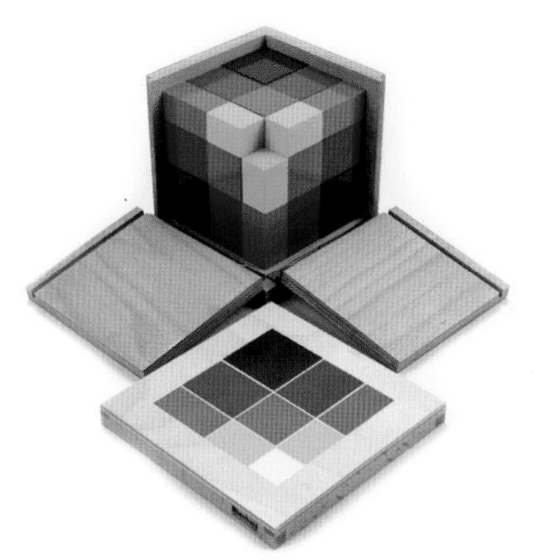

Place the three yellow prisms in the box.

Figure 88. The yellow prisms are now in the box.

home. The white king liked them especially, because they were bright yellow as he had once been. They went in and sat, when, lo and behold! A new high throne had been created especially for the white king to sit, just as he had hoped. The white king was so delighted that he joined the others and completed their cubical home.

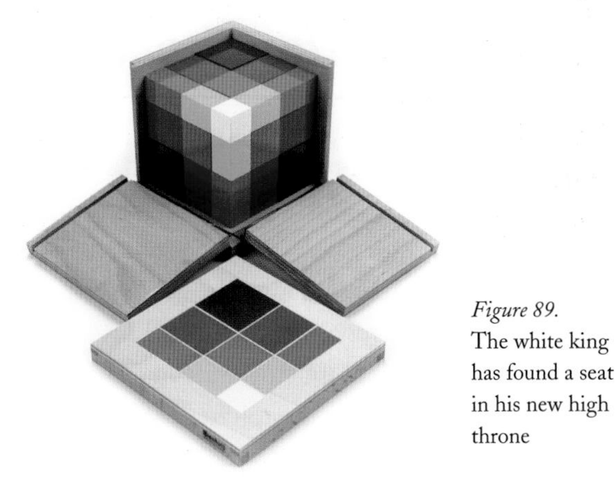

Place the white king in the box.

Figure 89. The white king has found a seat in his new high throne

And as far as anyone knows, they are living there still to this day.

Close up the box.

But something had changed. Now, the white king was bold and strong, so much so that when you work with this and you take the material out, he will be the first one and not the last

Put the lid on the box.

Figure 90. The door of the palace has been closed.

one to come out. He will be the first one to emerge, and no longer will he be frightened of being first. He's so strong and brave at this point.

This is how the trinomial cube changed from one color to another, and the three kings and all of their attendants and all of the parts changed from the land of letters to the land of numbers.

But do you want to know something interesting? This entire story took place in one afternoon!

Archimedes and the Hollow Sphere

INTRODUCTION

This is a curriculum story to be told when beginning work on the volume of the sphere. The study of the spherical volume actually begins with calculating the area of the spherical surface; only then can the actual volume be calculated. This is a very big study and needs a lively introduction. This story fits the bill.

Like many curriculum stories, it may also be told again after the unit on the sphere is complete. I often like to do this, book-ending the work with stories.

Archimedes (c. 287 BCE–c. 212 BCE) was possibly the greatest ancient mathematician. He lived in one of the most famous cities of ancient times, which we call by its very old name of Syracuse, on the Italian island of Sicily. That same city today is now called *Siracusa* and it is a popular tourist destination. In Archimedes' time, Sicily was a Greek colony, and its people considered themselves to be Greek.

The Romans besieged Syracuse from 214–212 BCE, finally conquering the city and ending Greek rule. It is said that a Roman soldier killed Archimedes at this time, despite a strict order of protection from the Roman leader, Marcus Claudius Marcellus.

In telling this story, you will need a large sphere or ball as a prop. Montessori upper elementary classrooms usually have a large, blue ten-centimeter sphere. That is perfect for this story. You could also buy a wooden ball in a craft shop and paint or varnish it. Blue is the traditional color, although the color does not affect the mathematics, so feel free to substitute, if needed.

Be sure to measure the diameter of your sphere. You will need to make at least four *great circles*. These are simply circles that have the same diameter as your sphere. Cut them out of heavy card stock or poster board of the same color as your sphere.

To begin the story of *Archimedes and the Hollow Sphere*, bring out a globe or map to locate the Mediterranean Sea and Sicily. Syracuse is located on the southeastern coast of Sicily.

Source: *Archimedes and the Hollow Sphere* is an original story that I wrote to complement a traditional Montessori geometry lesson on the surface area of the sphere. This presentation begins the study of the volume of the sphere.

STORY

Long ago in the land of Greece, there was a man who was a famous mathematician named Archimedes. He was born in about 287 BCE and lived until 212 BCE.

Archimedes lived in the area that is now called Sicily, which is no longer part of Greece, but it was ruled by Greece at that time. In Sicily, which is an island in the Mediterranean Sea, there was a city that was called Syracuse, and that is where Archimedes made his home.

Show Sicily on the map/globe.

Archimedes was a great mathematician, and he is known for many, many wonderful things that he did. He measured the volume of objects that were floating on the sea. He used that knowledge to measure the true weight of a crown of gold. That's another story, but it's a very interesting one.

Archimedes also figured out various ways to protect his city when the Romans decided to attack it, even though the Romans eventually did conquer the Greeks. Because Sicily is an island, when the Roman general Marcellus attacked, he did so by ship. Archimedes helped the king to find many ways to defend his island, but we'll come back to that story.

Hold up your large sphere.

Before that happened, Archimedes was approached with a problem, a problem which puzzled many people. This is a sphere, as you know, and the problem was, how could we measure the skin of this sphere? The surface of the sphere is curved—every part of it is curved. If we could skin that surface off and flatten it, it would break and split up. It won't become perfectly flat, that just doesn't work. It is like skinning an orange and trying to flatten that. There will be breaks in it, or possibly tears. Is there any way to find the area of the surface of the sphere? People had a very hard time with that idea.

So, they went to Archimedes and said, "Can you help us with a way to measure the surface of the sphere and then show us so we can do it, too?" Archimedes may have tried many things; we don't know how many different things he tried, but we do know that he was capable of taking an everyday experience and translating it into a mathematical principle.

He was known to suddenly crouch down in the middle of town and start drawing figures in the dust when he suddenly came across a geometric principle he had to explore right at that very moment. He was even known for trying to draw geometric figures on his own abdomen, with olive oil, in the middle of a meal! He would suddenly think of something and have nowhere else to put the figure, so he would draw it on his own belly!

Archimedes was an unusual person, but he was the right person to go to with this sphere problem, to try to figure out how to measure it. And he came up with a solution—I don't know if it was because of drawing with olive oil or with dust—but he did come up with a solution.

What Archimedes did was to approach a metalsmith. A metalsmith is a person who can make fine work out of metal, such as brass, copper, iron, or tin. Archimedes asked the smith to make a hollow sphere out of very fine, very thin metal. He also had the smith make several circles out of the same very fine, very thin metal. These were not ordinary circles; they were special circles with exactly same diameter as the sphere. They were what are called *great circles*. Great circles are simply circles with the same diameter as their corresponding sphere.

Display the four cut-out circles.

Once his sphere and the great circles were made, Archimedes came back to the king with a balance scale, which he proceeded to set up. In one pan of the balance, he put the hollow sphere. In the other pan, he put one of the great circles made of exactly the same metal, and *boink*, the balance went down in favor of the sphere—the sphere was heavier.

Use your hands as though they are a balance scale. In one hand, hold your sphere, and in the other hand, start stacking the great circles.

So, Archimedes started again. He took a second great circle made of the same metal and he put that on the balance scale as well. Again, the balance went down in the favor of the sphere—the sphere was still heavier than two great circles.

Archimedes did not give up. He took a third metallic great circle and he added that to the others on the balance scale. Once again, *boink*, the balance went down in the favor of the sphere—the sphere was still heavier even than three great circles.

Still, Archimedes tried again. He still did not quit. Instead, he took a fourth great circle made of the same metal and put that on the pan of a balance and—aha—they balanced. The sphere perfectly balanced the four great circles!

This showed Archimedes, and everyone else, that the four great circles were exactly equivalent to the surface area of the sphere. And do you know, what? Archimedes was right. Four circles *are* equal to the surface area of the sphere if they are actual great circles, the ones with the same diameter as the sphere.

Archimedes was very, very famous—not only for this, but also for the way in which he died, so let me tell you about that.

Eventually, Marcellus did succeed in invading Syracuse. But, because of all of the noble things that Archimedes had done to try to defend the city, Marcellus said, "Spare this man. He must not be killed; he must be saved because he is a great genius."

However, it is said that Archimedes was computing in the dust as he liked to do—drawing geometric figures—and in fact, the legend says that he was trying to work out a new proof of the Theorem of Pythagoras, of which we've already heard.

Well, as he drew in the dust, a Roman soldier appeared at the door and demanded that he give himself up. Archimedes ignored him because he was deeply concentrating upon his drawing.

Again, the soldier demanded that he give himself up, and again Archimedes ignored him and kept to his work. For a third time, the Roman solder demanded that he give himself up, but again, Archimedes ignored him. At this point, when Archimedes would not get up and leave with him, the Roman soldier killed him, even after his general, Marcellus, had told him not to—had told them all not to.

Some people think that perhaps the soldier didn't recognize who Archimedes was, and others say that maybe it didn't happen that way at all. But we do know that at that time, Archimedes passed away.

What Archimedes gave us to use for our work here is a way to find a surface area of a sphere. Even though we can't peel, can't skin, and can't flatten it, we can make four great circles. Archimedes gave us a great gift, a gift of a way to solve a problem that seemed like it couldn't be solved.

Well, whether it was false or true, the tale has spread far and near, because the tale was fun to hear.

Comment: *Later, after telling the story, you may want to tell the children something like this:*

Now, we will solve the problem with this particular sphere and find exactly what the surface area is of this very sphere that I am holding. Then you will be able to find the surface area of a basketball, a baseball, a soccer ball, even a ping-pong ball. You will be able to find the surface area of any sphere you like because Archimedes gave that gift to all of us who come after him.

Personal Stories

> "I believe your Story is a powerful connector. Your Story helps illuminate your uniqueness and makes you inherently relatable. Telling your story is what makes you real."
>
> —Christian Marie Herron, storyteller and brand strategist

I include some of these personal stories in this collection to show how events in one's own life can be made into stories. Of course, you will not want to tell these stories taken from my life. Instead, you will find the greatest satisfaction in creating simple narratives from the everyday happenings of your own life. You will likely find that your own personal stories become beloved by the children.

Sources: All of these *Personal Stories* are completely original stories, written by me.

Fishing With My Grandfather

Introduction

My grandfather and I loved to fish. Probably, the truth is that my grandfather loved to fish, and I loved my grandfather, so I spent time with him wherever I could, and this time often involved fishing.

Now, to my grandfather, there was only one fish worth seeking—trout. He referred to all other fish as "rough fish." Even though some of them were actually excellent fish, we very seldom fished for them. Nearly all fishing expeditions with my grandfather involved trout.

This personal story is a true tale of a fishing expedition that stands out in my mind. It took place near the Whitewater River in Minnesota's lovely southeastern bluff country, one of our favorite piscatorial destinations. This area is rich in trout streams and beautiful scenic country as well.

I try to lace this story with as many sensorial words as possible. I want to emphasize colors, shapes, and certainly sounds. This story has worked best with my older Children's House students and younger elementary students, but is appropriate for any age. I have even had great success telling it to adults. Even if they do not know any of the jargon of fishing—creel, hip boots, fly rod—they still enjoy the element of surprise in the tale.

I cannot help but feel that this story works much better orally than in print. I hope that you get the excitement and surprise from the print version.

STORY

When I was a boy, my grandfather and I used to love to go fishing. We loved to fish for trout. Now, he said that trout were the only fish worth catching. All other fish, he said, except possibly the catfish, were "rough fish"—not worth fishing for and not worth eating, either.

The only fish worth catching were trout, so we went trout fishing; if I wanted to go fishing with my grandfather, that's what we fished for. I loved my grandfather, so together, we would go fishing for trout all the time.

Now, to go trout fishing with my grandfather, the first thing I needed was a fly rod. A fly rod is a long kind of fishing pole or rod that is very, very thin and light in weight. It comes in several pieces that fit together. My grandfather taught me to take one piece of the rod, just where it is supposed to join to another piece, and we'd push that part along the sides of our nose before putting the pieces together to assemble the rod. By doing this, it would pick up enough oil that the pieces could come apart easily later on. That's how we always did it.

After we got our fly rods together, we would put them in the back seat of my grandfather's car and roll down the back window so that they stuck out the back on my side as we drove along with them. My grandfather had a two-door green Ford. Then we'd drive down to the stream where we'd go fishing for trout.

We always went fishing in a river or a stream, not out in a lake, but in a river or a stream. Some of them were very small, just creeks really.

We would get out of his car and take off our shoes. Then we'd put on thick socks and we'd pull on tall boots that came all the way up our legs—tall rubber boots that came way up our legs and clipped to our belts, called *hip boots*. Then we would walk around with tall rubber boots on. I loved that. I always loved having those tall rubber boots. I fancied myself looking especially interesting with the hip boots on.

On my right side, I would also clip to my belt a container for flies and artificial bait, and even worms sometimes, so I could carry those around. It was a little box with moist dirt in it so the worms would stay cool.

Then, on my other side, my left, we would clip a thing called a *creel*. The creel was a sort of box made of bamboo, split thin bamboo. It was like a basket, with many little holes in the side of it for air to flow through. In that creel would go the fish—that is, if we caught any. We would put the fish in there and the air would keep it cool as we walked around. But, at the beginning of the day, we put our lunches in our creels!

Finally, I put on a big hat to shade myself from the sun, and we were ready with our rods, our hip boots, and our creels to fish. Then we would walk down to the stream and wade right in.

One day, we stood together like this, hip deep in the cold rushing water. It was a beautiful warm day, and early in the morning, as I began to cast my bait out into the stream, hoping to catch a fish. It was just a nice day to fish.

My grandfather always said, "It doesn't matter whether you catch any fish. It matters that you're just there and enjoying the day." I never understood that. I always thought, "Why bother, unless you can catch a fish? That's the really important thing."

As the day wore on, we worked our way downstream. That means that we waded along in the direction that the water was flowing. I didn't catch a thing. Neither did my grandfather. But, we kept fishing until we eventually had to stop and have lunch, even though I still hadn't caught a fish. I was feeling kind of disappointed, because I didn't care what he said; it mattered to me to catch a fish!

After lunch, we kept on going downstream, and eventually, my grandfather said, "Now, it's time that we better start heading back upstream because it'll be dark before too long and we'll want to get supper." Upstream means that we would turn around and wade back the way we had come, against the flow of the water.

So, we turned and started wading back against the current to go upstream. Needless to say, we kept fishing as we did that. It got to be really disappointing because I had been fishing all day long and I couldn't catch a darn fish. We had been out there in nature, in what most people would think was just beautiful, on a nice day, but that didn't matter to me because I didn't have a fish.

I never got a fish. I got all the way back up to the point where high on a bank, a little ways back, I could see the pale-green color of my grandfather's old Ford two-door car sitting in the shade as the evening came on and the light dimmed. When I saw the car sitting there, I grew even more disappointed that I hadn't caught a fish the whole day.

I started walking the last few steps up, and right about where there was a place on the stream bank where we could walk up from the water to the higher ground where his car was, there were a lot of bushes. There was also a willow tree, which is a kind of a tree that likes to grow where it's wet. This willow tree had a lot of branches bending down toward the water and some other bushes grew right in there, so it was thick and sort of dark.

As I walked up to that area to go up to the car, suddenly, right up out of the bushes, WHOOOP! came a great big blue heron. It was a big bird that was very close to me, and with its wings spread out, they made a sound—WHOOO—and I was really frightened!

But I wasn't the only scared one. So was the heron, I suppose, because it flew up, and when it got just a little bit above my head, it opened its mouth to screech and out of its mouth dropped a beautiful rainbow trout! Right at my feet! From the sky came a trout to my feet!

I couldn't believe it! I grabbed that trout and put it in my creel, and I had had a good day fishing after all. Maybe the heron didn't, but I had an especially good day fishing. We went home with my trout, and we had it for supper. What a day! That was my day fishing with my granddad. And that's a true story!

The Pump and the Outhouses

INTRODUCTION

Possibly one of the most astonishing nostalgic tales that I tell children about my elementary school days involves the fact that our little rural school did not have running water.

It is extremely difficult for today's young children to imagine a school without any drinking fountains, washbasins, or flush toilets. The concept is completely foreign to most of them.

This is a fun personal story to tell, as it leads to speculation about what else we are used to that might not have been present in the past. While the children may understand that some modern electronic devices like computers did not exist, it is harder for them to accept the idea that we had a school without a toilet.

Remarkable!

STORY

A very long time ago, I was a child in school.

As I think you may know, I went to much of my elementary school in a little, white, one-room country schoolhouse. It stood on a low hill, as country schools often did, and there at that school, out in front, there was a water pump.

A pump is an iron contraption with a big handle that you

have to push and pull, up and down. Moving that handle up and down causes water to come pouring out of a spigot. That is called pumping.

We couldn't get water by turning on a faucet in our school; we had to go outside and pump it. During the winter, when it got very cold every night, we'd pump water in the late afternoon and bring it into the school. Then, the next morning, if the pump froze, our teacher could heat the water on a hot plate. When it was boiling hot, we'd take it out and pour it down the pump to break up or melt the ice so that we could pump water again. We had to do that fairly often in the wintertime when it was very, very cold.

Now, you may not know this—you may not even think about it—but if you don't have water in your school, it's very hard to have bathrooms, because there is no way to flush a toilet without water. Right? Water is used in bathrooms—there is no point in having a faucet or a toilet if there's no water!

Well, what did we do? How do you think we went to the bathroom in our school? Some people might think that you just had to wait all day long until you got home at the end of the day, but that wouldn't really work now, would it?

Instead, behind our school, there were two little buildings. One little building was for girls and one little building was for boys. We called those outhouses, because that was the name that was given to an outside bathroom, but they weren't like any bathrooms that you probably know. When you went in this outhouse, there was a board with two holes cut into it, and that board covered two deep holes that had been dug into the ground; and that's where people went to the toilet. There was no flushing. There was no special seat. There was no heat. There was a smell, though—a very bad one. It was a very simple place; there wasn't anything special to mark it as an outhouse.

When we wanted to go to the bathroom, we had to hold our hand up until the teacher let us go; then we would have to put on a coat and go outside and walk around to the back of the school where the outhouses were. This actually worked out pretty well except for one day in every year. And that day was Halloween.

For some reason, there were always some boys in our area who thought it was funny to come to our school and tip over the outhouses on Halloween night, so when we came to school the next day, we couldn't use them at all. They didn't just come to our school—they did it to all the schools! It would usually take the people who lived in the city and ran the school a day or two to drive around to all the different country schools and stand up the outhouses.

Of course, there was no telephone in our school, so we couldn't just call the people to come stand them up. Instead, our teacher would have to wait until the end of the day and call them from home; then they'd come driving out in a truck and set the outhouses back up.

Schools sure are different today, and sometimes we don't think of the little things that make a school today really a good place to be. To my way of thinking, and probably because my school didn't have one, one of the best things that schools have now is a bathroom with running water and flushable toilets! Isn't that a good thing?

Gathering the Seaweed

INTRODUCTION

The story of *Gathering the Seaweed* is a short personal story about my youth.

This story, like all personal stories, is based upon actual fact. This means that it could be a good little tale to tell to a preschool, or Montessori Children's House, age group, although I have also used it with elementary children and, sometimes, even with adults. It goes well when we are studying certain parts of biology, foods, gardening, or nutrition.

I often follow personal stories like this by asking children to talk about things in their own lives. Perhaps, some of them have gardens or parents who are avid gardeners. Many schools now have school gardens that also make this story applicable. Others may have gone swimming in a lake in the late summer and have discovered the thick, soft, greenish growths of lake weed. I ask them to talk about this, and soon, others who do not have these same experiences also join in to speak about events in their lives.

Of course, this discussion soon leads to the idea that they, too, can tell a story and that there are stories in all of our lives. The children can become storytellers in their own right. I like to help them see that everybody has stories to tell. Sometimes, it can be something that seems very small, like seaweed, but that doesn't matter—it can still make a good story.

It is incredibly valuable for children to begin writing and telling their own stories. Thinking about children as storytellers, Martha Hamilton and Mitch Weiss (2007, para. 1) wrote, "Why teach students the craft of storytelling? Because it is one of the most important life skills one can learn." Hamilton and Weiss continue by listing nine "reasons students should be given the opportunity to tell stories":

1. Storytelling increases self-esteem.
2. Storytelling, unlike some arts or sports activities, can involve all youngsters, regardless of ability level.
3. Showing poise and confidence when speaking in front of others comes with practice and experience.
4. Storytelling improves listening skills.
5. Learning a story, rather than memorizing, ensures a much better sense of story, sequence, cause and effect, and character traits.
6. Storytelling encourages creative writing.
7. Storytelling stimulates inventive thinking and imagination.
8. Telling stories instills a love of language in children and motivates them to read.
9. Perhaps most important of all, storytelling is fun (para. 7–15).

STORY

When I was a child, we had a couple of very big gardens, and I've mentioned my gardens to you before. I was sort of in charge of a lot of the gardening when I was a child and had to go out every summer to work in the garden. We needed to lay out long rows and plant our seeds. Later, the little plants came up and I would need to hoe to get rid of weeds. A hoe is a long tool with a sharp end that you use to break up the earth and dig up weeds.

Weeding was a lot of work! I had to do it, oh, probably every day for several hours to be able to keep up with the garden. Once a year, at the end of the harvest, we had to dig up the soil and till it. My father would come in with a tractor pulling a tool called a disc, which would break up and mix the soil so that the next spring, we could plant our garden all over again.

One thing we liked to do, because we lived where there were many, many lakes around us, was to go down to the lakes in the fall and look at them. There on the side of the lake would be a long row of seaweed that would have been washed up from the lake. Now, it's really not seaweed, it's lake weed, but we didn't know that. We called it seaweed. It seemed as if, in the late fall, it would die and be washed ashore, or maybe the lake just pushed it out.

The people who owned that stretch of the lakeshore, who lived there, were very happy if my father would drive his truck down and take some of the seaweed away. We would get a pitchfork, each of us, and we would fork that seaweed into the back of the truck, and drive back to the garden and lay a thick layer of it all over the garden in the fall. Then he would come out with a tractor pulling that special tool called a disc and mix the seaweed in with the soil. In the spring, it would be entirely gone. Completely! You couldn't see any sign that that seaweed had been put there. It was gone completely, eaten up by tiny helper microbes in the soil. Eaten up and made into fertile soil so that our garden would grow *so* beautifully the next summer.

Every year, we put on a nice, thick layer of that seaweed, or lake weed, and it was always a surprise that we never, ever, ever saw any sign of it the next spring. But, oh, did we ever have good gardens!

Hot Lunch at My School

Introduction

This is another small personal story about my own youth. As a child, I attended a rural one-room schoolhouse for a time. That was an incredible experience. I had initially grown up in the city and attended a city school. But when my mother remarried a rural man from the north, we moved into a very different world. The school was especially different. It was another world to me.

In that school, there was no real hot-lunch program like most schools have today. Instead, as the story tells, we had hot soup only, made upon a hot plate. We all also brought something else to school to eat, such as a sandwich.

It is also true that my teacher in those days believed that we should vote on any controversy. She explained that we lived in a democracy, and the democratic thing to do was to vote. This story tells how that affected our lunches.

Children to whom I have told this story find it interesting that we actually voted every day on what to have for lunch. After hearing this tale, they have held food elections to pick their favorites as well, and to no one's surprise, mushroom soup never has appeared on the list. Too bad!

Story

As I already told you at another time, I think, I grew up in the rural countryside in northern Minnesota. I lived in an area about ten miles from a town, and I went to a little country school with only one room.

Now, my little one-room country school was not quite half a mile from our house, so it was really a country school, in which kids from all sorts of different grades all sat in the same classroom and worked together, kind of like a Montessori school, actually!

Our school was very small, so we didn't have a hot-lunch program. There was no cafeteria. There was no cook. There were no lunch ladies. There was no hot lunch at all.

Our teacher, Mrs. Nelson, decided that a good thing to do would be to get a hot plate, which she did, and we could have hot soup as part of our lunch every day. So, we all pitched in a little, all of the kids pitched in money every month, and Mrs. Nelson bought condensed soup by the case. We would get several big cases, and they were filled with very big cans, family-size large cans of condensed Campbell's soup. One or two of these large cans with water in a big pot would make enough soup for all of us. Delish!

Mrs. Nelson was a big believer in voting for everything, even on subjects in school. We would vote on many things in the school, and one of those things was which kind of soup we would eat each day. Every morning, we would have a vote for the kind of soup we wanted to have for lunch.

All of the cases of soup were mixed, so there'd be many large cans of chicken noodle, several cans of turkey noodle, some cans of cream of tomato soup, and there would always be a few cans of mushroom—cream of mushroom—and that was it.

Every single time we opened a new case, the first variety that the students would all vote for—and I was okay with this—was always chicken noodle. We loved it—we would eat all of it. In fact, we would eat the chicken noodle soup every day until it was all gone from every case, because we children would vote for chicken noodle every day until all the cans of chicken noodle were eaten up.

Okay, then the next one was usually turkey noodle, because nobody could tell the difference. It tasted, or seemed, just the same as chicken noodle, so we'd eat all that up, too. Sometimes, the second soup would be the cream of tomato.

We would certainly come soon to that cream of tomato soup, which I absolutely never cared for. I simply never cared for cream of tomato soup at all, although I couldn't tell you why.

I would think, "Oh no, I paid my money, I helped buy the soup, so I have to eat it, but it's tomato." I never liked it much, but of course, I would eat it anyway. After all, I had paid for it.

The only soup I especially liked in the whole case was the cream of mushroom. I loved mushroom soup. To tell the truth, I still like cream of mushroom soup. But, I always had to wait until the very end to eat the mushroom soup because it would always be the last soup of the month. No one else would ever vote for it, so we finally ate it at the end just because it was all that was left. If, by any chance, a new shipment of soup arrived before we ate the cream of mushroom, the other children would vote for the new soup and we would start all over with chicken noodle. Again, we would eat everything else first and leave the cream of mushroom until later.

That was the first time I ever saw anybody make cream soup by mixing the soup and a can of water. In our house, my mom always used milk, but Mrs. Nelson, I guess being a frugal public school teacher, sent us out in the front yard where there was a pump, which was how we got water in the school, and we'd pump it out and bring in water and make the soup that way.

The good news—there is good news—was that there was something fun about the cream of mushroom soup. No one else ever voted for it until they had to, because nobody else liked mushroom soup. So when it came to the mushroom soup at the end, I could eat all I wanted, and I really loved that part. That's true—a true story. That's the way we had our lunch back in the day. And, that's all there is.

Frozen Fun—Bubbles and Maple Syrup

Introduction

This is another small personal story from my childhood. Northern Minnesota, where I was reared, is a place of strongly contrasting seasons. Although many people do not believe it, the area experiences a wonderful, warm, and even hot summer. During the summer, the days are long, and the sun is bright. The region also has two dramatic seasons of change and transition, spring and autumn. These are spectacular seasons of natural wonder and beauty that offer contrast to that which came before and that which is to come.

There is little doubt, however, that winter is the best-known season of the northland. For most people, the mention of living in northern Minnesota conjures up arctic visions, replete with ice, evergreens laden with snow, and a permanent chill. Actually, that is not so wrong.

To me, as a young person, winter was a great and beautiful season, bringing special treats unavailable at any other time. I loved the brightness of winter nights with the reflective white snow, the Aurora Borealis (Northern Lights), the sledding, and the ice-skating. Somehow, it never seemed so cold as it does now.

This short personal narrative introduces children to some of those special winter moments that marked my life. It brings to the fore the idea that winter is actually one of our wonderful seasons. It is not to be regretted, but to be celebrated and enjoyed.

Story

You know that I grew up in northern Minnesota. In the north, it gets very cold in the wintertime. It was often very, very cold, freezing cold, especially at night. But, sometimes in the day, it would get really, really cold as well. We would have days where it would be thirty-five or forty degrees below zero. That was really, really, very cold. That's *so* cold—very, very cold.

Now, there are things that we can do when it's cold out that are really a lot of fun. Many people don't know that. They think the most fun you can have when it's cold is to be indoors and make a hot fire or drink cocoa or do something like that, but there are fun things to do outside. When you live in the north, you want to come up with some things to do. Here are two of them that are a lot of fun.

One thing that we enjoyed doing when I was a boy, when it was really so cold out, was to get some maple syrup and take it out to where there was fresh, white, cold snow on the ground outside—it was best when the snow wasn't really fluffy. It has to be a little bit settled, as if it melted and crystallized a little. That makes a nice, hard snow. So, when we had this right kind of hard snow and it was really cold out, we would fill a big, ice-cold bowl with this cold snow, packing it down quite a bit. Then we would pour some of the maple syrup onto the snow and it would freeze just like that—it's instant ice cream or sherbet, in a way. Some people called it taffy or candy, because it can be hard or chewy.

We called it *Maple Freeze*; so fun to eat. That really was a lot of fun for us, even though it really isn't ice cream—it's more like a snow cone without the cone, or maybe maple candy. It doesn't really have the whole taste of ice cream, but a little maple syrup on the ice-cold snow was just so much fun. We'd have fun sitting around and eating it, right there.

Another thing we enjoyed doing a lot when I was young, in the same kind of cold, cold weather on a still day, was blowing bubbles. This is what you can do. You get a jar of bubble solution, the regular kind that comes with a little wand for making the bubbles.

It's nice to have a real bubble jar here and take it out and demonstrate, but you can also mime the experience.

When it's very, very cold, way below zero, the bubble freezes in the air instantly. Presto—frozen bubble!

You have a beautiful frozen ice bubble, but you can't hold it in you bare hand or your body heat will melt it instantly. But, if you have mittens or thick gloves, that bubble might sit right there in your hand, and it's just a frozen, crystal bubble, and you can then go "pshk" and it'll break. Some of these bubbles will just crack like an egg, while others may simply deflate.

Make a breaking sound.

What a clever thing. It has to be really cold. "Whoo" goes the bubble, and there it is.

Make a blowing sound

Now, all of that is past, this story, too, but you can bring it back to life yourself in your own winter celebrations.

A COMMENT ABOUT
Frozen Fun—Bubbles and Maple Syrup

That is the story that I tell to small children, but elementary children are fascinated as well. They are just amazed that you could do these things. Even their parents, when they talk to me, express amazement that we used to go outside in such cold! But, when you are children in the north, that's what you do! It was a lot of fun.

If you want to experiment with the maple syrup "ice cream," it is important to let your snow get very cold. Chill it well in the freezer so that it is very cold. The snow should be packed well in a clean pail or bucket.

Set the bucket outside when it is very, very cold. For me as a boy, that meant thirty-to-forty degrees below zero. Let the bucket sit out in the cold for a day or so. Then, pour the maple syrup on it. The result is simple "ice cream" or, possibly, maple candy.

I have been asked if you can do the same thing in a freezer. I have never tried it, but you probably can. Just be sure to set the freezer as cold as possible and let the snow sit there for a day to be really chilled.

Other Stories

"The universe is made up of stories, not of atoms."

—Muriel Rukeyser, American poet and political activist

Go, My Child

Introduction

The Botany work in Montessori classrooms is unique in the way it engages the children's creative imagination while also offering them basic information. This is done with impressionistic charts, as well as with stories.

One fascinating set of Montessori material is a collection of posters or charts called the Plant Physiology Charts. Although these charts bear an intimidating name, they actually include several attractive charts that serve as the central artifacts in very appealing object stories.

These posters are an example of what Montessorians call Impressionistic Charts. That name is used to suggest that they appeal to the imagination of children, creating an impression. They are not simply to convey facts, but to bring excitement to the work.

This curriculum story, *Go, My Child*, is told to emphasize the biological rule that life forms reproduce only their own kind. While most of us understand this, the notion that it could change radically has been made into very some interesting literature, such as E.B. White's masterpiece *Stuart Little*.

Figure 91. The tree says, "Go, my child. I have given you all the necessary provisions. Go and create new colonies to spread our principles throughout the world. Always remember that you belong to the noble stock of monocotyledons (or dicotyledons)."

There is a special chart that goes with this story, which I have included. You can make a poster like this yourself. Be sure to use it—it adds so much to the tale.

The speaker on this botany chart is an anthropomorphized tree with a human face. It is speaking to its seed, telling it to maintain its noble lineage and always remember what it is—that is, what it will become.

Source: *Go, My Child* is an original story, which I wrote to accompany the Montessori Plant Physiology Chart.

Story

Everything has babies.

Every kind of plant and animal has little ones. They have to reproduce. We know that reproduction is one of the vital functions that both plants and animals have. When they reproduce, they bring new beings into the world, and that's how they can go forward.

Now, there is something really important that we have to talk about. When plants or animals reproduce, they can only reproduce more of what they are. A plant can't reproduce and turn itself into an animal, and an animal can't give birth to little plants. Somebody's laughing because that's so funny.

Can you imagine an animal giving birth to a plant? Or a plant having a seed like an acorn, but when the acorn sprouts, out jumps a mouse? It just doesn't work that way!

Animals can only have animals, and plants can only have plants—and furthermore, only certain kinds. Here on this chart, we have a beautiful picture of a tree talking to its baby. See its little seed down here, with its backpack on, ready to go on a trip? Ready to go on a life's journey. Off to become something.

This young baby plant is ready to go and undertake the task of its life: to grow up. The great work—if you want to call it that—of its life.

The mother tree says to it, "Go, my child, I've given you the necessary provisions." In the backpack, in the seed, is all the food that's needed to sprout.

"Go and create new colonies, in order to spread our principles throughout the world. Never forget that you belong to the noble stock of the dicotyledons."

That mother tree is telling its seed, "Don't forget what you are. You can go and spread the idea of being an oak tree throughout the whole world, but you'll always be an oak tree. You can only have seeds that will be oak trees, because that's what you are." The little seed, the child, stands here listening, ready to go and spread its kind everywhere throughout the world. Point to the little seed on the chart.

This is an important message, and it is a message that all mother trees, and all animal mothers also, give to their young. They may not actually say it, but the message is still passed along. When you were born, your mother was able to look at you and know that you were a human being just as she is. If she'd given birth to you and you'd been an oak tree, she would have been very, very surprised.

Luckily, that didn't happen for anybody here in this room. We all followed our kind, just as the tree is telling its baby to do.

So the story is told, and here it begins. The story is told, and here it ends.

A COMMENT ABOUT *Go, My Child*

This is an example of a "story" that is less a story, more an introduction. However, the children do perceive it as a story.

It works beautifully as a creative dramatic piece after the children have heard the first presentation. Someone becomes the mother tree, another child is the seed, and a third child can act as a narrator. I have had many instances in which the resulting sketch is very humorous as the seed pleads to become a kitten or something else. The children have also done this same sort of skit using life forms other than a tree. If it is a dog, for example, then the mother may have a whole litter of babies to address. Go, my children!

The Little Red Spoke

Introduction

Jonathan Wolff is a Montessori consultant, trainer, speaker, and author with deep experience as an educator and administrator. More importantly (to me), he is also an inspiring master storyteller. His wonderful stories have enthused teachers and children across the country. Among his original works, Jonathan has created marvelous stories that focus on character development.

A great example of this genre is his masterful story *The Little Red Spoke*. Utilizing anthropomorphism, Jonathan creates a metaphorical story leading to introspection and self-discovery.

I am very grateful to my friend Jonathan Wolff for allowing me to use this story, which I print here now along with Jonathan's own introduction to it.

Jonathan Wolff's Introduction to *The Little Red Spoke*

Children, like adults, at times struggle to remember the underlying unity of life and our shared connections to the past and our planet amid the bewildering diversity of individual experience and cultural expression. This simple metaphor is an attempt to help young people realize that, beyond the constant flux and stimulation of the world, there is a place of quiet comfort and connection for those willing to look away from the sensory tumult of daily life and see the spiritual, moral, emotional, and ecological threads that bind humanity together as one universal family.

Story

There was once a Little Red Spoke that lived inside the great circular rim of an old wagon wheel. Day and night, night and day, the little spoke whirled and twirled at great speeds round and round and round as the old wagon traveled back and forth along the dusty country roads.

Because he looked only at the outside rim of the wheel, the Little Red Spoke saw the world most times as a blur of colors and shapes. The sky, the trees, and the road looked to him to be not much more than whirling, twirling streaks of blue and brown and gray.

There were times, of course, when the Little Red Spoke would stop whirling and twirling, times when the wagon needed to pick up or deliver whatever it was carrying to town. But even then, even in that stillness, the Little Red Spoke kept his eyes only on what was closest to the outside rim of the wheel—a rock, a patch of grass, an occasional family of ducks that waddled from one side of the road to the other.

One night, a great rainstorm blew throughout the countryside. The wind howled. Branches fell from the trees and scattered across the road. The next morning, when the wagon rolled into town, a big branch that had fallen to the ground in the middle of the night banged against the Little Red Spoke at the very spot where he was fixed to the outer rim of the wheel.

Thump! Crack! Snap! The Little Red Spoke felt a great pain in his long body! He looked at the outside rim of the wheel and saw, to his great surprise, that he was no longer attached to the rim of the wheel.

"Help! Help," he cried! "I'm broken! If something doesn't happen soon, I will fall off the wheel and be lost and left behind on the road forever!"

"There, there now," said a kindly voice. "You're all right. You're safe. You won't fall off the wheel or be lost."

The Little Red Spoke was very surprised to hear such a kindly voice; he was surprised to hear any voice at all! He had always believed he was alone as he whirled and twirled along the country back roads.

"Who are you?" he said. "What are you saying to me? If you look at the rim, you will see that I am no longer touching the wheel. I will soon fall onto the road and be left behind and lost forever in the dust."

"Look behind you," said the voice, "to the center of the wheel and you will see you are not alone. You will see, too, that what I am telling you is true. Look to the center of the wheel and you will feel so much better! I promise!"

Never in all his years had the Little Red Spoke ever thought to turn his eyes away from the outside rim of the wheel. He was afraid to look at the center of the wheel. He didn't know what to do.

"Behind me? Why there's nothing behind me," he said.

"Look behind you," said the soft, sweet voice. "Look to the center of the wheel."

So he gathered his courage and for the first time in his life, the Little Red Spoke turned his eyes from the outside rim of the wheel and looked at the center of the wheel—at the hub. To his great surprise, nine brother and sister spokes looked at him and smiled!

"Hello Brother," they said! "Hello! Hello!"

For a few moments, the Little Red Spoke couldn't speak. All these years, he had whirled and twirled along the back country roads thinking he was alone, thinking the world was nothing more than a blur of sky and trees and road. He was not alone! He was connected to all his brother and sister spokes at the hub of the wheel! He was safe! He would not fall off the wheel! He would not be lost and left behind.

The Little Red Spoke looked at his brother and sister spokes. "Oh my," he said! "H-h-h-hello." The peace he felt in the center of the wheel, the silence and calm at the hub, was so unlike the clatter and churning he had always known at the rim of the wheel. For the first time in his life, the Little Red Spoke felt connected and calm. He belonged. He was not alone.

The Little Red Spoke began to smile. "Hello," he whispered to his brother and sister spokes. "Hello."

The Story of Soap

INTRODUCTION

Everything has a beginning, and soap is no exception. The question with everyday things is how and when they began.

When I was a child, my grandmother made soap at home every year. She combined fat and lye into a distasteful, foul-smelling mixture in the kitchen. I did not understand the process, which I now know is called *saponification*. I did know that it worked, and we had homemade soap each year. It meant another clean year.

My grandmother had also mastered the technique of scenting her soap so that the odiferous brew transformed into delightfully sweet-smelling suds. She also made it float. At that time, only Ivory soap was known to float, but my grandmother's soap did just as well.

What event or happening could have first led to the discovery of the saponification process? Well, it just so happens that fat drips from roasting meat, and ashes are a source of lye. Put these together in the presence of water, and that could be how soap was discovered.

I wrote this origin story with the idea that soap may have been discovered in a primitive village, more or less by accident.

Note: Saponification is the process that produces soap from fats of various sorts and lye. The fat may be animal fat, as in this story, or possibly a vegetable oil. Lye is a strong base, which can obtained by leaching ashes with water, the happy accident described in the story. This ashes and water method was also used by the Babylonians.

The ancient Babylonians may have first made soap as long ago as about 2800 BCE. They made their soap from fats boiled with ashes, not completely unlike the Mount Sapone method.

A further note on pronunciation: In the name of the mountain in the story, Mount Sapone, the word *Sapone* should be pronounced as sa-Pone-ai, with the accent on the *pone* and the final *e* in the word pronounced *ai* as in Maine.

Source: *The Story of Soap* is a completely original story, which I wrote.

Story

It is told that long ago and far away, somewhere in the Mediterranean area, there was once an island. It may still be there for all I know, but its name has probably changed many times. Now, on this island, there was a great mountain, and the mountain was named Mount Sapone. A little way up the mountain, there was a village, though with only a few houses, it was hardly much of a village at all.

The people in this tiny village lived in that exact spot because of something very nice: quite close by, there was a spring with gushing water that emerged to start a small stream. This small stream entered into a still pool of water right below the village. What a nice place for a small village on Mount Sapone.

Now, something very interesting happened with that pool. People had a village fire in front of their homes. This small fire was used for many things. Among other things, it was used for roasting meats that the people found when they went hunting. They would bring back animals, roast them over the fire, and fat from the animals would drip over the ashes. That made a sticky mess, which nobody would touch or eat.

Now, people have to eat every day, so there was a lot of roasting going on. They didn't eat meat every day, but each time they did, more fat would drip over the ashes. This happened many times over and over. Sometimes, it would rain. When it rained, the fat and ashes would mix up in a watery solution, and some of that would wash into the nearby stream and pool. When that happened, something magical seemed to occur. All the clothing that was washed in that pool became extra clean. It was as if there was something special about the water in that pool whenever the fatty ash mixture had dribbled in.

One day, somebody came up with a very interesting idea. "Maybe, if we took a barrel and put all the fat and ashes in there, we could let it rain on them." So they tried that. The special thing that happens when the fat and ashes mix together in the heat of the fire is that they make soap. It's true.

There's something in the fat and something in the ashes that made the first soap. It may not have been the cleanest looking soap; it may have been a little ashy or greasy. But, the soap cleaned things better than anything else. Even to this day, there are two main ingredients in soap. One is fat, which may be oil, fat from plants, or fat from animals. The other is lye, which comes from ashes.

What a fabulous discovery there on Mount Sapone: the first soap. It is a wonderful thing because with soap, we all have the opportunity to be clean. That is the story of soap. And now the story is yours.

Stories from Etymology

INTRODUCTION

Properly speaking, this is not really a story, but a set of little "storylets" about etymology. Etymology, the history of words, should be a part of many lessons in the elementary class. It helps that etymology is fascinating to children. As a sort of origin story for a word, etymology is tremendously valuable for elementary vocabulary building.

There are hundreds of little etymology stories; the examples that follow are just samples of what can be offered in the elementary classroom—many other etymologies should be given to children. The best thing you can do is to get a good etymological dictionary or two. Then you can look words up and say, "Oh I wonder why? Why is that called *congruent*?" Or, "Why is that word named an *adjective*? Aha! Of course, that goes to a Latin word *adjacere*, which means to be thrown near." That's what the adjective typically is—a word usually in the middle between the article and the noun, and often near to the noun.

Source: *Stories from Etymology* represents a group of small anecdotes or narratives, which I wrote after consulting a number of etymological sources.

Story

I'm not going to share a specific story, but I wanted to tell you that there are hundreds of little stories that we can tell from etymology. Let me just mention a few so you get an idea. These are mini-stories—I call them *storylets*—like the story of a circle.

~

You know what a circle is? I have one right here. I think everybody knows what a circle is; here is one. Now, where did the word *circle* come from? Well, maybe you didn't know that it comes from the Roman word, the Latin word, *circus*, or *circulus*, because the Roman Circus—where they raced their chariots around and around—was in this shape. Because of that, we've taken the name of the Roman Circus; that round and round gives the notion of what a circle is. There were circles before that time, of course, but our word goes back to Roman times. So, that's an etymology story, and that's the whole story of the etymology of the circle—that's the whole thing.

Show a circle from the Geometry cabinet, or one which you have cut out.

~

One of my favorite etymologies is the story of the rodent. A rodent. Now, maybe you know what a rodent is. A squirrel is a rodent. A rat is a rodent. Beavers are rodents. A capybara is a South American rodent.

One of the most important things that you need to know about rodents is they gnaw with their teeth. Every rodent nibbles or gnaws throughout its life. The word *rodent* goes back to a Latin word *rodere*, which means "to gnaw," or "to eat away."

This would be a good time to display some pictures of rodents. Be sure that at least one prominently shows their teeth.

The really interesting thing is, that our English word *erosion* comes from the same Latin root. Why? Because erosion gnaws away at the land; it wears the soil away. So when you think of erosion, you really should think of a rodent at the same time—because that is what struck people when they named it. That is the rodent. Interesting story, don't you agree? Chew on that one.

Display one or more pictures of eroded fields.

~

Here is another little etymological tale. If you live in Ohio or some other states, you might have the cardinal as your state bird. It is the state bird of six different states: Ohio, Illinois, Indiana, North Carolina, Kentucky, and West Virginia. But why is the cardinal called a cardinal, I wonder?

Show a picture of a cardinal.

Well, when early European settlers came to America, they noticed the bright-red songbird and were reminded of the churchman, the Roman Catholic cardinal, who dresses in red robes, and has since the 1200s. They thought, "There is a bird dressed in red up in the tree. He looks like a cardinal." So it was named after the cardinal in the church. The cardinals were given that name not because the flying cardinal is actually a priest of any sort, but because his coloring reminded people of that.

Show a picture of a Roman Catholic cardinal in colorful red vestments.

Another interesting thing is that there are *cardinal numbers*, the numbers that count or tell how many of something there are, such as one, three, five, seventeen, or one hundred. These are not priests or churchmen, nor are they birds, but they are related. That is because the word *cardinal* comes from a Latin word *cardinalis*, that means "principal," "chief," or "essential." These numbers are so important, so essential, that they are called cardinal numbers. That is the same sense in which the church cardinals were named. They were considered important enough to be called cardinals.

Now, we have discovered that state birds, mathematics, and religion might be linked through the etymology of one word!

~

One of my favorite geometric etymologies is the word *pyramid*. We all know what a pyramid looks like. The first great pyramid in Egypt was built sometime between 2589 BCE and 2566 BCE.

The first part of the word pyramid is the prefix *pyr*, followed by *mid* meaning "middle" which combine to make "fire in the middle." That's because the pyramid is a place of fire.

A pyre is a funeral place where, in some cultures, bodies

were disposed of by burning in a big pile. Sometime in the past, when words were shifted from Latin to Germanic languages, there was a change in consonants, so words that started with a "p" like the Latin *pater* shifted to an "f" like the Germanic *father*. Pyr became fire.

So, a pyramid is really a place of fire; it's a little fire spot. It tells us something interesting about the Egyptians—I think I could guess what they may have done with their dead before they built that first pyramid! Some of them may have used a funeral pyre, which is why that shape is called a pyramid, a pyre. I think that's one of the most interesting etymologies, and I think it will help you to remember the name of the pyramid shape.

Pyramid note: Even though I like this etymology, it isn't accepted by everybody. There are other different histories done by various etymologists.

~

I will give you another little story because I just want to illustrate how much fun we can have with etymologies. This one I like: *acute*.

Do you know what an acute angle is? Or an acute-angled triangle? Well, the word *acute* goes back to a Latin word that means "needle:" *acus*—needle. What is the special thing that we should know about a needle? Just this: it's sharp! So, an acute angle is pointed like a needle. It's sharp and pointed, so from that we get a special geometry word. Maybe some of you have heard of *acupuncture*, which uses needles. It is called that because it starts like acute. *Acu*, just like the word *acute*, from the word for needle.

Even our word *acid*, which is a liquid that is sharp and burning, starts with the same sound as the word acute, except that the C has a soft sound. But it still has the same sharp beginning.

By the way, if you are very smart, if your thinking is quite brilliant, you might also be thought to be acute. That means that your thinking is sharp, like a needle. That's better than the opposite, which is *obtuse*. That word goes back to the Latin word *obtusus*. That word means "dull" or "blunt," dulled down. By about

1500 CE, it had also come to mean dull in thought. And we'd rather not have our thinking be thought of that way, we'd rather think of it as being like that needle—sharp and pointed and going right to the idea.

~

Here's another one. I'll tell you this one, which I think is fun, about the etymology of the word *angle*. This is a great one to do now since I just told you about *acute* and I mentioned acute angles. The word *angle* means "a corner," or something bent. It also comes from a Latin word, *angulus*, which means "a sharp bend." So, when we come to a corner in a figure, that's called an angle because it has a sharp bend.

Now this word means some other things. For instance, there is a group of people that were called the Angles, who lived, once upon a time, in Northern Germany. Why could they have been called that? Well, because they lived near Denmark, where the land makes a sharp bend. So the people were called Angles.

Later, some of them moved and they conquered an island that lay off the coast. That island became known as the Land of the Angles or Angle Land. We still call it that, except that the word has slightly evolved—now call it *England*. So, the acute angle and England are related by their etymology. They both go back to the same source—the sharp bend.

~

Now, for the very last one of these little etymologies. A common concern for teachers is discipline. You may have heard teachers say they're concerned about discipline, which can describe the good, self-controlled behavior that comes from the students as well as the efforts from the teacher to correct unacceptable behavior. Discipline comes from the same root as the word *disciple*, which means to follow or to become a pupil.

A disciple follows any great spiritual leader, not because of the fear of punishment, but out of love. True discipline is true love. Discipline comes from love and following from love. So, when we talk about punishment, we should not be speaking of discipline at the same time, because discipline is a following out of love.

By the way, that's why when we study a particular thing like chemistry, somebody might say that that's an academic discipline, because the chemist loves it. History is a discipline because it's loved by the historian. Do you understand? Math is also a discipline because the mathematician loves it. The mathematician doesn't study math for fear, the mathematician studies math for love.

That's it. Stories from etymology. Now, I've had enough. If you want any more, you can tell it yourself.

SOME COMMENTS ABOUT *Stories from Etymology*

This is really a set of little stories that suggest the kinds of things to have in mind when you want children to fall in love with words. You want them to become excited about more than the meaning of a word alone: you want them to get excited about how we came to be the way we are and how it is that we got to say the things we say! Then, they can be inspired to think, "Maybe I should look that up, maybe I should find out more."

When we suddenly find out that things that seem so different, like the country of England and the angle on the corner of a triangle, actually are related to each other and they're related through a people that once lived in Northern Germany, it becomes a much more interesting little story.

I gave the story of the word *discipline* because I think it's one of the things that helps us to understand that when we forget etymology, words can become distorted and we can suddenly be talking about them wrongly. When we do think of the real meaning, it can help us to refine the way that we work with young people.

Remember that we don't always have to tell a whole story unto itself. Sometimes, it can be beneficial to emphasize just one special little something about a word.

The Gifts of the Phyla

INTRODUCTION

This is a story about gratitude. It is somewhat scientific, but it actually directs children toward the idea that we are what we are because of all of the living things that have come before us. It proposes the idea that all of the various groupings of life have given us gifts for which we should be grateful.

This is usually presented with a sheaf of pictures illustrating each group that is mentioned. As each new group is discussed, bring out that picture and display it.

These are the groups that are needed:

Plants
Protozoa
Coelenterates (often called Cnidarians)
Annelida
Flatworms
Roundworms (also known as Nematodes)
Arthropods
Fish
Amphibians
Birds
Mammals
Human beings

For each group, you should have at least one, and preferably two or more, pictures. Have the same number of pictures for each group. You also should make labels with the names of each group. The pictures are available on the Internet, with very little searching required.

Please note that there may be slightly different terminology that you use. For example, the coelenterates or coelenterata are frequently called *cnidarians*. Cnidaria is, in fact, the more modern term. So, if you want to use the term cnidarians, just substitute it in whenever the text says coelenterates.

Also, the roundworms are frequently referred to as *nematodes*. Again, if you want to use the term nematodes, just substitute it whenever the text says roundworms.

Source: *The Gifts of the Phyla* is a classic Montessori story lesson, although it may have had its origins elsewhere. I have revised and altered it to emphasize narration and the element of gratitude.

STORY

Does everybody here like to get a present sometimes? Isn't it nice when someone gives you a gift? Maybe at Chanukah you receive a gift, or perhaps for Christmas, or perhaps at some other time, like your birthday. Or, maybe it's just because someone felt like giving you a present or a gift for some reason because they were just being nice to you. You might even give one to yourself every once in a while! Maybe you like it when you can give a gift to somebody else, and that makes you feel good as well. I know I like that.

I'm happy because I found out that I've received many, many presents—many, many, gifts from the past. I've received gifts from animals and plants that live all around us, and that lived before, and so have you! You might not even know that you got these presents. We should say *thank you* when people give us presents. So, we will do that. Because we've gotten wonderful presents from these other living things.

We're going to talk today about gifts of the phyla. Gifts that each phylum, each group, each kingdom, has given us so that we can live the way we do. We are able to live with what we have because of all those who came before us. Here we are, let's see what gifts I am talking about.

Show the picture(s) of the human beings.

Let's talk first about the gifts that the plants have given us. Plants are really an important giver of gifts for us. We could not live the life we live if plants didn't give us the gifts that they do. I take a deep breath because oxygen is a gift from the plants. Plants give us oxygen, and without the gift of oxygen from plants, we

Show the picture(s) of the plants.

would have a hard time—an impossible time. Plants give us life, food. First, plants give us life because plants came before animals, and our whole life emerged from early plants. Plants give us food. They are the only things that capture solar energy, the energy of the Sun, and transform it into something that we can use, that we and other animals can eat. If it weren't for plants, we would starve. Because we get food from them, we also get energy, not only our own energy, but also the energy that makes our cars run. That's another gift from plants. The energy that we can use to warm our homes, that's a gift from plants. And the energy that you may burn when you have your fireplace going, that's a gift from plants as well. Plants give us food, life, energy, and you know what? They give us beauty as well. If it weren't for plants, we couldn't live the life we live.

Show the picture(s) of the protozoa.

Think about something else, then. Let's look at one of the smallest living things: the *protozoa*. What kind of things can we get from the protozoa? Cells, the very cells that form the basis of life. It all starts with the protozoa. We need to have an animal cell on which we build our lives, and that's where it starts; it's the basis of all animals. Thank you to the protozoa.

Show the picture(s) of the porifera.

Now we'll look at the next one, which is the *porifera*. The porifera are sponges, they are pore bearers, and their gift is a colony of cells that show us how life can become complex and we can live with others. All the different parts of us can live together. Thank you to the porifera.

Show the picture(s) of the coelenterates.

Next, the *coelenterates*. The coelenterates are very interesting animals. The jellyfish is a coelenterate. They give us a cavity. Their gift is the opening in their center where digestion takes place. Instead of having each cell individually go out and get food and serve itself, the coelenterates give us a system. The coelenterate is layered with an outer layer and an inner layer. We also keep that helpful feature. It's nice to have an inside, and an outside. It helps to keep things like food on our inside! Now, the coelenterates gave us a bad idea that we didn't keep, which is that they're shaped like a bag. So, all of their food goes into the opening in the bag and all of their waste comes out that same opening. That's sort of a bad-breath idea—it's not a good idea in the long run for us. But that opening in the center, where the food goes, that's a great idea. Thank you to the coelenterates.

There are three main different kinds of worms. One kind of worm is the *annelid*, like an earthworm. These are worms that have little segments in them, and that's one of their big gifts. Your body and the bodies of all higher animals are segmented with various sections that go back to this animal right here. These animals also have blood vessels. They gave that idea to us—they gave the idea of blood vessels. What a great notion, a system that allows our blood to get from place to place.

Show the picture(s) of the annelida.

Then there are flatworms. A flatworm is a worm that is very, very flat. It is an absolutely flat thing, but they have what we call bilateral symmetry, which is an interesting thing. Bilateral symmetry means that if you draw a line down the middle of the animal, they're symmetrical on either side of the line. They're the same on both sides. Not all animals use this plan, but we do. We keep that notion. Starfish don't, but we do. In fact, all of the higher animals kept that idea.

Show the picture(s) of the flatworms.

Roundworms are another type of worm. They are easily the most common kind of worm, with about one million species. However, more than half are parasitic. Their digestive systems are their great gift, as we will see.

Show the picture(s) of the roundworms.

And now—this is one of the most important ones—both the annelids and the roundworms give us this: a tube-like digestive system with an opening at one end for food to go in, and an opening on the other end where waste products come out. Fundamentally, that's what you are, a tube with an opening on one end for your mouth where food goes in, and an opening on the other end where waste products come out—the rest of you is built around that!

That's the center of our bodies, and everything else is built around it. Some things, like our feet and hands, help to move our body so that the intake end can be close to something that we want to get to and eat. So really, that's a fundamentally important idea, it's a great gift for us, and it makes us able to use our bilateral symmetry to move us to a place where we can put something into our mouths so that we can live and eat. Thank you to the worms, both annelida and roundworms.

Show the picture(s) of the arthropods.

Next let's look at the *arthropods*. They represent most of the animals on Earth. It's true, most of all the animals that live are arthropods. One gift that we don't use from the arthropods is an exoskeleton. They wear their skeleton on the outside, like a suit of armor. Then, all of the soft internal parts sort of hang inside. That is a gift that has gone to many animals, but it is not one that we use.

What do you think that the arthropods did give us? Well, they gave us the idea of stiff and jointed legs on which we could walk. With these jointed legs, we are able to transport ourselves in a way much superior to the worms. Thank you to the arthropods.

Show the picture(s) of the echinoderms.

Now, let's thank the *echinoderms*, like the starfish. Their name means "spiny skin." They give us one of the most interesting things of all; they were the first animals to have any sort of skeletal structure on the inside of their bodies. It's not a skeleton, and it's not even bone, but it's cartilage. Cartilage is like what's in the very end of your nose; you can kind of move it around but it's stiffened a little bit, so it gives shape to your nose. It's also in your ears. It gives a little shape to your ears but it's not hard like bone. Cartilage comes first, and then, in higher animals, bones developed. Thank you to the echinoderms.

Show the picture(s) of the fish.

Now the next group to look at is the fish, and in fact, fish are responsible for giving us bones. If you've ever gone fishing or eaten fish, you may know that they can be bony. Those bones aren't just here and there. There is a very important bone that must be mentioned. The most important bone is their backbone, their spine. That's the bone that they have given us that's so important, because all of our nerves and bones come off that hugely important bone structure, our backbone. The fish is responsible for giving us this. The next time you have a piece of tuna or gefilte fish, you can thank a fish for the backbone that you have. Thank you to the fish.

Show the picture(s) of the amphibians.

Now, the amphibians, what have they shown us? What have they given us? You may not know, but ears are an important part that amphibians came up with first. They gave us the notion of an external ear, an ear to hear things and listen. There's something else that amphibians give us: lungs to breathe oxygen. Our lungs are based on the model that goes back to the amphibians—not to the fish, because they use gills and do not have lungs to breathe oxygen. Thank you to the amphibians.

Now, to the reptiles! Well, you wouldn't be surprised that their biggest gift to us is the egg, the developed amniotic egg, since we already heard about the egg earlier in the story of *The Chicken or the Egg*. In fact, this becomes the gift to live anywhere on Earth, since we are no longer bound to the water. The amniotic egg has freed us. Thank you to the reptiles.

Show the picture(s) of the reptiles.

Then we have the birds. Birds are so advanced, and they've given us so much: warm blood, the care of their young, and love. We see with the birds, suddenly, the evolution of caring and love, which is so important. The birds are warm-blooded and show advanced nesting and care. Thank you to the birds.

Show the picture(s) of the birds

Now, finally, let's thank the mammals. We must thank them for three important things: The free hand; stereoscopic vision, which means being able to look with two eyes and see things in certain ways; and intelligence, the special intelligence that we have. We can also thank them for hair. Our hair is a trait of the mammals. Finally, they give us milk. Thank you to the mammals.

Show the picture(s) of the mammals.

It's interesting that so many animals, and even the plants, have given us gifts. These gifts are important parts of what make us human. So we can look back at all of these species, all of these phyla, all of these things, and say thank you; thanks for the ears, thanks for the eyes, thanks for the gut that I use for digestion. Thanks for the legs that allow me to move so that I can get from place to place. Thanks for this tube that things go in and out of that becomes my digestive system. Thanks for the lungs. Thanks for the egg. Thanks for the brain and for intelligence. Thanks for all of that.

Show the picture(s) of the human beings again.

When we think about living things, we need to think that way—thankfully. We need to think that animals and plants have brought so much to all of us and given us so much. This story tells us the gifts that the phyla have given us, but you know what? It doesn't tell every single thing. Not at all. It can't. Because there are so many more things that we've gotten from plants and animals that have come before us for which we should be grateful—so many more things that this little story just gets us started on thinking about them. These are the gifts that make us who we are, the gifts of the phyla.

The Great River

Introduction

The story of *The Great River* is a highly imaginative introduction to human anatomy. Using a geographical metaphor to discuss the human body, it really fascinates the children.

In presenting this story, be sure to offer a sense of wonder and amazement. Let your voice convey your awe at some of the ideas, like "This country has *six billion inhabitants*!" Use your face to show astonishment as well.

Figure 92. The Great River.

There is a chart or poster, also called The Great River, shown here in Figure 92. This is an essential support in telling the story. It certainly adds to the imagery.

The Great River is a curriculum story because it introduces the curriculum on human anatomy. In Montessori schools, this is usually explored in the last year of the upper elementary class, roughly equivalent to grade six. Of course, the story and chart may be used whenever the study of human anatomy is begun.

Source: *The Great River* is a classic Montessori story lesson based on an impressionistic chart. I have developed an updated chart, and also revised and altered the story to emphasize narration and the storytelling aspect.

Story

I want to tell you about a very, very strange and odd country. This is a country unlike any that you've ever seen before. It's especially different. It is an unusual country in many, many ways.

First of all, it is extraordinary and different, curious and odd. At the same time, it will be very familiar—you might realize that you know it after all, in a way that you may not imagine. That may be one of the strangest things of all—how can this country be both strange and familiar? How can it be both different and the same? How can it be these two things at the same time?

Well, I said it was strange, and it is strange; it's a strange country. It's a country that's watered by a river, a Great River that flows through this land. This Great River reaches every place in the land. The Great River makes its way to every single inhabitant and every single location. This land is a wet one, watered completely by the Great River that flows through it.

Now, let's talk about the inhabitants who live there. The citizens who live in this land are, themselves, quite strange. How many are there? Well, let's say there are more inhabitants in this country than there are people who live in the entire world today. There are more than six billion of them all living in the land with the Great River. *Six billion!*

And what do you think they do? They work. That's all they

do. They work and they work, and they work, and then they work. They don't take any breaks. They don't pause. They don't have vacations. They don't take rests. They simply work all the time. They get all of the nutrition that they need directly from the Great River. Then, they put all their waste products right back into it. Right back into that same river! In fact, they work and work and work, and when they die, they simply slip into the river. They don't have any funerals; there's no mourning, there's no crying. They just simply slip into the river without any tears.

The Great River that waters all of this land is the center of everything that is there. It's a marvelous nation, isn't it? It's an amazing thing. It's unusual. It's so different.

Now, here's something else that you may not know. All of the citizens live in perfect harmony. They get along with each other. Each one, though he works for himself, is actually working for the benefit of the whole. So, every single one does the best he can for himself or herself, but at the same time, everyone gains from everyone else's work. This is strange because it seems that the inhabitants are filled with both selfishness and love. They are selfish in that they want what they can get for themselves, but all that they do for others is like a kind of love.

This country does have a government. It has a president. The president lives in a great palace that has a dome. This dome is very protective. It's strong and acts like a shield. It's actually like a castle where the president lives. The citizens of this strange nation around the Great River are perfectly obedient to the president. There are no protests. No police force or army is required to make the inhabitants do exactly as they should. They are completely obedient and they always work. They work for one another.

Like any government, there are many different departments that serve the president in this land of the Great River. The most important department is the Department of Transportation, which is run by the Great River itself. The other departments are the Department of Nutrition, which deals with food; the Department of Air—I think you know that must deal with air; the Department of Sensations—that's an interesting name; the

Department of Defense; and the Department of Purification.

These departments are all separate, but they're all joined to the president's palace so that they take their orders from the president. They can communicate very rapidly with the president's office and some of them, like the Department of Sensations, are specialists in rapid communication. Very rapid communication. The president issues orders, and each department follows orders, exactly as they should.

I happen to have a map, so let's take a look at this very strange country. Though it doesn't show all six billion inhabitants, it is a map that we can look at, and here it is.

Show the Great River chart.

This is a map of this very strange country that I'm talking about. Let's look at each department and see what they are and see how they fit.

Here, at the top of the hill, is the president's palace. The president's palace has the great dome on top. That fortified dome protects the president and keeps them safe. It is from the president's office that all orders are issued and that everyone follows these orders.

Point to the president's palace atop the hill on the chart.

Here's the Department of Transportation. The Great River has its headquarters in this area right here. This is the headquarters. This great pump moves the river around. It has four pumping stations—four chambers that move the river from place to place. That's the Department of Transportation.

Point to each department on the chart as it is mentioned.

Point to the red central building.

Down here, this is the Department of Sensations. As you look at the Department of Sensations, you'll notice there are five gateways to its office building. One of them is labeled with an eye. One of them is labeled with a nose. One is labeled with a hand. One gateway is labeled with an ear. Finally, one is labeled with a tongue. A strange building—but the Department of Sensations has instantaneous communication with the president's office!

Point to Department of Sensations building at the bottom center of the cart.

Way up here is the Department of Nutrition. The Department of Nutrition is a mill, and it is a mill that grinds things finely. This mill is not like any other mill; it doesn't just grind grain, though it actually can grind grain. This mill grinds vegetables, fruits, even meats. It will grind anything, and you see people carrying food to and from it. Then, when the foods are ground

Point to the windmill at the upper left of the chart.

up, they go into the Great River, where they're carried to all of the other departments so anyone can benefit from the food.

Point to the Department of Air on the lower left of the chart.

Here is the Department of Air. The Department of Air is a building that has a flexible top that can expand and contract. Here's a man with a bellows pumping air into it. At the same time, some gases are being pumped out from the Department of Air. The Department of Air is also connected directly to the Great River, so that it can bring in special gases and put them directly into the Great River itself.

Point to the hospital building with a red cross on it on the upper right of the chart.

Then, we have the next department, the Department of Defense. The Department of Defense is in charge of with defending the entire nation of the Great River and it is filled with medical personnel, all in white, who will rapidly fly to wherever they are needed. If their intervention is required, they will be there to defend the Great River by helping save and cure anyone who is ill. They can repel an invasion.

Point to the brown building on the lower right of the chart.

Finally, we have the Department of Purification, this brown building down here. It's also connected to the Great River, and there it separates the waste from the products that must be recycled. Some things, both liquids and solids, are being dumped out of the area for purification, but others can be recycled. By dumping and recycling, the river is always kept pure even though the inhabitants do put their wastes into it. The Department of Purification is always busy cleaning the river so that it stays pure.

Now, after all of this about this Great River, you may wonder, where is this country? Why haven't I heard of this country? Where could it be located with its six billion inhabitants? If there is such a place, then where is it?

Well ... it's right in this room! It's actually with us at all times. This great land never leaves you; it is with you wherever you go. It is the human body! Your body! The human body is the land of the Great River. And the Great River is the river of blood that pulses through us at all times. Be silent for a moment and see if you can hear or feel it pulsing through your body.

If you can feel it or hear it, or even if you can't, it's there inside you pulsing away, the Great River. And the Department of Transportation, this great pumping station, is your heart. Your heart is the pumping station with its four chambers that drive blood through your body and carry it to every inhabitant. And who are these inhabitants? Cells. Cells that work together in a marvelous way and fill your body with work because that's what they do. The cells in your body work all the time.

And what about this president's palace with the dome that's fortified on top? Well, that's your brain. Because it's from your brain that the orders are issued to all the other parts of your body. You may not even be aware of the orders being issued, but they are, continuously. They are constantly being issued to every department.

Look again at the Department of Sensations, with its five gateways that open up. That department is your senses. Your senses of sight, smell, touch, hearing, and taste that bring in information to your body. They communicate instantaneously with the office of the president so that you can immediately see, smell, taste, hear, and feel all that comes from the five gateways of sensations.

Of course, our lungs make up the Department of Air. Just like this picture, they can expand and bring air in like the man with the bellows. Then they contract, and some of the gases are expelled. They come back out. Those gases don't stay with us because we don't need them. But, the oxygen from the air does go into the Great River and then it can travel all throughout our bodies.

We must also look at the Department of Defense. These are the white cells of your blood that race madly to cure or help whenever there's an infection. These specialized cells are like little doctors and nurses that go from place to place as rapidly as they can, as if they were in an ambulance. They race to get there to try to help cure anything that happens within your body.

Finally, there's the Department of Purification. This department includes your large intestine and your kidneys, the areas where waste is separated from that which can be retuned to your body, and then it's expelled from your body when you go to the bathroom.

This is a marvelous country. Isn't it fabulous? It is very strange, but it's also very familiar, because it is within every one of us.

There are two great principles or laws in this nation besides work, which is the overpowering principle. The other two are love and selfishness.

Love is the principle that perpetuates the species. It's the principle that is revealed by the obedience that each cell shows, by the care that they take for themselves and one another, by the way they fulfill their responsibilities.

Then, there's the selfishness. For each of the cells wishes to exist and continue its own life. But, while it perpetuates itself, without knowing it, each one helps the whole body, the whole person, to survive. We live in a marvelous country. A country that is our person. A country that is us. Every one of us has this Great River inside of us.

That was just the beginning.

Now we're going to learn much more about the human body and many more things about all of those departments and some other secret departments that we haven't even heard of yet. We'll learn about all parts of the body. When we do, remember the Great River and how it waters our entire nation.

The Story of Pythagoras

INTRODUCTION

The *Story of Pythagoras* is a traditional activity in Montessori schools. His biography may also be told in many other schools as well. Of course, Pythagoras was a great Greek mathematician and philosopher. He is credited as the originator of the well-known Pythagorean theorem, which is usually written as $a^2 + b^2 = c^2$.

By telling the life of Pythagoras, this story gives a human figure to this man who lived more than two millennia ago.

The story of Pythagoras is a biographical story. It can be a model for many other stories of biography.

Source: I wrote *The Story of Pythagoras* based on widely available biographical information from many sources, even including my own math classes going back more than fifty years. Information about Pythagoras can easily be found in a variety of texts, as well as on the Internet.

Story

I want to tell you a story about a most extraordinary man. A man that some people think accomplished great and wonderful things. A man that some people think did terrible things. A man who lives in the mind of mathematicians every day, even though he lived over two thousand years ago. This man was named Pythagoras. Pythagoras—what a name!

Pythagoras was a scientist and a mathematician. Some people believe that he could predict the future. Some people believe that he could remember what happened in a former life. They even said he could read sealed letters without opening them. They told many fabulous stories about him. Pythagoras had many friends and students, but he also had many enemies as well.

Pythagoras was born about 582 BCE. The place of his birth was an island named Samos, off the coast of Turkey, near the Turkish city of Smyrna. It is said that his mother, Pythais, was the most beautiful woman on the island, and she, too, had gifts: she could tell the future. Sometimes, maybe many times, she was right. Eventually, Pythagoras began to do this himself. Because of this, it appears he was banned from the island, sent away, banished by the ruler of the island at that time.

So Pythagoras traveled. When he traveled, it's reasonably sure that he traveled to Syria and to Palestine. We think he may have traveled all the way to Babylon, where he met with the priests who measured the stars and the circles. Some people think that the scientists of India influenced him. Perhaps, he may have even traveled there as well. But, it is certain that he traveled to Egypt. Oh, Egypt! What a land that must have been! Long and narrow. Some places were as narrow as only a mile. Some places, near the delta, were very wide. The land was fed throughout from one great river, the Nile. The Nile River, emerging from central Africa, fed all of Egypt, gave Egypt its water, its food. It made the country of Egypt. Without the Nile, there would be no Egypt.

When Pythagoras arrived in Egypt, he was struck by something wonderful and terrible. Every single year, in the spring, the waters of the Nile would rise up and up. In a good year, the river would begin to flood, all across the land. Don't think of this flood being beautiful, clear, refreshing water. Coming out of central Africa, it was murky, thick, muddy water. Water clogged with silt and sticky mud. The water was filled with insects that had drowned, fish swimming desperately. There were sticks, leaves, and branches, maybe the occasional tree. There were the bodies of various other animals, too, animals that had fallen into it or had been swept away. Some were tiny like ants; some may have been the size of dogs or even larger.

This murky, sticky, mucky mess spread across the land of Egypt. It inundated everything and covered the land. When it finally went away, it left anywhere from a few inches to a few feet of mud and silt and other things behind it, covering everything.

You may think this was terrible, but to the Egyptians, this was the gift of the Nile. Because in that mud was great fertility, fertility that allowed the Egyptians to raise wonderful crops and farm every year for thousands of years. The gift of the Nile was the mud left behind by this inundation, the mud that could be plowed and planted for rich crops. It also did something else: it erased the borders between various peoples' property so that those lines had to be recreated somehow.

As Pythagoras looked at the results of the flood, he saw a team of Egyptian priests come out carrying a golden chain with twelve links in it. The priests stood at an obelisk, which is a stone tower, and they would line up. One priest would march down the chain three links, and then turn the chain at that point. Another priest would do the same thing four more links down, and then a priest would take the end of the chain to meet the priest holding the first link. Amazingly, a triangle with a right angle would be formed. They made a corner at perfect right angles. They did this again and again and again, making parallel lines, marking the fields off again. Their method, they said, was a secret from the gods, which they would reveal to no one. Pythagoras realized that it was not a secret of the gods but a property of the numbers three, four, and five. With those three numbers, he thought he could always make a right-angled triangle, and he was right. Those numbers are called a Pythagorean triple. Pythagoras stayed in Egypt for more than twenty years, gathering their wisdom, and this idea about three, four, and five is one of the most important things he took from the Egyptian priests.

Then, in about 525 BCE, Cambyses, the king of the Persians, conquered Egypt and took Pythagoras as a prisoner to Babylon. At court in Babylon, Pythagoras became an acquaintance of all the great people there. He must have learned so much more, and perhaps he also taught at the same time.

Eventually, in about 520 BCE, he did return all the way back to his island of Samos, where he formed a school that he called *The Semicircle.* For some reason, Pythagoras left Samos again after only one or two years and went to the place we know now as Italy. Back then, it was called *Magna Graecia,* or Great Greece, because it was owned by Greece—there was no country of Italy in those days. All of southern Italy was a colony of Greece. There, Pythagoras, at the age of seventy, founded a new school, and it appears that he had as many as six hundred students. It was a secret school! The students at the school were known as the Pythagorean Society or the Pythagorean Brotherhood. His students studied arithmetic, geometry, music, and astronomy. It's thought that Pythagoras taught them the secret of the triple that he had learned in Egypt, and he also taught a famous theorem: the Theorem of Pythagoras, or the Pythagorean theorem.

Some people also think it was there, in Magna Graecia, that Pythagoras discovered the special intervals in music that we call octaves. Some people even think that it was there that the foundation was laid for astrology as well as astronomy.

Pythagoras's followers were vegetarians who ate neither meat nor beans. They believed that the souls of their departed friends might live in animals or even in beans, so therefore they could not eat them.

Now, it turns out that in about the year 508 BCE, the countrymen around the city where Pythagoras had his school were very suspicious of what was going on there, so they attacked the school. Nearly all of Pythagoras's followers were massacred, but most accounts say that Pythagoras escaped and fled, possibly to a city called Metapontium, which means "beyond the port." Some people believe that Pythagoras died there with some of his brotherhood. Others believe that he starved himself to death. We probably will never know for sure.

Pythagoras is given credit for discovering so many things. We don't actually know which things he actually discovered and which things someone else discovered, but Pythagoras was given the credit for lots of things. Odd and even numbers, the description of the point, irrational numbers, the various lengths of string that create the musical octaves, the Pythagorean Triples, the beginnings of astrology—so many things. Pythagoras, however, was very, very secretive, and only certain knowledge could escape from the Pythagorean Brotherhood. They did not share their secrets with others, and no documents exist from Pythagoras himself, but he was probably the scientist of his time that had the greatest influence on the future. At the same time, he's a person about whom we know very little. Compared with other Greeks, such as Euclid, we know almost nothing about Pythagoras. This great man, however, founded many things and we owe so much in geometry, mathematics, music and science, to Pythagoras, the great, great Greek.

Afterword

> "People think that stories are shaped by people. In fact, it's the other way around."
>
> —Terry Pratchett, American novelist

Stories change lives. Properly (and frequently) used, stories transform people. This transformation is positive and can be long-lasting or even permanent.

Our educational system is in crisis. We face challenges from many other nations in struggling to measure up to a world standard. Schools struggle to effectively educate all students. Increasing ethnic diversity, poverty and economic disparity, and cultural differences pose challenges to educators at all levels.

Our science and mathematics scores suggest to many educators and lay people that much more emphasis must be placed there. This may point toward additional weight being placed on technology and engineering, leading to programs such as STEM (science, technology, engineering, and mathematics). However, progress also is imperative in literacy and language arts. Other fields such as the humanities, social sciences, and the arts also need significant reinforcement.

In the United States, we face the "achievement gap"—the disparity in academic performance related to race, poverty, home languages, or a variety of other suggested causes.

> The "achievement gap" in education refers to the disparity in academic performance between groups of students … It is most often used to describe the troubling performance gaps between African-American and Hispanic students, at the lower end of the performance scale, and their

> non-Hispanic white peers, and the similar academic disparity between students from low-income families and those who are better off. (*Education Week,* 2004, para. 1)

There is a tremendous amount of discussion about how to solve the problem of this gap, but it seems evident that although many changes and adjustments could offer meaningful and powerful assistance, no one single change can provide a complete answer. Yet, I suggest that stories have an important role to play in the solution to this crisis.

Stories are a powerful vehicle to reach children who are completely literate, while simultaneously reaching those who are struggling with the basics of reading and writing, or mathematics. Stories can connect children to essentials from science, the arts, and social studies. Stories appeal to typical children, as well as to many with special needs. Stories are color-blind—they reach listeners of all races and ethnicities. Finally, stories can reach children of wealth, children of poverty, and children in between.

I will not suggest that stories are a panacea. I will argue, however, that the power of story can reach learners in ways few other media can accomplish.

We can fully incorporate stories into every unit, in almost every subject. Furthermore, constructing a variety of narrative structures in which basic curricular components can be embedded can expand the format well beyond stories to a complete program organized around the stories.

I call this complete program the *Story-Centered Curriculum.* Stories like *The Chicken or the Egg* (p. 184) and *The Noun Family* (p. 145) are but two examples of using a narrative structure to embed elements of a school curriculum. In other words, the oral stories that we use need not have plot, characters, or a dénouement. Anecdotes, historical tales, and even little bits of information can be placed in a narrative format.

For example, in discussing the first element, hydrogen, a teacher might say, "You know, the story of the name of hydrogen is interesting. It was named from a Greek word *hydros*, which meant 'water'; and from French *–gène*, which means 'producing.' So, hydrogen was named because it produces water, along with oxygen. It has a valuable task to perform. Can you imagine the world if there were no hydrogen to produce water?"

A little tidbit like that is hardly a fully-fledged story, but it provides valuable information in a short narrative form. It involves science, etymology, and history all at once. It ends with an invitation to speculative higher-order thought. I point this out to indicate that stories need not be formal or structured, even though many are. In a Story-Centered Curriculum, there is room for many kinds of stories, varying in length, subject, intensity, structure, or formality. The important thing is to start telling.

For many, that is, indeed, the exact problem. In several storytelling workshops that I have led, I have encountered people who link storytelling to public speaking and let their fears of "giving a speech" infect their view of storytelling. I am frequently told, "Oh, Michael, I could never do that. I'm not good at that kind of thing." I can see that it's really more than that, that they're frightened—of failure.

The good news is that seldom will anyone meet a more appreciative and forgiving storytelling audience than children. Of course, practice is necessary, but when we make errors, as we all inevitably will, children are happy simply to "go with the flow."

Really, the trick, for me, has been to lose myself in the tale, focusing on the telling and the enjoyment that comes from that. In this way, it's no longer about me. Instead, it becomes about the spiritual connection to the listeners that story is offering.

In the beginning of this book, I offered a tale about a mystical source, a well providing a limitless flow of sacred golden water. This source was called the Deep Well of Time, and it served as the inspiration for the title of this book. Think once more about that image and reflect with me on how it speaks to the transformational power of story in the lives of children.

Narrative stories are motivating. They can involve children in the life, culture, and work of the classroom. Even reluctant learners can be captivated by the enchanting power of a fascinating fable or creative story.

Story allows us to time-travel. It can take us from the adult world and link us to childhood. It can carry us to the world of the dinosaurs, the first farmers, or ancient civilizations. With story, we can also travel in space to any place, real or imagined. Stories involve us in imagination, conceptualizing, visualizing, reasoning, and speculation. Stories can lead to probabilities, possibilities, and the seemingly impossible.

Story can also carry us to the future, to imagined worlds, and to plausible (or implausible) lives yet to be lived. Of course, the magic of story can transport all of us, children and adults alike, throughout the universe.

Story is nearly unique in the way it can simultaneously harness and stimulate the imagination, leading both to the fanciful and to deeper understanding of common curriculum elements. Other arts, such as music and visual art, have the same capabilities, but even these are magnified when linked with story.

Go to that deep well. Drink deeply of the sacred waters. Share the intoxicating beauty of the world—imagined and real—with children. Build it throughout your curriculum and lesson plans. The children will love it and learn from it. Importantly, so will you.

Welcome to the world of the Deep Well of Time.

Appendix A

The Triangles of the Detective Triangle Game

This is a list of all sixty-three triangles that are included in the Detective Triangle Game (p. 150), a commercial material. If you prefer, you may make your own from colored card stock or heavy construction paper. To do the game correctly, each of these triangles will be needed.

small	red	acute-angled	scalene	triangle
small	yellow	acute-angled	scalene	triangle
small	blue	acute-angled	scalene	triangle
medium	red	acute-angled	scalene	triangle
medium	yellow	acute-angled	scalene	triangle
medium	blue	acute-angled	scalene	triangle
large	red	acute-angled	scalene	triangle
large	yellow	acute-angled	scalene	triangle
large	blue	acute-angled	scalene	triangle
small	red	right-angled	scalene	triangle
small	yellow	right-angled	scalene	triangle
small	blue	right-angled	scalene	triangle
medium	red	right-angled	scalene	triangle
medium	yellow	right-angled	scalene	triangle

medium	blue	right-angled	scalene	triangle
large	red	right-angled	scalene	triangle
large	yellow	right-angled	scalene	triangle
large	blue	right-angled	scalene	triangle
small	red	obtuse-angled	scalene	triangle
small	yellow	obtuse-angled	scalene	triangle
small	blue	obtuse-angled	scalene	triangle
medium	red	obtuse-angled	scalene	triangle
medium	yellow	obtuse-angled	scalene	triangle
medium	blue	obtuse-angled	scalene	triangle
large	red	obtuse-angled	scalene	triangle
large	yellow	obtuse-angled	scalene	triangle
large	blue	obtuse-angled	scalene	triangle
small	red	acute-angled	isosceles	triangle
small	yellow	acute-angled	isosceles	triangle
small	blue	acute-angled	isosceles	triangle
medium	red	acute-angled	isosceles	triangle
medium	yellow	acute-angled	isosceles	triangle
medium	blue	acute-angled	isosceles	triangle
large	red	acute-angled	isosceles	triangle
large	yellow	acute-angled	isosceles	triangle
large	blue	acute-angled	isosceles	triangle
small	red	right-angled	isosceles	triangle
small	yellow	right-angled	isosceles	triangle
small	blue	right-angled	isosceles	triangle

medium	red	right-angled	isosceles	triangle
medium	yellow	right-angled	isosceles	triangle
medium	blue	right-angled	isosceles	triangle
large	red	right-angled	isosceles	triangle
large	yellow	right-angled	isosceles	triangle
large	blue	right-angled	isosceles	triangle
small	red	obtuse-angled	isosceles	triangle
small	yellow	obtuse-angled	isosceles	triangle
small	blue	obtuse-angled	isosceles	triangle
medium	red	obtuse-angled	isosceles	triangle
medium	yellow	obtuse-angled	isosceles	triangle
medium	blue	obtuse-angled	isosceles	triangle
large	red	obtuse-angled	isosceles	triangle
large	yellow	obtuse-angled	isosceles	triangle
large	blue	obtuse-angled	isosceles	triangle
small	red		equilateral	triangle
small	yellow		equilateral	triangle
small	blue		equilateral	triangle
medium	red		equilateral	triangle
medium	yellow		equilateral	triangle
medium	blue		equilateral	triangle
large	red		equilateral	triangle
large	yellow		equilateral	triangle
large	blue		equilateral	triangle

APPENDIX B

The Algebraic Trinomial Cube

For reference purposes, this is how the twenty-seven pieces in the Algebraic Trinomial Cube are distributed:

- One red cube, four centimeters on each edge. This is called the first red king.
- Six prisms with the square faces painted red. These are divided into two sets of three. These two sets are called the attendants to the red king.

  First set: Each prism in the first set of three measures 4 x 4 x 3 centimeters.

  Second set: Each prism in the second set of three measures 4 x 4 x 2 centimeters.

~

- One blue cube, three centimeters on each edge. This is called the first blue king.
- Six prisms with the square faces painted blue. These are divided into two sets of three. These are called the attendants to the blue king.

  First set: Each prism in the first set of three measures 3 x 3 x 4 centimeters.

  Second set: Each prism in the second set of three measures 3 x 3 x 2 centimeters.

~

- One yellow cube, two centimeters on each edge. This is called the yellow king.

- Six prisms with the square faces painted yellow. These are divided into two sets of three. These are called the attendants to the yellow king.

  First set: Each prism in the first set of three measures 2 x 2 x 4 centimeters.

  Second set: Each prism in the second set of three measures 2 x 2 x 3 centimeters.

~

- Six black prisms measuring 4 x 3 x 2 centimeters. These are called the bodyguards.

Appendix C

The Arithmetic Trinomial Cube

For reference purposes, this is how the twenty-seven pieces in the Arithmetic Trinomial Cube are distributed:

- One blue cube, four centimeters on each edge. This is called the new blue king.
- Three green prisms. Each green prism measures 4 x 4 x 3 centimeters. These become the first attendants to the new blue king.
- Six brown prisms. These are divided into two sets of three.

    First set: Each brown prism in this set of three measures 4 x 4 x 2 centimeters.

    Second set: Each brown prism in this set of three measures 3 x 3 x 4 centimeters. These also become attendants to the new blue king.

~

- One red cube, three centimeters on each edge. This is called the new red king.
- Six red prisms, each measuring 4 x 3 x 2 centimeters. These were called the bodyguards, and will now become the bodyguards of the new red king.

~

- Six orange prisms. These are divided into two sets of three. These will be the attendants to the white king.

First set: Each orange prism in the first set of three measures 3 x 3 x 2 centimeters.

Second set: Each orange prism in the second set of three measures 2 x 2 x 4 centimeters.

- Three yellow prisms. Each measures 2 x 2 x3 centimeters. These are also attendants to the white king.
- One white cube, two centimeters on each edge. This is called the white king.

Bibliography

This bibliography is a list of all of the sources I have consulted or otherwise used (whether referenced or not) in the process of researching and preparing this work.

Baring-Gould, S. (1876). *Curious Myths of the Middle Ages*. London: Rivingtons.

Bettelheim, B. (2010). *The Uses of Enchantment: The Meaning and Importance of Fairy Tales*. New York: Vintage.

Brett, D. (1988). *Annie Stories: A Special Kind of Storytelling*. New York: Workman Publishing Company.

Brett, D. (1992). *More Annie Stories: Therapeutic Storytelling Techniques*. New York: Magination Press.

Campbell, J. (2008). *The Hero with a Thousand Faces*. Novato, CA: New World Library.

Campbell, J. & Moyers, B. (1988). *The Power of Myth*. (1988). Betty S. Flowers (ed.). New York: Doubleday.

Cassidy, V. (1951, January). Jack and Jill. *Modern Language Notes*, 66 *(1)*, p. 38–39.

Christian, D. (2004, reprinted 2011). *The Maps of Time*. Berkeley, CA: University of California Press.

Coleridge, S. T. (1817, reprinted 1834). *Biographia Literaria*. New York: Leavitt, Lord & Co., p. 174.

Corbett, P. (2008). *Jumpstart! Storymaking*. Oxfordshire, UK: Routledge.

Cox, M.R., (1893). *Cinderella: Three Hundred and Forty-Five Variants*. London: Published for the Folk-Lore Society by David Nutt.

Crawford J. M., Translator. (1888). *The Kalevala*. Cincinnati, OH: The Robert Blake Co.

Czaja, P. C. (2003, November) Story Telling in Montessori Education. *Montessori Leadership*, pp. 69–71.

Denning, S. (2011). *The Leader's Guide to Storytelling: Mastering the Art and Discipline of Business Narrative*. San Francisco, CA: Jossey-Bass.

Denning, S. (2007). *The Secret Language of Leadership: How Leaders Inspire Action through Narrative*. San Francisco, CA: Jossey-Bass.

Dorer, M. J. (2005a). *Montessori's Cosmic Curriculum: The Legacy, Practice & Future.* CD Recording. Fort Worth, TX: Egami Inc.

Dorer, M. J. (2005b). *The Cosmic Café.* St. Paul, MN: St. Catherine University.

Duffy, M. & Duffy, D. (2002). *Children of the Universe: Cosmic Education in the Montessori Elementary Classroom.* Altoona, PA: Parent Child Press.

Green, R. & Smith, S. (Producers). (1997-April, 2006). *The Red Green Show.* [Television series]. Toronto, Canada: CBC Television.

Harrigan, P. (1994, May 28). Tall Tales and Deep Truths. Colombo, Sri Lanka: *The Island.*

Harvey, H. B. (2012). *The Art of Storytelling: From Parents to Professionals.* Chantilly, VA: The Great Courses.

Haven, K. (2007). *Story proof: The science behind the startling power of story*. Santa Barbara, CA: Libraries Unlimited.

Karia, A. (2015). *TED Talks Storytelling: 23 Storytelling Techniques from the Best TED Talks*. North Charleston, SC: CreateSpace Independent Publishing Platform.

Kipling, R. (1907). *Just So Stories*. New York: Doubleday.

Lang, A. (1903). *The Crimson Fairy Book*. London: Longmans, Green and Co.

Leitman, M. (2015). *Long Story Short: The Only Storytelling Guide You'll Ever Need.* Seattle, WA: Sasquatch Books.

Lillard, P. P. (1996). *Montessori Today*. New York: Random House.

Lipman, D. (1999). *Improving Your Storytelling: Beyond the Basics for All Who Tell Stories in Work and Play*. Little Rock, AR: August House.

Lipman, D. (1994). *Storytelling games: Creative activities for language, communication, and composition across the curriculum.* San Francisco CA: Oryx Press.

Lipman, D. (2006). *The storytelling coach: How to listen, praise, and bring out people's best*. Little Rock, AR: August House.

Lönnrot, E. (1888). *The Kalevala.* J. M. Crawford, translator. New York: John B. Alden.

MacDonald, M. R. (2006). *The storyteller's start-up book: Finding, learning, performing and using folktales.* Little Rock, AR: August House.

Mellmann, K. (2012). Is Storytelling a Biological Adaptation? Preliminary thoughts on how to pose that question. In: Carsten Gansel, Dirk Vanderbeke (Eds.): *Telling Stories: Literature and Evolution.* Hawthorne, NY: Walter de Gruyter, Inc., pp. 30-49.

Marbin, B. (2006, January 27). In *The Literacy of Learning* by Jake Ten Pas. Corvallis, OR: Corvallis Gazette-Times.

Miller, J. P. (1996). *The Holistic Curriculum.* Toronto Ontario Institute for Studies in Education.

Miller, S. & Pennycuff, L. (2008, May). *The Power of Story: Using Storytelling to Improve Literacy Learning.* Journal of Cross-Disciplinary Perspectives in Education. Vol. 1, No. 1. pp. 36–43.

Montessori, M. (1996, first published 1948). *To Educate the Human Potential.* Oxford, England: Clio Press.

Montessori, M. M. (1976). *Cosmic Education.* Amsterdam, Netherlands: Association Montessori Internationale.

Morgan, J. (2002). *Born With a Bang: The Universe Tells Our Cosmic Story.* Nevada City, CA: Dawn Publications.

Morgan, J. (2003). *From Lava to Life: The Universe Tells Our Earth Story.* Nevada City, CA: Dawn Publications.

Morgan, J. (2006). *Mammals Who Morph: The Universe Tells Our Evolution Story.* Nevada City, CA: Dawn Publications.

Perrow, S. (2012). *Therapeutic Storytelling: 101 Healing Stories for Children.* Gloucestershire, England: Hawthorn Press (Hawthorn House).

Pottish-Lewis, P. (1994). *Story Telling.* A speech delivered in Washington, D.C., July, 1994 at the AMI-USA Summer Conference.

Pottle, J. (2015). *Science Through Stories.* Gloucestershire, England: Hawthorn Press (Hawthorn House).

Pratchett, T., Stewart I. & Cohen, J. (2002). *The Science of Discworld II: The Globe.* London: Ebury Press, pp. 325, 327.

Ramsden, A. and Hollingsworth, S. (2012). *The Storyteller's Way: Sourcebook for Inspired Storytelling.* Gloucestershire, UK: Hawthorn Press.

Sawyer, R. (1942). *The Way of the Storyteller*. New York: Viking.

Scalise Sugiyama, M. (2001). Food, Foragers, and Folklore: The Role of Narrative in Human Subsistence. *Evolution and Human Behavior*, 22(4): pp. 221-240.

Schiro, M. S. (2004). *Oral Storytelling and Teaching Mathematics: Pedagogical and Multicultural Perspectives*. Los Angeles: SAGE Publications, Inc.

Shepard, A. (1990). *Tell a Story! A Guide to Storytelling*. Arcata, CA: Simple Productions.

Smith, C. (2014). *The Storytelling School: Handbook for Teachers*. Gloucestershire, UK: Hawthorn Press.

Smuts, J. C. (1926). *Holism and Evolution*. New York: J. J. Little and Co.

Strauss, K. (2006). *Tales with Tails: Storytelling the Wonders of the Natural World.* Westport, CT: Libraries Unlimited.

Wallis, D. A. (2005, April). *History of Angle Measurement*. Paper presented at the FIG Working Week 2005, Cairo, Egypt.

Welch, A. S. (1862). *Object Lessons: Prepared for Teachers of Primary Schools and Primary Classes.* New York: A. S. Barnes & Company.

Online Bibliography

This online bibliography is a list of all of the online electronic sources I have consulted or otherwise used (whether referenced or not) in the process of researching and preparing this work.

Breyer, M. (2013). *Finally Answered! Which Came First, the Chicken or the Egg?* Mother Nature Network: Earth Matters, Animals. Retrieved from: http://www.mnn.com/earth-matters/animals/stories/finally-answered- which-came-first-the-chicken-or-the-egg

Crandall, S. (2007). *Sally Crandall, Storyteller*. Retrieved from: http://www.sallycrandall.com/index.htmlc

Darling, D. (n.d.). *Babylonian Astronomy*. Retrieved from: http://www.daviddarling.info/encyclopedia/B/Babylonian_astronomy.html

Education Week. (2004, updated 2007). Achievement Gap. *Education Week (electronic version)*. Retrieved from: http://www.edweek.org/ew/issues/achievement-gap

Elliot, T. (2009). *Story Activities in Montessori*. Retrieved from: http://www.ehow.com/video_4403219_story-activities-montessori.html

Ellis, B. & McAndrews, S. (2014). *Storytelling Magic: Enhancing Children's Oral Language, Reading, and Writing*. Fox Tales International. Retrieved from: http://www.foxtalesint.com/library-1/82-articles/259-storytelling-magic-enhancing-children-s-oral-language-reading-and-writing

Farrell, J. (2007). *What is a Myth?* Retrieved from: http://ccat.sas.upenn.edu/~jfarrell/courses/myth/topics/what_is_myth.html

Forest, H. (2000). Why Storytelling? *Story Arts Online*. Retrieved from: https://www.storyarts.org/classroom/index.html

Hamilton, M. & Weiss, M. (2007). *Why Children Should Be Given the Opportunity to Tell Stories.* Retrieved from http://beautyandthebeaststorytellers.com/Handouts/whychildren.pdf

Hansen, H. (2010). *Story-Telling Basics: 7 Powerful Steps to Telling Great Stories!* Retrieved from: http://www.content4reprint.com/speaking/story-telling-basics-7-powerful-steps-to-telling-great-stories.htm

Jennings, T. & Ponder, L. (2009). *Folktale Closings: Alternatives to 'Happily Ever After.* These were originally collected by participants of the listserve "Storytell," originally compiled by Sharon P. Johnson, augmented and organized by Stefani Koorey & further augmented, and prepared by Betsy Bybell. Retrieved from: http://www.folktale.net/endings.html

Jennings, T. & Ponder, L. (2009). *Folktale Openings: From Storytell.* These were collected by participants of the listserve "Storytell," originally compiled by Sharon P. Johnson, augmented and organized by Stefani Koorey & further augmented and prepared by Betsy Bybell. Retrieved from: http://www.folktale.net/openers.html

Lendering, J. (2015). *Astronomical Diaries.* Retrieved from: http://www.livius.org/articles/concept/astronomical-diaries/

Magoulick, M. (2006). *What is Myth?* Retrieved from: http://www.faculty.de.gcsu.edu/~mmagouli/defmyth.htm

National Council of Teachers of English. (1992). *Guideline on Teaching Storytelling.* Retrieved from: http://www.ncte.org/positions/statements/teachingstorytelling

National Literacy Trust. (2015). *Storytelling Tips.* Retrieved from: http://www.literacytrust.org.uk/assets/0000/0865/Storytelling_tips.pdf

Nolan, L. (n.d.). *Confessions of a Montessori Mom.* Retrieved from: http://www.confessionsofamontessorimom.com/2011/08/montessoris-history-of-creation-physics.html

O'Hara, C. (2014). How to Tell a Great Story. *Harvard Business Review.* Retrieved from: https://hbr.org/2014/07/how-to-tell-a-great-story

Oxford University Press. (1989). *The Oxford English Dictionary.* 2nd ed. 1989. OED Online. Oxford University Press. Retrieved from http://dictionary.oed.com

Scalise Sugiyama, M. (2009). *Home.* Retrieved from: http://pages.uoregon.edu/mscalise/index.html

Silver, S. H. (2002). Review of The Science of Discworld II: The Globe, in *Steven Silver's Reviews*. Retrieved from: http://www.sfsite.com/silverag/globe.html

Switek, B. (2012). *Hooray for Dinofuzz!* Retrieved from: http://phenomena.nationalgeographic.com/2012/12/31/hooray-for-dinofuzz

Switek, B. (2015). *10 Ways to See the Dinosaur in a Bird.* Retrieved from: http://mentalfloss.com/article/57763/10-ways-see-dinosaur-bird

Vanderbes, J. (2013, September). The Evolutionary Case for Great Fiction. *The Atlantic.* Retrieved from: http://www.theatlantic.com/entertainment/archive/2013/09/ the-evolutionary-case-for-great-fiction/279311

Widrich, L. (2012). *The Science of Storytelling: Why Telling a Story is the Most Powerful Way to Activate Our Brains.* Lifehacker. Retrieved from: http://lifehacker.com/5965703/the-science-of-storytelling-why-telling-a-story-is-the-most-powerful-way-to-activate-our-brains

Illustration Credits

Thank you to everyone who provided the illustrations for this book.

Graphic design by Cheri Citrowske from originals ©Michael Dorer, Montessori Leadership Group: Figures 1-7, 29-31, 33-39, 91 and 92.

Graphic design by Cheri Citrowske: Figures 8-27, 41, 42, 46-49, 51-59.

Photographs provided by GAM Gonzagarredi Montessori srl and used with permission: Figures 32, 40, and 50.

Original art by Robert Jacobson: Figures 43-45.

Wikipedia Commons image: Figure 28.

Photographs by Andy Vevang: Figures 60-90.

Author photo (p. 355) by Rebecca Zenefski.

Acknowledgements

This book only really came together because of the wonderful support and backing of my family. My wife, Rose, and our children, Jacob, Benjamin, and Margaret, spent countless hours listening to these stories and the ideas behind them. They were always patient and encouraging, even with stories they had heard several times, or stories that did not work. Jake, Ben, and Meg even acted as inspirations for the first story I ever wrote down, *Measuring the Farm.* They made this possible.

I am greatly indebted to my grandfather, Richard J. Dorer, for his inspiration and imagination. He was the first to make storytelling come alive for me. His genius at writing, his visionary leadership, and his genuine warmth have deeply influenced my life.

I also owe a very big debt of thanks to all of the exceptionally brilliant people who helped work on this book. A huge *Thank You* to my talented editor, Molly Foran Yurchak. She really has an eagle eye and a great ear for stories, and offers frequent expert advice. I also owe many thanks to Cheri Citrowske for her exceptional work on the graphics; to the extraordinary and detail-oriented work of Carey Jones, my copy editor; and to Erik Jacobson for the design of the book.

I am very grateful to Camillo Grazzini, Eleonora Honegger, and the entire talented and gifted faculty at the International Centre for Montessori Studies. They helped me to see and understand the role that storytelling could take in Montessori education.

Thank you to my friends Jonathan Wolff, Larry Schaefer, and Syneva Barrett, and my wife, Rose Dorer, for contributing stories and ideas to this book. I have edited and somewhat updated some of these contributions, so any errors are my own.

A special thank you to Jane Campbell, owner of the Parent Child

Press, the publisher, for her support, and for giving me this opportunity to spread the word about storytelling.

Many Montessorians around the world listened to these stories and volunteered their enthusiasm and input. Thank you. I am also very grateful to the sponsors of a variety of conferences who encouraged and supported me in presenting these stories to adults around the world. Finally, I am thankful for all of the children in so many classrooms who listened to these tales and brought me such cheer. I sincerely thank them.

About Michael Dorer

Michael grew up listening to stories but didn't start telling them until he was in his thirties, beginning with a few tentative yarns for children. Even though the stories were a bit makeshift, they worked wonders with their audiences. That started a lifelong love of stories and storytelling. Today, Michael continues to appeal to children through his storytelling.

Michael has a background as an internationally trained Montessori educator. After training in America and Europe, he specialized in Montessori curriculum and materials, focusing on storytelling. He has also worked with adults in teacher education for almost thirty years.

Michael has had a diverse background working with children from toddlers to middle schoolers, beginning in 1969. Today, you can frequently find Michael speaking to school groups and at professional conferences, presenting a variety of workshops, consulting for schools, or telling stories.

After receiving Montessori credentials from the American

Montessori Society and the Association Montessori Internationale, Michael completed a doctorate in Instructional Leadership.

Michael has been active professionally, having served as a Board Member of the American Montessori Society as well as its president. Additionally, he is a senior consultant for the Montessori Foundation. Michael also wrote the charter for the nation's first Montessori charter school.

Michael has written and published seven Montessori teacher manuals in a variety of subject areas.

At home in Minnesota, Michael and his wife, Rose, enjoy visiting schools, cooking, and playing with their grandchildren and their black Labrador. Whenever he can, Michael likes canning and preserving foods. If you're lucky, you may get to try his homemade jam while listening to a story.